# The Power of Language and the Language of Power

*A Linguistic Perspective on Power Dynamics in NATO*

Isabela-Anda Dragomir

# The Power of Language and the Language of Power

## A Linguistic Perspective on Power Dynamics in NATO

CEEOLPress 2022

# The Power of Language and the Language of Power
*A Linguistic Perspective on Power Dynamics in NATO*

*Author*

**Isabela-Anda Dragomir**

*Department of Applied Social Sciences and Humanities,
Faculty of Military Sciences,
"Nicolae Balcescu" Land Forces Academy of Sibiu*

© 2022 by CEEOLPress
Published in 2022 by CEEOLPress, Frankfurt am Main, Germany



Typesetting: CEEOL GmbH, CEEOLPress Frankfurt am Main
Layout: Alexander Neroslavsky

ISBN:      978-3-949607-12-7
E-ISBN: 978-3-949607-13-4

# *Preface*

This monograph is based on the doctoral thesis defended in 2019. Along the journey, my research endeavor has benefited from the advice of expert observers and professors whom I would like to thank for their extensive and valuable contribution: first and foremost, Mrs. Silvia Florea, dr. habil., my thesis coordinator, who provided timely advice and constant assistance throughout my endeavor; Dr. Eric Gilder and Dr. Radu Drăgulescu, my doctoral advisors, who brought pertinent comments on the earlier drafts of the work and offered relevant feedback and encouragement; the ReaderBench masterminds, especially Dr.Eng. Mihai Dascălu and Dr. Ștefan Trăușan-Matu, who believed in my work and added incommensurable value to my research.

I would also like to express appreciation to Dr. Donald Abenheim and to Dr. David Yost, professors at the Naval Postgraduate School of Monterey, California, my host institution during the nine-month Fulbright grant as a visiting researcher, who gave me a great sense of freedom and latitude, not only to conduct research on a broader topic than originally intended, but also to place the study in the context of theories of international political order, such as collective security and the balance of power.

The finalization of this thesis would not have been possible without the help of BG Dr. Ghiță Bârsan, Commandant and Rector of "Nicolae Bălcescu" Land Forces Academy of Sibiu, who kindly took interest in my project and was most supportive with all connected professional activities and goals.

Several other people offered assistance that was sincerely appreciated, particularly COL (r) Carmen Teodorescu, Adriana Dumitrescu, Brândușa Niculescu, Florina Maier, Viviana Sărac, Anca Tomuș, Tanya Herfi, Jovan Drones and John R. Morgan.
Finally, I would like to thank my family, for their boundless patience and encouragement, as well as for their practical assistance in making it all possible.

# Table of Contents

# Introduction

## The Rationale Behind a Linguistic Analysis of Power Dynamics in NATO Military Discourse

Since the dawn of modern history, maintaining a power balance as an underlying condition for international order has been one of the most constantly pursued endeavors of humanity. Starting with the ancient Trojan War and ending with the contemporary "war on terror", leaders all over the world, in isolation or alliance, have struggled to uphold power and play a determining role in keeping a power balance that would serve national and global interests and secure international peace and prosperity. The interpretation of international relations through the theory of balance of power involves a high degree of abstraction, reified into the visual representation of Powers, i.e., states holding the status of, as the weights in a pair of scales.

Regardless of the investigative entry point (whether it is social, cognitive, historical, or linguistic), any discussion about power must assume the existence of an equilibrium of forces; nonetheless, the balance of power has never been rigid nor static. The inherent instability of the international power balance, stemming from consistent social changes, generates a dynamic configuration of the relations between the agents involved in this mechanism. The resulting power dynamics have traditionally been explained in terms of structures, dimensions, patterns, or frameworks of power. But while patterns of power substantiate strategy, the concept of power balance leads to considerations of military potential, diplomatic initiative, and economic might.

Against a continuously changing environment, one feature that is constant throughout recorded history is the formation of alliances, tasked with the well-defined role of pursuing goals that individual states cannot achieve on their own. Maintaining international order and keeping a global power balance while securing peace and stability is one endeavor traditionally undertaken by alliances. The North Atlantic Treaty Organization (NATO) makes no exception.

The challenges that NATO (in its dimension as community of powers) has faced throughout its evolution have reshaped the concept of "balance of power" and replaced it with the more appropriate concept of "power dynamics", so as to illustrate the continuous tendency to slide away from the notion of an even distribution of power and rather express the endless shifting and regrouping of power within the Alliance. As a consequence, the "balance of power" has become a respectable and indeed indispensable part of the diplomatic lexicon, but the real object of scientific contemplation should be the concept of "power dynamics".

Although language is not power, it encodes power. Power is embedded in the ideological workings of language, and ideology is invested at all levels of language. When exploring language in the context of NATO discourse – defined here as official policies and positions assumed in text and talk at the level of the Alliance's different planning groups, councils, and committees – the investigation starts from the premise that the discussions and debates that create official documents occur against a background where forces in agreement or opposition generate meaning negotiations between social actors invested with power, conventionally related to topics pertaining to military strategies and politics and manifested away from the public view. Nevertheless, the resulting policies are reified in open, official documents, which are invested with the role of making sense of the world and constructing social actions in relation to everyday realities. As a result, the discourse analysis includes historical, social, cognitive, and linguistic explorations of texts, interactions, and practices at local, institutional, and societal level.

The diverse excursions into the language that illustrates the dynamics of power in NATO discourse are informed by a discourse analytical approach founded in the theory and method of critical discourse analysis as applied to the field of International Relations. The methodology lays strong emphasis on language and how the inherited structures of language frame the discourse of power in military communication. Both the theoretical and analytical core of the paper pivot on the importance of language and discourse for the social construction of the ideology of power.

Every so often, linguists and analysts from all fields have given attention to what is being decided to the detriment of analyzing how the decisions are made and why there is opposition or consensus. The manner and the reason for decision-making have more to do with framing than with anything else. The most significant part of framing is the relationship between words and actions, with a strong emphasis on the power of

10

language to galvanize military and political will and reify it into action. While this investigation tries to fill the existing gap between the "what" and the "how", I cannot claim it completely fills it. Nowhere is there a comprehensive account of how the balance of power operates, and perhaps none can be constructed, given the ever flexible and eluding character of power. However, the current research aims to discover a pattern in power dynamics at the NATO level and to confirm this pattern. To do so, the practical chapter of the thesis conducts a critical analysis of the language of power used in typical NATO discourse.

Understanding the fact that the balance of power is never rigid, uniform, and unvaried, but rather instable and insecure, generates the following cogent deduction: the power dynamics resulting from the instability are actually generated by the interactions that take place between the weights of the balance. Taking the rationale even further in the context of current investigations of power dynamics in NATO, the conclusion is that the dynamics of power manifest in a multi-layered framework. First of all, there is a level of opposition that characterizes the relations between the United States and the Soviet Union, then between NATO and the Warsaw Pact states, and, after the end of the Cold War, between NATO and Russia, as well as between NATO and other state or non-state actors on the international scene. It has been framed as external bipolar balance, typified by a specific pattern of power dynamics, primarily substantiated by ideological opposition. Secondly, there is opposition at the level of NATO as an organization, generated by the conceptual polarization between member states in terms of doctrine and strategic concepts. This type of relation has been defined in terms of an internal multipolar balance framework, anchored on the background of NATO's ideological evolution and analyzed from the perspective of the challenges brought to the American leadership in NATO (by the so-called medium powers within the Alliance: the United Kingdom, France, and Germany) and of the dynamics of the relations between these powers.

The research question that draws all these premises together is framed as follows.

**How is power dynamics operationalized through language in NATO discourse?**

The practical section of the book, which documents a critical analysis of the selected NATO discourse samples, brings together the results of an in-depth description, interpretation and explanation of the contexts that foster the discursive manifestation of power and the linguistic tools used to construct them.

Extensive research conducted during my Fulbright grant at the Naval Postgraduate School in Monterey, California, has generated an in-depth analysis of the ideological evolution of NATO. Although this investigation has not been the principal aim of the paper, it has offered a detailed perspective and understanding of how power dynamics function within and outside the organization. Furthermore, such an approach has proven to be extremely helpful in locating the patterns of power most prevalent in NATO military discourse. Accordingly, of the varieties of power typically deployed in discourse, three emergent types have been selected, on which to base the ideological-driven analysis: adversarial, integrative, and predominant power.

Undoubtedly, the background elements that inform the analysis are very complex and diverse. The approach undertaken by this paper relies on various concepts of power, defined at the intersection of language and ideology; it pivots on a multi-layered historical, social, cognitive, and political structure which is constructed based on the dynamics between the actors both within and outside NATO; it investigates language as the primary tool of operationalization of power and the dynamics associated with it. Given the complexity of the framework in which power dynamics are examined, the main research question has been detailed into three secondary research questions:

1. What kind of power rhetoric is employed to ensure cooperation both within the Alliance and with external actors?

2. How is internal and external opposition materialized in NATO military discourse?

3. What kind of discursive patterns of power does the United States use in order to assert its (pre)dominant role in NATO?

In order to address these research questions, three hypotheses that frame the notion of power and thematize the linguistic investigation have been formulated:

1. The rhetoric of integrative power has kept the Alliance coherent and cohesive under the umbrella of common values, granting the success of NATO's enduring role in international security. The validity of

this assertion has been explored by looking at discourse strands of integrative power, in the framework of external bipolar relations and of NATO's internal structure.

2. NATO is the most powerful alliance in history and, in addition to action, it has fought opposition by using language. This hypothesis has been evaluated through an analysis of discursive manifestations of adversarial power relations in both the external bipolar balance and the internal multipolar balance frameworks.

3. When the internal power balance tilts, it does so in favor of the United States, in virtue of its predominance in NATO. The hypothesis that the United States has a predominant role in NATO rests on the discursive materialization of three types of power: referent, expert and legitimate.

The link between language and power provides the point of departure for the elaboration of a systemic method of interpretation. The methodology used in this paper relies heavily on Critical Discourse Analysis (CDA) as a qualitative method aimed at analyzing the causes and effects of different social and political issues, by offering a detailed account of the relationships that exist between text, talk, society, power and ultimately ideology. Military policies, as the main object of investigation, can be better understood by analyzing the various issues of a community, as well as the language and texts that express them.

A flexible paradigm of analysis, CDA involves a shift of perspective. Language is no longer seen as an abstract construct but becomes an instrument that carries the meaning of what is being said under specific historical, social and political conditions. This particular methodology has been selected with the aim of systematically exploring interconnections between discursive practices, events and texts, and wider social organizational structures, the relations within and outside them and the processes associated with them. Further investigation will also reveal how such practices, events and texts are ideologically molded by relations of power and power dynamics. In addition to describing the relationship between texts, interactions, and social practices, CDA is used here to understand the structure of discourse practices and then combine description and interpretation in order to explain why and how power dynamics and the discourses associated with them are constituted and manifested the way they are. Starting from the premise that discourse is socially constructed as well as socially conditioned, the main task of the present paper becomes one of understanding and revealing the social dynamics that are generated by mainstream ideology and power relations and propagated through the use of written texts.

In order to offer a more comprehensive account of how power dynamics are represented in NATO discourse, a quantitative research has also been conducted, aimed at validating the qualitative analysis and supplementing it with statistically reliable and generalizable results. Approached from a statistical entry point, the main research question generated a fourth secondary interrogation:

1. How are the concepts of integrative and adversarial power linguistically operationalized in NATO discourse between 1949 and 2018?

The theory that informs this supplementary investigation produced a fourth work hypothesis:

1. The operationalization of the concepts of integrative and adversarial power has suffered discursive modifications visible in NATO documents produced during the Cold War and in the years after the end of the Cold War.

The two periods investigated with the help of quantitative analysis tools cover 184 official texts produced between 1949 and 1990, and 1991 and 2018, respectively, with specific emphasis on the summit and ministerial meetings final communiqués which are imbued with discursive conceptualizations of integrative and adversarial power. The end of the Cold War was chosen as a reference point given its importance for the social and political changes it propagated. With the USSR fading away from the international scene, the Warsaw Pact dissolved and the Berlin Wall falling, the configuration of the security environment at the beginning of the 1990s was typified by radical modifications that bore a significant impact on the manner in which the Alliance positioned itself on the world map. Without waiving its core tasks and values, NATO had to adapt and reinvent in order to successfully cope with the new challenges occasioned by the shifting of the power balance in Europe and beyond. The quantitative analysis sets out to examine how these strategic changes impacted the manner in which the concept of power was reified in discourses by locating language variations, if any, at the level of the NATO texts produced before and after 1990.

14

The methodology used for the quantitative analysis stems from the investigative framework proposed by ReaderBench and is based on a corpus-assisted discourse analysis that follows a number of analytical steps and depends on the automated application of specific indices.

The results of the quantitative research methodology enrich the discussion of the results yielded by the qualitative analysis. The validation of the quantitative analysis hypothesis is a complementary indication of the fact that not only is NATO discourse a legitimate locus for the manifestation of power dynamics, but that noteworthy revisions of the discourse have also been operated, illustrated through diverse linguistic operationalizations of power, a notion that has suffered conceptual amendments during NATO's ideological evolution.

While well-aware of the fact that no method, investigation, or conclusion will provide an absolute answer to a specific issue or depict an exhaustive image of the object under scrutiny, the rationale behind this exploratory journey is to provide a better understanding of the manner in which language can become a tool for ideological expression and of how discourses can be tailored to become more efficient, straightforward, and transparent instruments that shape social reality.

By and large, the book sets out to examine the problem of power as a construct in communicative theories and the way in which it relates to and is constituted by NATO discourse. By way of an extended example, it investigates the way in which the dynamics of types of power (integrative, adversarial, and predominant) impact social, political, and military relationships between the members of the North Atlantic Organization and between the Alliance and external actors.

# Chapter 1

## A Flexible Analytical Framework for the Linguistic Investigation of Military Discourse

The theoretical scaffolding on which this section is constructed compromises two distinct sections that converge toward a rich and ample approach of the investigative portion of the paper. It specifically defines the analytical framework that has informed both the qualitative and quantitative analysis, with particular emphasis on the method and instruments used during the investigation.

The qualitative examination is approached from three entry points, on which is anchored the examination of the three different types of power dynamics (integrative, adversarial, and predominant).

The chosen analytical framework is based on a flexible architecture designed to facilitate an ideological investigation of language, by integrating social, cognitive, and discursive approaches into the examination of ideologies and their communicative articulation. It espouses the qualitative interpretation of discourse with the quantitative analysis resulting from the application of lexical, semantic and cohesion indices utilized by the Reader Bench framework[1]. Based on the utilization of a validated textual complexity model, the quantitative analysis is aimed at supplementing and validating the qualitative exploration, by offering additional information about and a more in-depth insight into the manner in which the linguistic operationalization of power dynamics has changed throughout NATO's ideological 70-year evolution, from a lexical, semantic and structural point of view.

Starting from the premise that discourse analysis contributes extensively to the comprehension of the manner in which social, political and even cultural contexts coexist, cooperate and sometimes even influence social

---

[1] ReaderBench is a text processing framework relying on advanced Natural Language Processing techniques that encompass a wide range of text analysis modules available in a variety of languages, including English, French, Romanian, and Dutch. ReaderBench is the only open-source multilingual textual analysis solution that provides a unified access to more than 200 textual complexity indices including surface, syntactic, morphological, semantic, and discourse-specific factors, alongside cohesion metrics derived from specific lexicalized ontologies and semantic models. (Source: ReaderBench: A Multi-lingual Framework for Analyzing Text Complexity. Available from: https://www.researchgate.net/ publication/319474819_ReaderBench_A_Multi-lingual_Framework_for_ Analyzing_Text_Complexity [accessed August 28, 2018]).

change, discourse is broadly defined as "language in use" and is demarcated by social, political and cultural constraints that reflect and configure social order. Chris Barker and Dariusz Galasinski suggest that the struggle for social change is a matter of language, which is "an instrument … of intervention in the world, through mechanisms of description, definition and control" (2001:17). Ideologically wise, the discourse can be interpreted on the basis of three pillars (who speaks, what they speak about, how they speak), and an analysis that takes into consideration these parameters will undoubtedly offer a comprehensive perspective on the construction of the individuals, of the society and ultimately of the world itself.

Military discourse, is, in virtue of the proposed definition, a manifestation of socially-anchored communicative practices that transmit ideological values specific to this particular community of practice. In the words of Fairclough, social institutions (and the military is one example thereof) contain "diverse ideological-discursive formations" (IDFs) associated with different groups within the institution. … A characteristic of a dominant IDF is the capacity to "naturalize" ideologies, i.e., to win acceptance for them as non-ideological "common-sense" (1995:27). The critical dimension of the discourse analysis aims at "denaturalizing" ideologies. The author further defines the process of "denaturalization" by postulating that it "involves showing how social structures determine properties of discourse and how discourse in turn determine social structure" (27).

The concept of power can be traced at the intersection of language and ideology. There is definitely a strong dialectical relation between discourse, ideology, and power. A detailed discussion of different patterns of power has created the broader circumstantial perspective about the concept and was instrumental in the selection of the most prevalent categories of power relations manifested in discourse. Based on a secondary research question that has been explored in the background, formulated so as to identify the most salient patterns of power in military discourse, the analysis was focused on three types of power most frequently identifiable in NATO discourse: adversarial power, integrative power and predominant power, branched out in three subcategories: expert, legitimate, and expert power.

In analyzing the discourse of power, the approach calls for a holistic investigation, a focused interdisciplinarity, which explores the act of communication on several levels:

18

1. textually, by analyzing textual complexity in terms of surface indices, word density, syntactic and morphologic elements, and discursive structures that facilitate the dissemination of the message;

2. from the perspective of discursive practices, i.e., of the institutional processes that generate the production, transmission, and reception of the message;

3. in terms of socio-cultural practices, targeting the manner in which the military discourse of power contributes to social stability or social change.

The link between language and power provides the point of departure for the elaboration of a systemic method of interpretation. The methodology used in this paper relies heavily on Critical Discourse Analysis (CDA) as a method to analyze the fundamental causes and consequences of issues, by offering a detailed account of the relationships that exist between text, talk, society, power and ultimately ideology. The mechanism of understanding military policies, as the main object of investigation, can be enhanced by a thorough examination of the incumbent social issues, as well as of the language and type of texts used to construct reality.

## 1.1. The Qualitative Approach

CDA has been employed as a method of qualitative investigation, with a focus on the key terms involved in the deconstruction and interpretation of military discourse (criticality, text, and context). Against this background, the analytical framework espouses the socio-cognitive approach proposed by Teun A. Van Dijk, which reunites three different layers of analysis to describe discursive manifestations that occur at the intersection between language, ideology and the notion of power, with Ruth Wodak's Discourse Historical Approach (DHA).

Starting from Van Dijk's observation that "the point of ideological discourse analysis is not merely to "discover" underlying ideologies, but to systematically link structures of discourse with structures of ideologies" (1995c: 143), the proposed study of NATO military discourse is based on analytically explicit methods, employed in order to dissolve any intuition one may have about the meaning of language and targeted explicitly at the patterns of discourse that generate specific social representations.

The initial approach used for the selection and location of discourse of power in NATO official communication is drawn from Van Dijk's three-level framework that connects ideologies and language from the socio-cognitive perspective. The first level is a socially-anchored investigation of the organizational structures within NATO (members, governments, ministries, and NATO committees: the Nuclear Planning Group, the Defence Planning Committee, and the North Atlantic Council), the dynamics of their interaction (consensus, opposition, hegemony, predominance) and the shared characteristics (identity, tasks, goals, norms, positions, resources); the second level explores the values (unity, solidarity, partnership, cooperation) and the ideologies of the military organization; finally, the third level is dedicated to the analysis of military documents, by investigating specific structures of text and talk (syntactic constructions, semantic structures, pragmatics, formal and informal patterns, logic and composition of the discourse).

The proposed analytical framework is informed by a linguistic investigation conducted on two levels – the micro and the macro level – and has resulted in the unpacking of three types of power relations and the discourses through which they are deployed. As a product of this integrated approach, Van Dijk's three-level framework has been incorporated into a two-level examination. The micro level hinges on Van Dijk's discourse analysis of structures of text and talk, which provides a critical insight into the lexical choices, syntactic structures, the pragmatics, and the semantics of military discourse, with the intent of unearthing the power relations embedded in discourses and the dynamics associated with them. The macro level incorporates the social and cognitive perspectives in Van Dijk's model, with extended forays into the historical context, the communicative situation and the function the discourses are meant to perform.

The undertaken analysis will also assimilate Wodak's historical approach, centered on a two-directional timeline that will scrutinize military discourse both synchronically and diachronically (Reisigl and Wodak 2009). Following the concept of "context" proposed by Rheindorf and Wodak (2018), the following have been considered: (1) the immediate language or text and the internal co-text (specific NATO documents, Final Communiqués from Ministerial Meetings and Summits); (2) the intertextual and interdiscursive link between utterances, texts, and discourses (reformulations, recontextualizations); (3) the external social and political variables that create the specific situational context (the chronology of events); and (4) the larger sociopolitical and historical context in which the discursive practices are rooted and to which they are connected (the evolution of NATO's ideology and strategies).

Working within the broader framework of DHA, which places great emphasis on the importance of historical contexts, this section traces three specific discourse strands that have been identified in close connection with the type of power they illustrate. The integrative or relational power is located in the discourse of unity; adversarial power relations are exemplified through the discourse of opposition; finally, referent, expert and legitimate power manifestations have been collected under the discourse of U.S. predominant power. These strands have been singled out as forming a distinctive subdiscourse about power, illustrated through a corpus of documents well-defined by a common topic; demarcated by a beginning and an end on the timeline; produced by a specific group of social actors; and connected by strong intertextual links. The identified discourse strands and topical threads allow a clear delineation of the communicative events under investigation, thus defining the object of analysis in a more detailed manner. This in turn facilitates focused contextualization and better tracing of the dynamics of discursive representations of power.

In terms of modus operandi, the qualitative analysis starts with a summary of the historical context in which the investigated documents were issued as strands in the discourse of power, then provides a description of their more immediate context and finally explains and interprets the language deployed in the formulation of the texts. This methodological mélange allows tracing the salient features of discourse along a chronological evolution of relevant events and the communicative instruments associated with them. The conceptual analysis is supplemented by a language-focused investigation aimed at exploring the manner in which the syntactic, morphological, lexical, and semantic fields of power have changed in a particular type of discourse during the investigated period. A context-sensitive analysis was conducted in virtue of the fact that such an approach strongly relies on the multilayered representation and definition of context, whose understanding is essential in decoding the effect of varying sociopolitical conditions (the immediate and historical context) on the dynamics of power relations, illustrated through a comprehensive examination of appropriate texts.

The general descriptive approach described in this section proposes a flexible analytical framework for the subject under investigation from a multifold perspective: morphosyntactic, lexical, semantic, and structural. In order to create a more comprehensive avenue for investigating ideology and power, the linguistic analysis has been conducted within the broader historical, social and political context in which ideological values and the notion of power have been given substance through military discourse.

## 1.1.1. The Social Environment – NATO as an Organization

Permanently changing social environments require the formation of alliances, tasked with the well-defined role of pursuing goals that individual states cannot achieve on their own. Maintaining international order and keeping a global power balance while securing peace and stability is one endeavor traditionally undertaken by alliances. The North Atlantic Treaty Organization makes no exception.

The social level of analysis takes a close look at what NATO represents from a structural point of view. The underpinning question that informs this description is the following: What is NATO? In order to grasp the mechanisms of power and its dynamics within an organization, one must first structurally and conceptually define that organization. Scholars are united in believing that NATO may be one of the hardest institutions to understand. Part of the difficulty resides in the complexity of the structure and part in the difference between the formal and the actual processes of decision-making. To answer the question regarding a definition of NATO, one must take an adventurous step into the labyrinth of forms the organizations takes.

First of all, NATO is an alliance of 30 states. In each, the head of government's office, the foreign and defense ministries and the armed forces are the institutions most involved in its affairs. NATO is also those armed forces of the member states which have been committed into the integrated military structure. They are subordinated to one of three Major NATO Commanders, of whom the most major by any definition is the Supreme Allied Commander Europe (SACEUR), whose headquarters – Supreme Headquarters Allied Powers Europe (SHAPE) – is at Casteau near Mons in southern Belgium.

Second of all, NATO is a complex structure of committees. The most senior is the North Atlantic Council (NAC), which meets at least weekly

22

in permanent session – each Wednesday morning at 10.30 at the Brussels Headquarters. In the NAC, each member state is represented by an ambassador. Twice a year, the foreign ministers of the Alliance convene for what are called meeting of the Council at ministerial level. From time to time, the Council also convenes at the head of government level, usually known as NATO summits. The Defence Planning Committee (DFC), meaning the Council without France (for reasons that definitely pertain to power dynamics, and which will be explored later in the paper) meets twice-yearly at ministerial level. Defense ministers also meet twice a year as the Nuclear Planning Group (NPG) and deal with nuclear affairs.

Finally, NATO is an international bureaucracy situated in Brussels and divided into two categories: staff of the national delegations and the international staff. The latter is led by the Secretary-General who heads meetings of the North Atlantic Council and is the senior civilian executive in the organization. It consists of about 1,500 people who are tasked with servicing the committees and running the five organic divisions that generate papers, studies, and proposals.

This quick glimpse at what NATO stands for in its institutional dimension was aimed at clarifying the levers and levels from which the balance of power is operated within the Alliance. There is no doubt that NATO is the sort of organization for which the word "labyrinthine" was invented. The whole process of relationing is even more complex because decisions must be taken by consensus and because the powers of the committees and headquarters are a great deal more limited than most people understand. Needless to say, an institution with such a degree of complexity can run on its own steam forever, but the truth of the matter is not necessarily how long, but actually how far. The power dynamics that manifest inside the organization and outside of it allowed the Alliance to keep its course and avoid sidetracking from the initially established purview. The type of interactions that typify the relations between the members of the Alliance and between NATO as a security organization and other state or non-state actors has been the fuel that has propelled the institution on a steady course for almost 70 years.

Knowing what NATO is leads to the subject of what NATO does. There is no denial of NATO's role in international security. From its inception, in 1949, throughout the regional challenges of the Cold War and in the aftermath of the terrorist attacks that forced the Alliance into a new global security configuration, NATO was essentially an instrument of collective defense. Designed as a "community of powers" (and composed, throughout its evolution, of a diverse array of great, medium and small powers), the North Atlantic Treaty Alliance has been tasked with the objective of maintaining a balance of power in the world, initially as a counterweight to the Soviet Union, then to Russia, and, more recently, to the dangers of international terrorism. The doctrine of collective security that fundaments the existence of the Alliance starts from the assumption that the members of the organization have both a duty and an interest to cooperate in adverting the threats to international order. The famous Article 5 of the Washington Treaty, stipulating that "an attack on one is an attack on all", basically reiterates the ancient tenet representing the founding stone of every alliance: if a state threatens the balance of power, all the members of the international community must band together to restrain and reduce the threat.

## 1.1.2. The Cognitive Level – Strategy as Ideology

The discussion on the cognitive dimension of military discourse starts from the understanding of the importance attributed to the social-cognitive function of ideology, an aspect that has already been tackled in the previous chapter. Applied to NATO, ideology is refined in the form of military strategy, an element of paramount importance for the functioning of the organization. Paul Buteaux argues that, in virtue of its strategic policies, the North Atlantic Alliance can be defined as a "regional mutual security organization", whose cohesion is ensured by focused regional comprehensive political and military doctrine (1983:1).

For the purpose of our investigation about the ideology of power in NATO, the starting premise is that the strategic doctrine of the Alliance has always been a matter for debate, and at times, the occasion for substantial controversy among the members of the organizations. Allied differences have emerged not only over the content of the strategic doctrine itself but also on how that doctrine was to be interpreted and implemented in the actual military planning of the Alliance.

One illustrative example is the issue of détente, a controversial strategy that dominated NATO's agenda in the late sixties. The nuclear policies of that period were dictated by the terms under which the United States offered its nuclear guarantees to the allies. As a consequence, the declaratory strategic doctrine of NATO could be interpreted as a statement of the allies' understanding of the American terms and conditions and ostensibly as allied acceptance. However, such acceptance did not automatically translate as complete allied consensus on nuclear policy, nor even as a fully shared acceptance, but rather as a formulation of what the members of the Alliance publicly agreed upon at a certain time. Against the background of power dynamics, such issues generated tensions and opposition relevant for the investigation of how power was negotiated and discursively framed in NATO policy documents.

As demonstrated by the linguistic exploration of U.S. predominant power, a key factor determining the Alliance's strategic doctrine was the influence of the American policy on NATO's ideology. Much of the modifications of the Alliance's policies and of the doctrine underlying them have almost always stemmed from American initiatives. As the Alliance leader, the United States has traditionally assumed the task of attempting to reconcile its own strategic preferences with those of the allies. One way in which this has been achieved was either unilaterally, by means of changes in its own declared position, or multilaterally, by seeking allied acceptance of alterations in the Alliance's strategy. When the allies resisted such changes and tried to sway American policy to their own interest, the result was a varying degree of disjunction that reflected opposition between the Alliance's interest and those of individual members. For example, in the late fifties and early sixties, the strategy of flexible response was extremely controversial. The solution to its general acceptance within NATO was to create new institutions (e.g., the Nuclear Planning Group) through which allied consultation about nuclear policy could occur. The creation of this organism did much to lessen the tensions that allied divisions on nuclear policies had created and was a resourceful means of promoting sufficient consensus to sustain the Alliance's purpose.

As a cognitive tool that encompasses collective structures of ideas, notions, norms and values, NATO's strategic doctrine takes a number of different forms and serves a wide array of purposes. If we define it as a connected series of beliefs and related statements of what are thought to be facts about strategy, the Alliance's doctrine serves to substantiate relations of power within NATO by justifying, explaining, prescribing, and even predicting its dynamics. Consensus and opposition take different forms and are generated by diverse contexts, but what is also relevant about their manifestation is also the triggering mechanisms and the context where conceptual differences or consent stem from. Notions such as "deterrence doctrine", "arms control doctrine", "enlargement doctrine", or "war on terror doctrine" not only describe operational plans, deployment policies or engagement rules but also function as designations that entail changes in the existing policies or require the adoption of new ones. In order to communicate ideas about NATO policies, if the object of such communication is to affect policy, then the interests and particular characteristics of the audience must be considered. Thus, both the manner of its determination and the subsequent uses to which strategy is put become manipulative tools by means of which reconciliation of different and sometimes conflicting interests and points of view is sought, and by which the coordination of policy among member states is achieved.

At macro-level, the Alliance's strategy affects the policies and interests of all twenty-nine allies, by dictating the complexities of their interactions at a number of different levels. Power dynamics are typically encouraged by the degree of conflict existing between primary and secondary interests. Membership in NATO, for instance, may purchase security under the American nuclear umbrella, albeit at the expense of freedom in areas of significant concern. In the case of France, the constraints imposed on her policy by participation in the integrated military command of the Alliance eventually came to be considered an unacceptable infringement on her sovereignty and led to France's withdrawal from this structure in 1966. On the other hand, pressing political considerations may lead allies to pursue their security objectives in ways that may alter their ties with the Alliance. It was the case of the Federal Republic's Ostpolitik, interpreted as an attempt to break out of the straightjacket of existing policy by altering the nature of the link between German aspirations in Europe and the character of German participation in NATO. By seeking political agreements in Eastern Europe on the basis of their territorial integrity and, by extent, their political status quo, the Germans challenged the balance of powers within the Alliance and in the wider European geopolitical context, by trading the military support for their security, which they obtained through the Alliance for their political and diplomatic position within the continent. The dynamics resulting from this vacillation was not so much an issue of a conflict between the membership status and outer objectives but rather a matter of reordering priorities between the Alliance and broader concerns.

An additional cognitive function of military doctrine serves to define and structure the organization in terms of its common concern:

military security. Membership in an alliance implies a minimum degree of common agreement as to the source and character of the threat to which the organization must forge a collective response. In light of this task, the Alliance becomes a forum for policy clearing, creating diplomatic alignments, a means by which a coordinated response to international developments is attempted. The reverse aspect of this is that the Alliance can be used to resist allied policies that are considered undesirable or inimical to individual national interests. Consequently, there is always a latent potential for conflict between the requirements of alliance cohesion and the impact international development has on individual allies. In addition to other manifestations that have to do more with action than with theoretical debates, adversarial or integrative power is also located and manifested in discourse, a resourceful locus for the linguistic operationalization of military strategy and ideology.

Relevant for the present investigation of power dynamics is to understand the strategic doctrine within the political and social context in which it is formulated. In the case of NATO, the political context is that of an alliance. It means that efforts should be constantly made to secure and sustain the continued joint endeavor of the allies, which ultimately translates as a basic need for collective security.

However, since NATO is not made up of a homogenous group of states, it is inevitable that certain power plays manifest against the political and social background. Not all allies are equally concerned with questions of strategic policy, nor are they all equally affected by changes in it. As a consequence, not all allies are similarly influential in dictating strategies, which makes the power balance uneven and tilt in favor of more potent states. By way of example, the issue of nuclear policy divides the Alliance in "inner" and "outer" groups. This unequal distribution is generated by factors such as involvement in the crucial central front, military contribution, possession of nuclear weapons, and deployment of nuclear capable forces, all of which apply as characteristics that separate the allies. Although the United States may stand for a class in itself when it comes to nuclear issues, it is possible to argue that for the purpose of alliance consultation on nuclear policy, Britain and Germany are also legitimate candidates for the "inner" group.

Last but not least, strategy may serve another important ideological purpose. A typical function of ideology is to reinforce the legitimacy of institutions and policies by means such as the definition of values, norms and principles, and by demonstrating the efficiency of the institution in promoting these values, norms and principles, which actually validates the rationalization of policy based on them. In the case of NATO, the legitimacy of its institutions and policies must be demonstrated to a variety of domestic publics that reflect different traditions and characteristic attitudes toward alliance and alignment. Therefore, the rhetoric developed to accommodate these circumstances typically focused on notions such as the indivisibility of alliance security, common defense, joint commitment to the "free world", collective fight against communism, or terrorism.

NATO also operates outside its organizational boundaries, in what has been framed in this paper by the external bipolar balance framework. Against this backdrop, strategic doctrine is used to influence the character of the relationship with the adversaries, which reversely enables strategy to be used as a means of manipulating inter-allied relations. The manner in which the strategic doctrine is formulated can have an essential impact on policies. Defining concepts such as "parity", for example, or establishing the conditions of what "strategic stability" refers to, may influence the strategic objectives sought with respect to an opponent and hold out the prospect of bargaining advantages, or it may serve to nullify an opponent's preferred strategic options.

In sum, the determination and formulation of the strategic doctrine are among the most important tasks of NATO, and, as the history of the Alliance has shown, have been closely related to issues of cohesion, solidarity, opposition, or predominance. This detailed approach to what the cognitive dimension of ideology stands for in the context of power dynamics was aimed at validating the assumption that NATO's ideology is a fundamental pillar on which the organization constructs its discourse, as a materialized form of capturing the elusive shiftings in the power balance, inherently embedded in the Alliance's conceptual and linguistic construction of strategies and doctrine.

## 1.1.3. The Discursive Construction

In addition to the investigation of discourses from a social and cognitive point of view, the proposed analytical framework also takes into consideration the linguistic elements that construct the analyzed discourses, in terms of morphology and syntax, lexicon and semantics.

## 1.1.3.1. Morphosyntactic Elements

The military discourse is constantly changing so as to accommodate the evolution of social paradigms from a linguistic point of view. The postmodern tendencies that define the social discourse in general have also impacted the narrative materializations of contemporary military discourse, which is centered on the nucleus of conflict – war, national and international security, defense.

Against this backdrop, the morphology of communication involves continuous changes of meaning, reconstruction of linguistic elements, creation of new terms associated with the appearance of new types of weapons, military technique, and equipment, on the account of the emerging asymmetrical types of conflict. New military terms are created according to the rules of English morphology. Some examples include affixation (e.g., maneuverability, survivability, rotary, missilery, aerial), word junction (e.g., minehunter, warhead, firepower, target seeking, airbase), shortening (e.g. chute/parachute, cap/captain, rekki/reconnaissance, shrap/shrapnel, torp/torpedo, vet/veteran).

From a more complex perspective, the syntactic characteristics of the military discourse can be allocated implications that go deeper than the surface layer of the grammatical constructions and underline ideologies inherent in communication. For example, Kress and Hodge pointed out that word order, or transactional structures of sentences may encrypt underlying semantic or even cognitive agency. In English, the responsible agency is associated with the grammatical subject and initial positioning. Hence, different syntactic forms can convey ideologically monitored opinions on liability assumed for socially positive or negative actions. For instance, antonymic properties, attributed to opposition groups (positive for ingroups and negative for outgroups) may be heightened by concentrating on their responsible agency and by positioning them as subjects and topics of the sentence. Conversely, the responsible agency can be syntactically toned down by using passive sentences, or even completely veiled by agentless passives or nominalizations. In NATO discourse, a typical discourse location for this kind of syntactic management are the final communiqués and the summit documents, texts in which the accent is placed on the commonly-assumed responsibility for the action to be taken rather than on the subject initiating it.

Syntactic structures are also illustrative of ideology in the context of the connection between sentence complexity and the background of the individuals producing the discourse (education, position). As an institution, the military has the ability and privilege of restricting comprehensibility of its discourse and implicitly control public access to it. In the case of strategic decision-making, for example, the public is excluded from the process through the complexity of vocabulary and structures, but when military communication is attributed an informative role, the message may be expressed by various forms of "simplified language" (Ghadessy 1988:46).

This practice is demonstrative for the manner in which power, as an inherent characteristic of military discourse, is translated into language variables that are instrumental in getting symbolic access to the resources of public discourse.

## 1.1.3.2. The Military Lexicon

It is well known that lexicalization is a major domain of ideological expression. In order to refer to individuals, groups, organizations, institutions, social issues, or social relations, language offers a wide array of word choices, depending on discourse genre and context (personal – mood, perspective, opinion; social – formality, familiarity, power relations; sociocultural – norms and values). The representation of participants and their relations or their actions is achieved in ideologically bound context or event models.

Military ideologies are diversely expressed in polarized lexicalizations ("terrorist" vs. "freedom-fighter", "Western" vs. "Eastern"), or in slogans, such as "Pro Joining", "Pro Annexation", emphasizing the positive implications of the ingroup opinions and values. According to Geis (1987), the lexicon of military discourse also differentiates between the "peaceful" nature of our weapons and military operations and the catastrophic and cruel nature of theirs. Military propaganda and news reports about the Gulf War abound in euphemisms, such as, "coercive interrogation", "escalating sectarian violence", "friendly fire", "to neutralize", "surgical strike", "smart bombs", utilized in order to put comforting distance between the civilian population and the violence on the battlefield, by making the brutality or war sound somewhat lofty and poetic. In the aftermath of September

11, Bush's military campaign of transforming the Greater Middle East into a Pax Americana was referred to as "the Global War on Terror", a syntagm that was redubbed "overseas contingency operations" during the Obama administration. During the Middle East conflict, affiliation to the outgroup of the opponents is discursively materialized through terms such as "fundamentalists", "zealots", "fanatics". On the background of the intense phenomenon of migration in the aftermath of the recent Syrian war, the credibility of the refugees has been undermined in military discourse by the use of collocations such as "illegal aliens", "economic refugees". Euphemisms are installed in the discourse so as to veil the bitter realities of war, but also to assign overblown honorifics to depict America as an embattled protagonist on the international scene. "Exceptional", "indispensable", and "greatest" are some of the most commonly used words, which presidents, politicians, and military leaders prefer to frequently deploy in their discourse in order to label the objectives of the imperative armed intervention in the Arab Gulf.

Well-known phrases, such as "shock and awe", used to underpin the reality of the massive air strike on Baghdad, have entered the common pool of lexical choices the military discourse employs to describe the results of diverse armed interventions. In the same vein, the death of dozens of civilians is referred to as "collateral damage", brought about the attempt to "decapitate" a much-hated regime.

The language of 21st-century war on terror is not exclusively targeted at soothing the public opinion. Less familiar notions and terms are employed in military discourse to conceal certain evident realities. "Asymmetrical warfare", for example, hints at the unethical and systematically coward strategy of the enemy, who is habitually prowling behind and mingling with civilians (often referred to as "hostages"). As a result, armed forces must be properly equipped in order to be able to cope with deceitful tactics and underhanded weaponry, including ambushes and improvised explosive devices, as well as with a wide collection of "unconventional" procedures, quite frequently directed against "soft" targets (the civilian population). The "gray zone" is yet another ambiguous term used by the military to define the puzzling typology of lower-level conflicts that are not defined as full-fledged wars. These conflicts typically include "non-state actors", another formulation coined by the military to label individuals or groups partly or wholly associated with state-run entities.

The military discourse is also populated with idiomatic expressions, aimed at concealing the actual meaning of what is being transmitted while actively engaging the recipients in decoding the message and associating it with "civilian" manifestations of the same concept. Among the most popular such jargons, the following are worth mentioning as salient in the modern military discourse:

- Idiomatic expressions associated with the concept of "peace": *give peace a chance, peace at any price;*
- Idiomatic expressions associated with the concept of "war": *on the war path, a war of nerves, cold war;*
- Idiomatic expressions associated with the concept of "fight": *to fight a losing battle, fight hand to hand, a running fight, a fighting chance, to fight the good fight;*
- Idiomatic expressions associated with the concept of "shot": *a long shot, a shot in the dark, to call the shots, no more shots in the locker;*
- Idiomatic expressions containing tactical terms: *the best defense is a good offense, to go on the offensive, to be on the defensive, to throw someone on the defensive, to open (up) a new front, to beat a retreat, to steal a march on, to give someone his/her marching orders, to go over the top, a sitting target/a sitting duck, to use brute force;*
- Other military idiomatic expressions: *armed to the teeth, a chink in someone's armor, a Pyrrhic victory, hit the mark, miss the mark, no man's land, a thin red line, off (one's) guard, by main force.*

Another distinctive feature of military communication on the lexical layer is the extensive use of acronyms, which result from the abbreviation of the first components in a phrase or a word, usually individual letters or syllables. Depending on the amount of elements in their composition, acronyms may have one, two, three, four, five or even six components: A (Army), Ju (July), AC (Atlantic Council), AF (Afghan Forces), DPC (Defence Planning Committee), NPA (NATO Parliamentary Assembly), NPG (Nuclear Planning Group), TCC (Temporary Council Committee), NACC (North Atlantic Cooperation Council), NATO (North-Atlantic Treaty Organization), NRFA (NATO-Russia Founding Act), MRBM (Medium-Range Ballistic Missiles), SALT (Strategic Arms Limitations Talks), SFOR (Stabilization Force), PESCO (Permanent Structured

Cooperation), SACEUR (Supreme Allied Commander Europe), STANAG (Standardization Agreement) etc.[2]

One of the proposed objectives of this study at the lexical level is to investigate the manner in which ideological values are made public by consistent use of specialized lexicon and other vocabulary terms particularly coined for this purpose.

## 1.1.3.3. The Semantics of Military Discourse

Military discourse, like any other type of discourse (legal, economic, scientific, politic etc.), contains specialized terminology historically gathered alongside the development of military art, which is continuously changing, due to military (tactics, strategy, geopolitics etc.) and social, political, economic, technical, scientific factors. The evolution of language over time does not only influence military terminology at the structural level, but also brands the semantic content of the words.

The boundary between the common language and the military language is not impenetrable, so a linguistic form may be encountered in the common language and in modern military terminology at the same time. Specialists in the field consider that most of the military terminology is actually composed of the words taken from everyday language, which were "terminologized" and entered the military lexicon with the aim of expressing military notions and concepts (Ploae-Hanganu 1992:78)

The military metalanguage is systemic insofar as it is borrowed from the main lexical pool. This process is underlined by the resemblance existing between the form of military objects and, for instance, parts of the human body, or the logical and functional contiguity of military items and concepts with those already in use in the general language. This phenomenon emphasized the underlying relationship between the term and the linguistic context that generates it, as well as a semantic dependence on the specialized domain it is included in.

Terms such as *muzzle* (gun ~), *mask* (gas ~), *curtain* (fire ~), *vest* (bulletproof ~), *dog* (~ tag), *mess* (~ hall), *petty* (~ officer), *private*, *shell*, *star*, *branch*, are examples of vocabulary items that acquire a military meaning only when assigned to this particular domain. It is the specialized field that certifies their status as military terminology; outside it, they are just common words.

[2] A comprehensive glossary of abbreviations used in NATO documents and publications is AAP-15 (2010), retrievable online from http://www.dtic.mil/dtic/tr/fulltext/u2/a534294.pdf

In addition to the myriad of specialized words that characterize it (i.e., military terminology), the lexicon of military discourse is enriched through diverse modalities. For example, transference of meaning (Pentagon is the name of the House of Defense Ministry and the name of the Ministry itself) or change of meaning ("to acquire" traditionally means "to get", "to obtain", but the military meaning has widened its meaning to "to discover/locate a target").

As noted, military terms may become common words, losing their value as a specialized lexical unit and, conversely, general vocabulary words may become military terms, by borrowing the systemic features of the common terms. In addition, semantic evolutions of military terminology can renovate word meaning and generate polysemy. Terminologists Roman Golovin and Boris Kobrin (1987) argue that the polysemy of specialized language can be determined by the meaning-related changes undergone by the notion being reproduced (in terms of form, content, function, usage). The military discourse is quite populated with polysemantic terms, such as "unit", "security", "armor" etc.

Military discourse, in its dimension of scientific language, must be precise, homogenous, implicature-free, and devoid of wrong or ambiguous meanings. Although polysemy is an inadvisable phenomenon in modern terminology, we have to admit that specialized language is continuously enriched by receiving and validating modern military words that acquire additional meanings, becoming multifaceted within the macro-system of military terminology.

At the discourse level, semantic strategies, employed as a linguistic instrument of managing meaning, are aimed at legitimizing, justifying, naturalizing, rationalizing, authorizing, universalizing, or even denying ideologies. Ideologically-controlled representations (models) of different situations resort to discourse semantics in order to transmit "biased" presentations of standpoints and attitudes, i.e. positive self-presentations of the ingroups versus negative presentations of the outgroups. One stratagem of this kind is implicitness, manifested in that all information that is detrimental to the ingroup remains implicit, while information that is unfavorable to the outgroup is made explicit.

In military discourse, the semantic operation of hyperboles, under- and overstatements, irony, metaphor, euphemisms etc. is closely related to underlying models and social beliefs. Attitudes and positions embedded in the polarization "us" versus "them" may typically be expressed by exaggerating otherwise regular features or normal actions of "us" while using demeaning metaphors that marginalize and belittle "the others". The military discourse is replete with diversely depreciating metaphors that discredit and even dehumanize the "enemy".

Another important discursive materialization of local semantics is variation in levels of generality and specificity when addressing events. The mistakes or errors of the ingroup are presented in euphemistic terms, attributed uncontrollable circumstances, and blamed on external factors, and described in general, abstract terms. Oppositely, when the narrative focuses on the outgroup's attitudes and actions specific details are usually favored. The ideologically controlled purpose of this type of discourse is to transmit the preferred mental models (social cognitions) of the military organization delivering the message.

The strategic deployment of disclaimers in military discourse is yet another example of the manner in which communicative contexts are controlled by core ideologies. In their attempt to produce a good impression and avoid negative reception, the authors of the discourse practice the use of such semantic strategies in order to describe themselves in a positive manner while still transmitting the negative description of the "other", which is veiled in the discourse with the help of language.

When investigating military discourse, as a communicative expression of the values, beliefs and truths belonging to a community of practice, the issue of discourse coherence is critically relevant for anchoring the analysis in a broader setting of shared comprehension. As a semantic characteristic of discourses, Van Dijk argues, "coherence is based on the interpretation of each individual sentence relative to the interpretation of other sentences" (qtd. in Dascălu 2014:12). Within a discourse, there are a number of global semantic structures, which are not directly categorized in terms of links between individual propositions, but rather according to sets of propositions or entire sequences of propositions. According to Yuan Wang and Minghe Guo, who have dedicated extensive research to discourse coherence, "these macro-structures determine the global or overall coherence of a discourse and are in turn determined by the coherence of sequences" (2014:461).

Syntactic and lexical structures are elements that go into the linguistic make up of sentences. Related sentences and clauses express propositions and their properties, consolidate relations between arguments, predicates, modal operators etc. Macro-structures, on the other hand, are not so directly linked to actual sentences, since they are higher level properties characterizing sequences of propositions. In NATO communiqués, for instance, they are often directly expressed, in topical sentences, placed at the beginning or at the end of a passage. Their cognitive function is quite apparent: they deliver the macrostructure of a certain discourse and facilitate comprehension.

Coherence is not restricted to the progressive links between isolated or intercalated propositions. It also relates to the topic of discourse in a particular passage. Topics or semantic macropropositions of discourse outline, in a subjective manner, the most important or most relevant information to be transmitted. The above-mentioned conditions of semantic coherence are relative to the notion of topic. As a discourse feature, topicalization is also subject to ideological management. Ingroups topicalize information that emphasizes their positive self-image and is consistent with their agenda, while demoting negative presentations. Undesirable models of social events will generally be de-topicalized in their discourse. An analysis of the military discourse from this angle will definitely bring light on questions relative to the "aboutness" of sequences of sentences or even whole discourses. Systematic relations between the notion of discourse topic and the semantic representation of the sentences of the discourse can be established if we take into consideration the fact that discourse topics can be made explicit in semantic terms. The same passage or discourse can have one topic or several, theoretically potential topics. It will prove extremely purposeful to dedicate a consistent part of the investigation to underlining the possible topics emerging from the military discourse and to establish whether they are in line with the contemporary ideologies (synchronic analysis) or recurrent in different discourses at different times (diachronic perspective).

The overall meanings (macropropositions) are organized by super-structures, or conventional schemata that usually define an argument or support a point of view. Schematical categories define the order of discourse and signal importance or relevance. In virtue of their role within the discourse, these may also be ideologically manipulated. Variations of importance and relevance are materialized by either giving prominence to positive information within semantically subordinated topics, for example, or by downgrading damaging presentations to a lower level of the schemata.

36

Discourse semantics also involves the logical connection existing between the ordering of sentences and the chronological organization of facts. Van Dijk differentiates between discourse ordering in the case of actions and events and ordering pertaining to the description of states.

"For actions and events, the discourse ordering will be called normal if their temporal and causal ordering corresponds to the linear order of the discourse. For descriptions of states, where the facts all exist at the same time, it will be assumed that a normal ordering corresponds with the general-particular and the whole-part relations between facts." (1977: 97)

In addition to the organization of facts, the author argues, the structure of the discourse is also governed by the ordering of the perceptions and the knowledge about them. This perspective entails a cognitive dimension of semantic coherence, the so-called assumed normality, referring to the fact that the receivers' expectations about the semantic structures of discourse are determined by their own knowledge about the structure of world in general and about the state of affairs or courses of events, in particular.

All things considered, the targeted indicators of linguistic information entailed in the semantic representation of military discourse can be enumerated as follows: specific topical sentences, the relations between macro-propositions and the use of connectives for illustrating such relations, macro-structural presuppositions of sentences. In addition to such elements relative to discourse coherence, the entry point of analysis of military discourse from a semantic perspective should also consider investigating notions such as referential identity (pronominalization, article selection), information distribution (introduction, continuity, expansion, topicalization, functioning) and certain general constraints on the conceptual structure of mode/modality, or time/tense.

## 1.2. The Quantitative Analysis

The quantitative approach was chosen as a supplementary method aimed at enlarging the scope of the present linguistic investigation of military discourse. Coupled with the qualitative interpretation of language in NATO official documents, the quantitative analysis was conducted so as to supplement the critical discourse examination by offering visual and statistics-based representations of the manner in which language is employed in the targeted military texts. Working within the framework of the above-mentioned elements of the analytical pattern, the quantitative study integrates a flexible model of analysis constructed on the basis of specific lexical, semantic and structural indices[3].

## 1.2.1. The Model

The quantitative investigation preferred for this paper consists of an automated approach to discourse analysis, heavily drawing on the importance of technology to facilitate research on language. The selected model, designed with the help of the researchers who developed the ReaderBench multilingual framework, is an automated system that measures textual complexity, by integrating the most common indices from other systems such as *Lexile* (MetaMetrics), *ATOS* (Renaissance Learning), *DRP Analyzer* (Questar Assessment, Inc.), *REAP* (Carnegie Mellon University), *SourceRater* (Educational Testing service), *Coh-Metrix* (University of Memphis). The model proposed by Jessica Nelson et al. recommends both an abductive and an inductive experimental approach aimed at mapping discourses with focus on textual complexity, cohesion and semantics. In line with Nelson's model, Dascălu et al. designed a framework that consists of three layers: (a) linguistic resources that provide solid language background knowledge and can be used to train the semantic models and compute various measures; (b) linguistic services used to process and append semantic meta-information to text resources, and (c) linguistic applications that rely on machine learning and data mining techniques (2017:495-496).

Designed as a cohesion-based discourse analysis, the model facilitates the identification of the textual interconnection that enables the selection of discourse strands constructed on the basis of topical and semantic coherence at various levels. The model adopts a multi-layered approach consisting of three types of nodes: a central node (the document representing the entire reading material); blocks (a generic entity reflecting paragraphs from the initial text); and sentences, the main units of analysis, seen as collections of words and grammatical structures obtained after the initial processing. In addition to the focus placed on cohesion, the notion of topics also emerges as relevant for the construction and application of the model. Topics, identified as being the key concepts relevant for the

---

[3] An article entitled "Exploring Differences in NATO Discourses using the ReaderBench Framework" is going to be published in the following issue of the Transylvanian Review. The theoretical elements and the subsequent discussions included in the article originate in the section dedicated to the quantitative analysis in this paper.

discourse, are essential in facilitating a general perspective on the cognitive interface, but also in observing emerging points of interest or shifts of focus within discourse threads. The extraction of the topics from a specific discourse is underpinned by different elements of the analysis and is conducted at different levels (the entire document or separate paragraphs). The relevance of the concepts inherent in the analyzed discourse is discovered by identifying semantic similarities at the level of paragraphs or fragments of text (local coherence) or throughout the entire document (global coherence).

This specific model was chosen in virtue of its complexity and versatility. One of its biggest advantages is that the application of new and various analysis tools is the goal of the investigation, and not the starting point; consequently, accent is placed on the dynamicity of the language. The results of the proposed statistical model are expected to complement and substantiate the qualitative analysis with statistical data that validates the work hypotheses and offers a more comprehensive answer to the research question.

## 1.2.2. The Method

The method applied relies heavily on automated instruments employed so as to specifically address the secondary research question, specifically designed for the quantitative investigation. The statistical data aimed at showing how the concepts of integrative and adversarial power are lexically and semantically operationalized in NATO discourse between 1949 and 2018. The application of specific analysis indices targeted the identification of dynamicity at the level of discourse construction, in terms of readability, cohesion, syntactic dependencies, structure, lexical variation, and uniqueness. The main objective of the quantitative analysis was to demonstrate that the operationalization of the concepts of integrative and adversarial power has suffered discursive modifications visible in NATO documents produced during the Cold War and in the years after the end of the Cold War.

To this end, the corpus on which the analysis was conducted consisted of 184 independent documents extracted from NATO's discourses between 1949 and 2018, categorized according to two criteria – period and type. The first period covers the 41 years between 1949 and 1990, while the second focuses on the documents issued after the end of the Cold War until the present moment, 1991 to 2018. The documents selected for the investigation are summit and ministerial meetings final communiqués that are imbued with discursive conceptualizations of integrative and adversarial power. Table 1 presents the quantitative analysis corpus statistics.

**Table 1** Quantitative analysis corpus statistics

| Period | Integrative power | Adversarial power |
|---|---|---|
| 1949-1990 | 40 | 41 |
| 1991-2018 | 66 | 37 |
| No. of documents | 106 | 78 |
| **OVERALL TOTAL** | **184** | |

In Table 2, the corpus was generally described in terms of mean and standard deviations (Stdev) for paragraphs, sentences, and word counts.

**Table 2** General corpus statistics

| Type | Period | N | Paragraphs Mean (Stdev) | Sentences Mean (Stdev) | Words Mean (Stdev) |
|---|---|---|---|---|---|
| Adversarial | 1949-1990 | 41 | 17.71 (7.47) | 50.32 (21.46) | 1323.22 (571.86) |
| | 1991-2018 | 37 | 12.49 (6.02) | 47.16 (21.18) | 1233.22 (531.95) |
| Integrative | 1949-1990 | 40 | 16.08 (4.99) | 48.93 (17.03) | 1270.40 (416.79) |
| | 1991-2018 | 66 | 12.02 (5.38) | 43.53 (22.32) | 1168.88 (597.34) |

## 1.2.3. The Indices

The ReaderBench framework implements various metrics and categories of textual complexity indices, ranging from classic readability formulas, surface indices, morphology and syntax, semantics, and discourse structure. Figure 1 depicts an overview of the multi-layered textual complexity model that includes: a) the simplest surface measures that account only for the form of the text; b) syntactic indices computed at sentence level that consider the distribution of different parts of speech or of syntactic dependencies; c) semantics and complex discourse structure that are mostly derived from the CNA model; and d) word complexity focused on individual tokens and spanning across all previous levels by including different facets of the difficulty of each word taken individually, or within its semantic context.

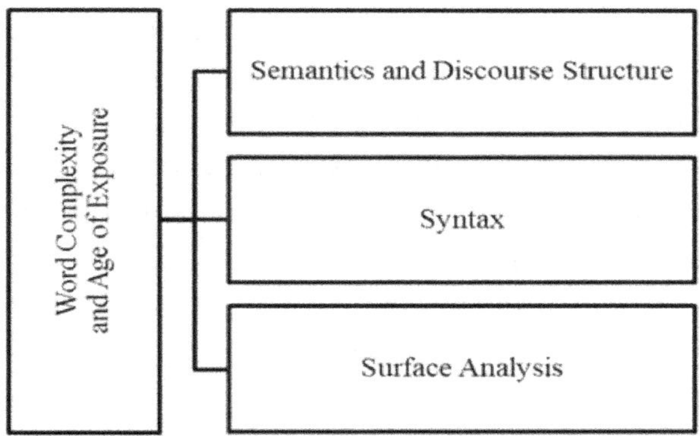


**Fig. 1** ReaderBench multi-layered textual complexity model

The aforementioned indices are language independent, and thus only specific semantic models need to be trained once the Natural Language Processing (NLP) pipeline is in place, whereas some indices are language-specific and require additional NLP techniques to be set up. ReaderBench includes a comprehensive NLP pipeline, originally drawn from Chris Manning and Hinrich Schütze, that considers: a) stop-word elimination, b) the reduction of inflected forms to their corresponding lemmas, c) named entity recognition, d) the annotation of each word with its corresponding part of speech tag, e) dependency parsing, and f) co-reference resolution (Manning & Schütze, 1999).

The indices applied to the current quantitative investigation are briefly described below.

*Surface indices* measure the form of the text. The analysis of the basic traits of texts is derived from initial studies conducted by researchers such as Ellis Page (1968) or William_Wresch (1993). The most relevant surface indices are word length, paragraph length and sentence length (average values and standard deviations), measured in terms of the number of characters, words or unique words; the number of sentences and paragraphs; the number of commas per sentence and paragraph; the number of unique content words per sentence and paragraph; word entropy. The underlying assumption for the interpretation of this category is that the more diverse concepts a text contains, the more complex the text is.

*Syntactic and morphologic indices* are calculated at word and sentence level. Word- and sentence-based analyses, including part of speech tagging and dependency parsing, are instrumental for providing two different complexity assessment schemes: a) normalized frequencies of each part of speech and b) structural indices derived from the parsing tree. Such indices analyze, for example, the morphological values of words (nouns, pronouns, adjectives, adverbs, verbs, conjunctions, prepositions) and the types of dependencies that typify their relation. According to Vicenzo Gervasi and Vicenzo Ambriola, an increased number of specific semantic dependencies or a higher maximum depth indicate a more complex discourse structure, yielding increased textual complexity (2002:212). Although nouns and verbs are the most prevalent morphological elements, the analysis is not limited to the investigation of these parts of speech but also takes under scrutiny prepositions, adjectives, and adverbs, considering that they are also indicative of a more elaborate and complex text structure. In addition, the use of pronouns might reveal a more intricate and connected structure of the discourse by revealing potential pronominal co-references.

*Word complexity indices* focus on the complexity of words but goes way beyond their form. The complexity of a word is assessed according to the number of syllables and the difference between various flectional forms or depending on the distance between the lemma and stem. The depth of the hypernym tree and the polysemy of content words are also indicative of the complexity of lexical ontology of targeted discourses. Under this indices category, ReaderBench considers the following individual word complexity measures: a) mean syllable count per word: longer, more complex words tend to be perceived as being more difficult; b) mean polysemy count per word: words with multiple senses are more difficult and require more contextual information for disambiguation; c) average and maximum distance within the hypernym tree to the ontology root: more general words are closer to the root, whereas more specific words tend to have a longer path; and d) differences between the inflected form, the lemma and the stem: words with longer prefixes and suffixes tend to be more complex. All word indices are averaged at document, paragraph, and sentence levels by considering only the lemmas of content words (i.e., dictionary words, not included in the stop-words lists, and having as part of speech one of the following: noun, verb, adverb or adjective).

*Semantic cohesion indices*, mostly focusing on the usage of diverse types of connectives and transitions (temporal, addition, contrast, opposition, condition, concession, reason and purpose, cause and effect etc.), on the complexity and length of lexical chains, and on different layers of cohesion (inter-/intra- paragraphs, paragraph-document, start-middle, middle-end, start-end) are extremely instrumental in identifying and explaining interconnection, intertextuality, consistency and uniformity of ideas, notions, concepts and cognitive elements that characterize discourse strands and validate their categorization. Cohesion relates to the perception of a text's overall quality and coherence, and may be present at both local (i.e., sequential relations between neighboring sentences) and global (i.e., relations between paragraphs) levels, according to Scott Crossley et al. (2011) and Danielle McNamara et al. (2010).

ReaderBench is based on the extensive use of the Cohesion Network Analysis, which provides an in-depth assessment of the interconnectedness of the discourse. From a computational perspective, Dascălu argues, cohesion is viewed as a relatedness measure between text chunks computed using multiple semantic models that complement one another (2014:69). Under the CNA model, local and global cohesion is explained in terms of the strength of intra- and inter-paragraph links extracted from the cohesion graph. Crossley et al. developed automated measures of global document cohesion flow based on a CNA that considers the adequacy of paragraph sequences – i.e., the degree to which one paragraph succeeds the previous one in a cohesive manner. The cohesion flow measures take into consideration the order of different paragraphs and the manner in which they combined to give the document a unified meaning. The more cohesive a text is, the easier to comprehend.

Entity-density features measure the manner in which the number of entities within a text influences the cognitive resources needed for their understanding. Named entities introduce conceptual information required for contextualizing the content of a document. Computing counts of unique or repeated entities help evaluate the degree of comprehensibility of a text, given that the larger the number of unique entities (per paragraph or sentence), the more complex the text is.

In addition, other indices such as dialogism, rhythm, or cue phrases have also been applied in order to identify and explain diachronic changes in NATO discourse.

The application of the polyphonic model represents discourse as an interaction between different points of view (i.e., "voices") that relate to each other, an approach pioneered by Ştefan Trăuşan-Matu et al. (2007). Voices are identified in the form of semantic chains of related words spanning throughout the text. A number of textual complexity indices are calculated in order to measure the effect of each voice and to establish the level of intersection between voices: a) distribution per sentence or paragraph, including span (distance between the last and the first occurrence of words from the same voice), b) recurrence (average and standard deviation of the distance between subsequent words pertaining to the same voice), and c) overlap measures (e.g., co-occurrences or mutual information). (Dascălu, 2014; Dascălu, et al. 2018).

Trăuşan-Matu et al. (2014) also consider rhythm to be an important feature of discourse. Text-wise, rhythm is measured in terms of its communicative purposes, with the help of several indices: a) the average number of stressed syllables and of rhythmic units in each sentence, b) the number of deviations from dominant structures divided by total number of syllabic segments, c) the rhythmic index, d) the frequency of the maximum rhythmic index, e) the maximum number of consecutive unstressed syllables, and f) the number of alliterations and assonances in a text searching sentence by sentence.

Cue phrases are used to quantify the usage of different types of pronouns (e.g., first, second, third, interrogative, or indefinite) and connectives (e.g., conjunctions, contrasts, sentence linking, or conditions), offering a more in-depth understanding of the structure of each sentence or paragraph, and their degree of complexity.

44

Last but not least, the ReaderBench framework integrates specific word lists that capture particular semantic valences, namely: General Inquirer (GI), Lasswell dictionary, SenticNet, Affective Norms for English Words (ANEW), Geneva Affect Label Coder (GALC), Linguistic Inquiry and Word Count (LIWC) and EmoLex or NRC Word-Emotion Association Lexicon.

For the present quantitative analysis, more than 800 complexity indices, including all word-list indices, were generated Using *ReaderBench* framework. The underlying semantic models were trained using The Corpus of Contemporary American English (COCA) corpus.

# Chapter 2

## The Corpus

The aim of this section is to explain the rationale behind the choice of the corpus, based on theoretical and empirical guidelines found in specialized literature. Although apparently facilitated by the transparency of the database, as the majority of the analyzed documents have been retrieved from NATO's online archives, the selection of the corpus was somehow hindered by the time span chosen for the analysis (70 years), by the comprehensive collection of documents (over 1000), by the size and accessibility of archives (some of which are outdated or contain missing links), and by the topical variety of the texts (over 25 thematic categories and more than 150 topics). Dealing with large files, navigating through a notable topic variety, and managing an impressive database were factors that needed to be dealt with by appealing to theory-related as well as empirical methods for organizing research.

### 2.1.1. Corpus-Related Issues

In the definition of Douglas Biber, "corpus-linguistics is a research approach aimed at supporting empirical investigations of language variation and use" (2012:1). The results of this practical approach have proven to be extremely relevant, valid, feasible, and pertinent. Linguistic studies typically employ two main research methods: "corpus-based" and "corpus-driven" techniques. Elena Tognini-Bonelli (2001) posits that the underlying distinction between the first two types resides in the difference between deductive and inductive approaches. While corpus-based research methodology essentially involves a deductive approach in which a given corpus acts as a catalyst helping to validate or reject a pre-set theoretical paradigm, the corpus-driven approach is inductive in that it chooses a targeted corpus and seeks to generalize a theory or to validate hypotheses. Discourse analysis, Paul Baker (2006) proposes, may use either or both. When the research circumstances allow for both corpus-based and corpus-driven analyses, the researcher may hybridize the two approaches combining the merits of deduction and induction at the same time.

Historically and methodologically related to the discipline of discourse studies, corpus-assisted investigations are particularly relevant when combining qualitative and quantitative interpretations. Especially relevant for supplementing the intensive critical examination facilitated by CDA with a computer-based architecture based on carefully selected algorithms of analysis, corpus-assisted discourse analysis investigates and compares characteristics of specific discourse types, while the analysis integrates the techniques and tools advanced by corpus linguistics. These include compiling specialized corpora and examining individual words or word-cluster frequency lists, comparing keyword lists and discursive concordances.

The choice of the appropriate corpus analysis techniques was mainly informed by the belief that the linguistic investigation of power dynamics in military discourse could greatly benefit from a combination of the three mentioned methods. Investigating power essentially means examining a social construct that is deployed, among other media, through discourse and language. Meaning is socially created as a cumulative effect of language use; by collecting and analyzing examples of a specific discourse construction (i.e., of power), the cumulative effect becomes visible and thus validates the meaning. Therefore, the qualitative analysis is both corpus-based and corpus-driven, given that the corpus data was used to validate or refute my hypotheses about the operationalization of power dynamics in NATO discourse and, at the same time, the corpus itself represented the sole source of my theories about power and NATO language.

The quantitative approach balances the critical interpretation in that it aims at validating the qualitative findings by supplementing them with statistically reliable and generalizable results. To this purpose, the corpus-assisted methodology was instrumental for describing and explaining language phenomena by identifying patterns or, conversely, mere occurrences. The algorithm used for the quantitative analysis emulates the model proposed by Reader Bench and has been described in detail in the following section of the paper.

## 2.1.2. Selecting the Corpus

Both qualitative and quantitative analysis have adopted an intertextual reading of the materials, which focuses on how texts relate to other texts by simultaneously constructing legitimacy for discursive re-presentation and re-interpretation. Much of the research has been dedicated to identifying patters among different interventions across a timeline, and therefore intertextuality here allows for a better documentation of how different discourses of power relate to each other.

First, the empirical material used as basis for the analysis is primarily composed of NATO official documents resulted from 114 Ministerial Meetings (63 at the level of the Ministers of Defence and 51 at the level of Foreign Ministers) and 30 Summits, which occurred between 1949 and 2018. I chose to investigate this type of texts in an attempt to locate specific communicative events through which official actors use language to express power. The timeframe that covers the material being studied starts with the Washington Treaty, the document that reified the military ideology of the emerging military organization that became the North Atlantic Treaty Organization in 1949 and ends in the present, with the latest NATO event, the July 2018 Summit. The timespan covered is of almost seventy years, an extensive period that has yielded a collection of approximately 1000 documents, in the form of Strategic Concepts, Final Communiqués, Declarations, Statements, Plans, Basic Texts, Official Texts, etc.

All the identified documents have been manually introduced in a table containing the temporal and spatial references of the communicative event (date and place of the Summits and Ministerial Meetings) and a list of all public texts produced on these occasions, with the official title of the documents and a hyperlink that traces them back to the virtual space where they were originally published (NATO's official site/online archives).

Secondary data is composed of a number of 100 speeches, addresses, statements, press conferences and articles, collected from mainstream newspapers and magazines (*Chicago Tribune, Washington Post, Wall Street Journal, The Economist, The New York Times, Foreign Policy, Foreign Affairs, International Affairs, International Herald Tribune*) or official sources such as the Department of State Bulletins (DOSB), Foreign Relations of the United States (FRUS) or United States Information Service (USIS). Although these texts are not necessarily analyzed using a methodical discourse analysis framework, they were used as references and discussed with the aim of reflecting and clarifying the historical, political, and social context that generated the discourses in the main corpus.

After having identified the patterns of power relations that are more prevalent in NATO discourse and after framing the research question and the sub-questions, all collected material was analyzed accordingly, in an attempt to validate or overturn the work hypotheses formulated in the introductory part. The main objective of the analysis was to examine the manner in which the three different patterns of power dynamics are operationalized through language, by sorting out common discursive configurations of unity, opposition or dominance and by discovering intertextual references that validate the existence of a communicative pattern representative for these discourses.

## 2.1.3. Sampling

Given the magnitude of the collection of both primary and secondary source documents, only texts that emerged as relevant for the analysis of power dynamics have been selected. Starting from the premise that context is of paramount importance, especially when conducting a three-level critical discourse analysis (social, cognitive, and linguistic), key events on the timeline were first identified; subsequently, the diachronic approach was supplemented with the synchronicity generated by simultaneous discourses.

The relevant examples were selected on the basis of topical categories, assembled after running keyword searches and extracting sets of key items that occurred with a relevant frequency. From these categories, pertinent samples have been carefully chosen in relation to the social, political, and historical context that generated them and used in the paper so as to illustrate the patterns that constitute the common thread in each type of discourse. These emerged as belonging to three categories of power relations: adversarial, integrative and predominant, exemplified in as many discourse strands.

More specifically, for the qualitative analysis, the discourse of power relations investigated in this chapter has been exemplified in detail by a sample of 70 primary sources, drawn from a comprehensive collection of 76 documents published after Summits and 606 official texts resulting from Ministerial Meetings. The specific discourses have been collected in multiple "discourse strands", each branching out into topical threads, subsequently analyzed as specific subcorpora, composed of the discourses they are part of or linked to thematically. Such a manner of investigation was selected because: it allows for topical continuity; it offers strong (and often explicit) intertextual links among the elements of the discourse strand; it provides relative temporal proximity when anchoring discourses on a timeline, which advantageously makes discourses not only temporally but also topically bounded.

Within the corpus, there are three discourse strands defined according to the type of power they illustrate. The discourse of unity is constructed on the concept of integrative or relational power; the discourse of opposition illustrates the dynamics of adversarial power relations; the discourse strand of U.S. predominant power pivots on manifestations of America's referent, expert, and legitimate power in NATO discourse. Each discourse strand is then split off into a number of topical threads, assembled on thematic and lexical bases, yielding 32 examples for the discourse strand of unity, 30 discourse samples for the discourse strand of opposition, and 33 illustrative documents for the discourse strand of U.S. predominant power (primary sources and secondary data). The discourse strands have been treated as separate communicative entities; however, they are often invested with more than one type of power relations. Furthermore, the topical threads overlap at times, meaning that themes such as nuclear issues, NATO enlargement, or terrorism have been approached from distinctive positions of power, either adversarial or integrative, or both.

Although the corpus is monogeneric, the quantitative investigation was aimed at offering a contrastive comparison of the manner in which the concepts of integrative and adversarial power were lexically and semantically operationalized before and after the end of the Cold War, a moment that is considered a cornerstone in the ideological evolution of the North Atlantic Treaty Organization. The quantitative analysis pivots on the study of integrative and adversarial power. In the case of the two types of power under examination, the discourses were again categorized on a timeline, according to two time periods: 1949-1990 and 1991-2018. The application of these criteria generated a corpus of 184 texts: 106 documents for integrative power (40 before and 66 after the end of the Cold War) and 78 documents for adversarial power (41 pre- and 37 post-Cold War).

The linguistic analysis envisaged the examination of a broad range of texts but conducting an exhaustive analysis of power dynamics in NATO discourse falls short of a realistic endeavor. This is due to both the limits set by the frames of the dissertation and also because it is close to impossible to locate and access all NATO texts, some of which are still classified to this day.

50

Chapter 3

# Representations of Power Dynamics in NATO Military Discourse

The most comprehensive section of the book is dedicated to the analysis of the power dynamics in military discourse, aimed at locating, identifying, explaining and analyzing discursive patterns of power relations with the aim of discovering intertextual references that validate the existence of a communicative pattern representative for these discourses.

The quantitative analysis of the NATO discourses is dedicated a special subchapter, consisting of an in-depth study of the manner in which integrative and adversarial power has been diachronically operationalized through language. The comparative approach focuses on two distinct periods (1949-1990 and 1991-2018) and targets the sorting out of the similarities and differences between the discursive configurations of unity and opposition, offering both a longitudinal and a transversal analysis of NATO language from a statistical perspective.

## 3.1. Diachronic Representations of Power Dynamics – A Quantitative Approach

As mentioned before, the purpose of conducting a statistical analysis in addition to the investigative dimension of the CDA was to validate the qualitative findings by supplementing the critical discourse analysis with statistically reliable and generalizable results.

The investigation of the differences in the writing styles of NATO discourses was based on statistical interpretations that targeted the type (integrative versus adversarial) and time period (two intervals between 1949 and 2018) in which they were produced. The study focused on the lexical, semantic and cohesive properties of the analyzed documents, by offering an answer to the quantitative research question: How are the concepts of integrative and adversarial power linguistically operationalized in NATO discourse between 1949 and 2018?

First, all variable indices reported by ReaderBench were verified for linguistic coverage (i.e., if an index is representative for at least 20% of the documents) and for normality, and those that were not representative or demonstrated non-normality were removed. Multicollinearity was then assessed as pair-wise correlations ($r > .90$); if writing style properties demonstrated multicollinearity, the index that demonstrated the strongest effect in the model was retained for the final analysis. Finally, three multivariate analyses of variance (MANOVAs) were conducted to examine whether the textual complexity features indicative of writing styles differed across discourse type and period.

In the first stage of the processing, 91 textual complexity indices generated by the ReaderBench framework were eliminated due to a low linguistic coverage. Most removed indices referred to specific elements which are not frequently encountered in NATO discourse, such as:

1. Words pertaining to specific word lists with low coverage of at least 1% and below 20%:

   - Pleasure/Enjoyment, Disappointment, Happiness, Gratitude, Feeling love, Disgust, Surprise, Relief, Anxiety, Lust, Pride, Sadness, Hatred, Desperation, Shame and Negative categories from GALC (Scherer 2005)
   - Affloss (words for affect loss and indifference), Wlbgain (gain in well-being), Notlw (denial), Rcrelig (religion), Wlbpt (concern for well-being), Anomie (anarchy, disillusion), Enlloss (enlightment loss) and Rcloss (rectitude loss) categories from Lasswell (Laswell and Namenwirth 1969)
   - Arousal dimension from ANEW (Bradley and Lang 1999)
   - Ipadj (adjectives referring to relations between people), Male/ Female (words referring to men/women and social roles associated with men/women; also used as a marker in disambiguation), Think (words referring to the presence or absence of rational thought processes), Ani (words referring to animals, insects etc.), Ought (words indicating moral imperatives), Food (words referring to food), Nonadlt (references to infants through adolescence), Card (cardinal words) and Say (word for say and tell) categories from the GI (Stone et al. 1966);

2. Words pertaining to specific word lists that have no occurrences:

   - Envy, Guilt, Joy, Contempt, Jealousy, Irritation, Compassion,

Admiration/Awe, Humility, Dissatisfaction categories from GALC;

- Self, Color, You and Our categories from GI;

3. Lexical dependencies according to the taxonomy used within the Universal Dependencies corpora v2, with a low frequency of occurrence: unspecified dependency (dep), describing a weird grammatical construction (19%), concessions (15%), clausal subject passive occurrences (csubjpass), (4%), and parataxis, which is a discourse-like equivalent of coordination, describing relations between a word, often the main predicate of a sentence and other elements (3%);

4. Lexical dependencies which are not encountered in any document: second person (reference to an interlocutor), case (case-marking elements treated as separate syntactic words – prepositions, postpositions, clitic case markers), copulas (function words used to link a subject to a non-verbal predicate), discourse (elements – interjections, other particles – that are not clearly linked to the structure of the sentence), dislocated (fronted or postponed elements that do not fulfill the usual core grammatical relations of a sentence), foreign (foreign phrases that cannot be given a compositional analysis), goes with (a relation between two or more parts of a words that are separated in a not so well-edited text), iobj (indirect object), list (usually characteristic for web or email signatures, where strings of items are listed and modify the previous one), mwe (multiword expressions), names (multiword proper names with no clear internal syntactic structure) remnant (relations that provide a satisfactory treatment of ellipses, where a predicational or verbal head gets elided), reparandum (overridden disfluency), root (grammatical relations indicating the root of a sentence) and vocative (marking a dialogue participant in a text – common to conversations, newsgroups, postings etc.).

Secondly, normality was checked in terms of Kurtosis and Skewness whose absolute values need to be below or equal to 2; all variables exhibiting higher values were disregarded in follow-up analyses.

Third of all, all variables were tested using Levene's test of equality of error variances and those indices for which the resulting p-values are significant (p < .05) were disregarded as they exhibited a difference between the variances in the population. Thus, 341 indices were retained and were entered into a Multivariate Analysis of Variance (MANOVAs) (Garson, 2015) that was conducted to examine whether the documents' properties differ across document's type (integrative and adversarial) and period (1949-1990 and 1991-2018). There was a significant difference, Wilks' $\lambda\lambda = .693$, $F(14, 167) = 5.274$, $p < .001$, and partial $\eta2 = .307$. The textual complexity indices from Table 3 present in descending order of effect size the variables that were significantly different between the two types and time periods. The most predictive indices explained considerably more variance in terms of period (partial $\eta2 = .473$, $p < .001$) in contrast to type (partial $\eta2 = .208$, $p < .001$), denoting that there were higher differences in time than between types.

**Table 3** Tests of between-subjects effects for significantly different indices

| Textual complexity index | Adversarial 1949-1990 Mean (SD) | Adversarial 1991-2018 Mean (SD) | Integrative 1949-1990 Mean (SD) | Integrative 1991-2018 Mean (SD) | F | p | Partial $\eta^2$ |
|---|---|---|---|---|---|---|---|
| Average number of words within a specific list per sntence (Means GI) | 0.84 (0.20) | 0.71 (0.20) | 0.77 (0.22) | 0.88 (0.24) | 12.459 | .001 | .065 |
| Sentence standard deviation in terms of unique content words | 6.70 (1.22) | 6.18 (1.45) | 5.77 (0.92) | 6.36 (1.28) | 8.819 | .003 | .047 |
| Average number of words within a specific list per sentence (Academ GI) | 0.06 (0.06) | 0.06 (0.05) | 0.08 (0.05) | 0.05 (0.04) | 7.844 | .006 | .042 |
| Average word length (characters) | 7.50 (0.16) | 7.72 (0.17) | 7.56 (0.15) | 7.64 (0.18) | 7.316 | .007 | .039 |

| Textual complexity index | Adversarial 1949-1990 Mean (SD) | Adversarial 1991-2018 Mean (SD) | Integrative 1949-1990 Mean (SD) | Integrative 1991-2018 Mean (SD) | F | p | Partial $\eta^2$ |
|---|---|---|---|---|---|---|---|
| Average number of words within a specific list per sentence (Space GI) | 0.29 (0.13) | 0.22 (0.12) | 0.25 (0.10) | 0.26 (0.10) | 6.423 | .012 | .034 |
| Average number of words within a specific list per sentence (Virtue GI) | 1.23 (0.34) | 1.24 (0.33) | 1.37 (0.33) | 1.65 (0.43) | 6.043 | .015 | .032 |
| Average AOA score per paragraph (Bird) | 399.43 (14.48) | 389.46 (14.38) | 390.96 (15.85) | 393.45 (19.73) | 5.987 | .015 | .032 |
| Weighted average start-middle cohesion (Wu-Palmer semantic distance in WordNet) | 0.57 (0.07) | 0.62 (0.06) | 0.52 (0.08) | 0.62 (0.07) | 5.867 | .016 | .032 |
| Average number of words within a specific list per sentence (Ovrst GI) | 1.06 (0.28) | 0.96 (0.33) | 1.06 (0.27) | 1.21 (0.4) | 5.648 | .019 | .030 |
| Average number of words within a specific list per sentence (Strong GI) | 2.88 (0.57) | 2.88 (0.52) | 2.75 (0.56) | 3.13 (0.59) | 4.978 | .027 | .027 |
| Average number of words within a specific list per sentence (Quan GI) | 0.33 (0.11) | 0.28 (0.10) | 0.28 (0.10) | 0.31 (0.11) | 4.842 | .029 | .026 |

| Textual complexity index | Adversarial 1949-1990 Mean (SD) | Adversarial 1991-2018 Mean (SD) | Integrative 1949-1990 Mean (SD) | Integrative 1991-2018 Mean (SD) | F | p | Partial $\eta^2$ |
|---|---|---|---|---|---|---|---|
| Average number of words within a specific list per sentence (Econ 2 GI) | 0.43 (0.14) | 0.50 (0.19) | 0.48 (0.18) | 0.68 (0.24) | 4.74 | .031 | .026 |
| Sentence relevance score standard deviation | 6.37 (1.38) | 6.35 (1.78) | 5.42 (1.28) | 6.39 (1.86) | 4.025 | .046 | .022 |
| Average number of unique verbs per paragraph | 8.48 (2.15) | 11.57 (3.35) | 8.97 (2.06) | 10.42 (2.96) | 3.992 | .047 | .022 |

In order to better understand the differences, Figure 2 presents the profile plots computed using the estimated marginal means of each textual complexity index.

Average number of words within a specific list per sentence (Means GI)

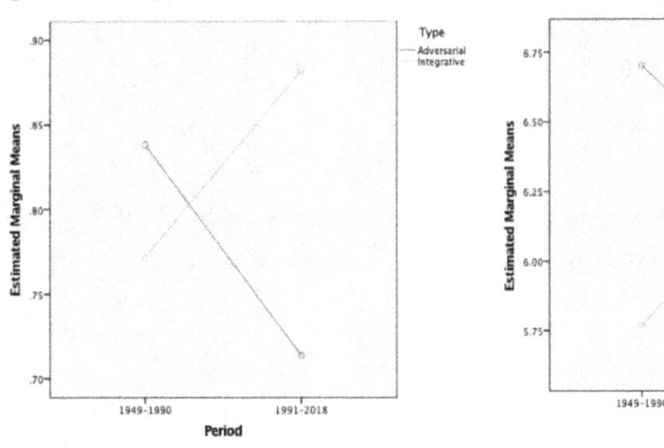



Sentence standard deviation in terms of unique content words

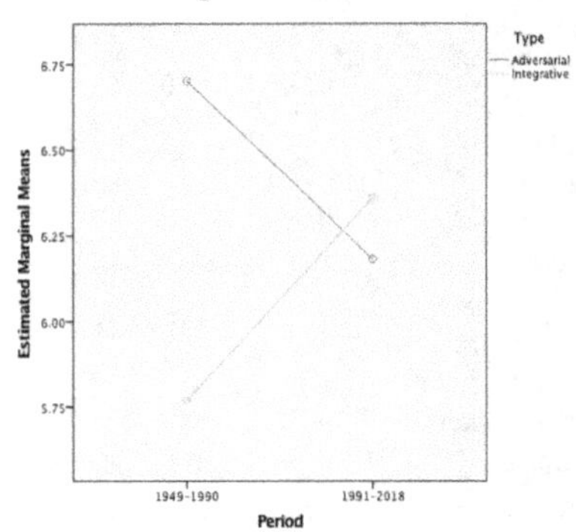

Average number of words within a specific list per sentence (Academ GI)

Average word length (characters)

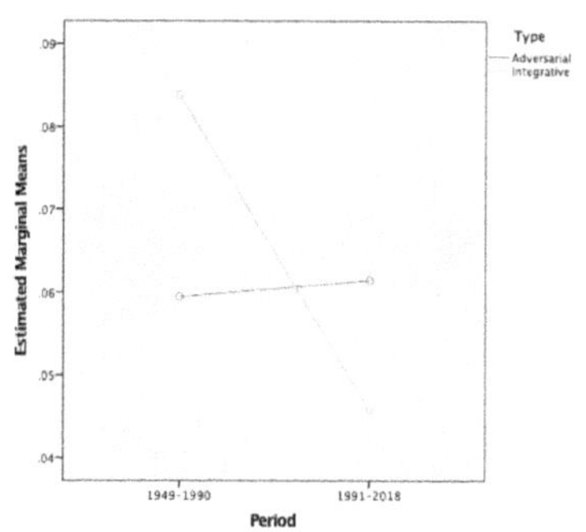
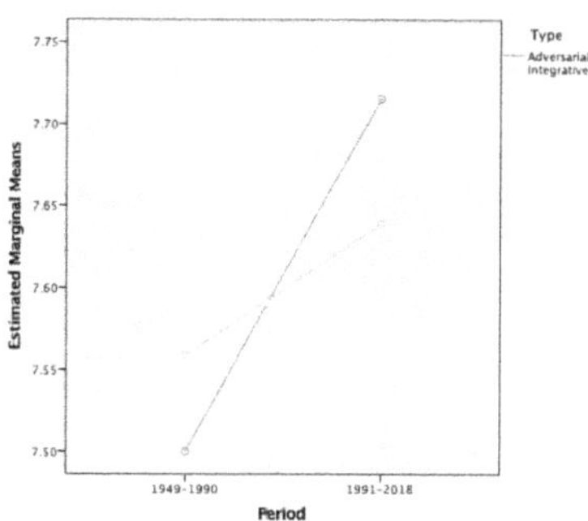

Average number of words within a specific list per sentence (Space GI)

Average number of words within a specific list per sentence (Virtue GI)

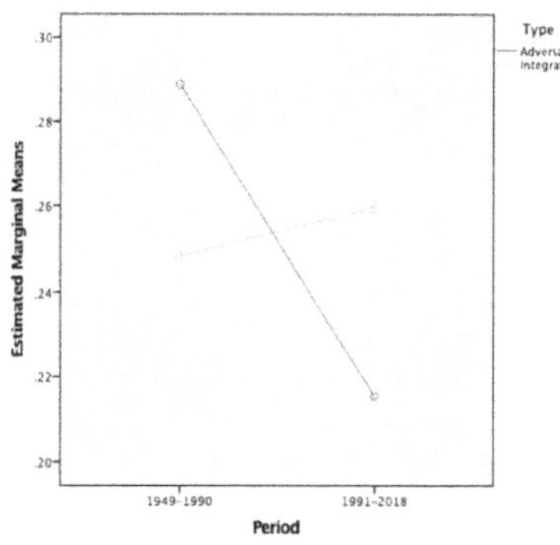
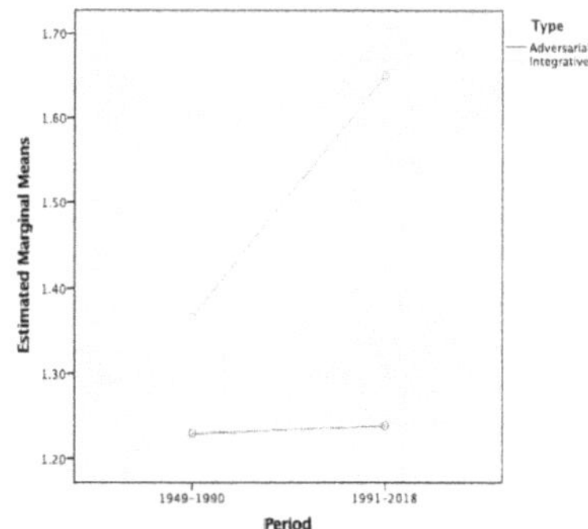

Average AOA score per paragraph (Bird)

Weighted average start-middle cohesion (Wu-Palmer semantic distance in WordNet)

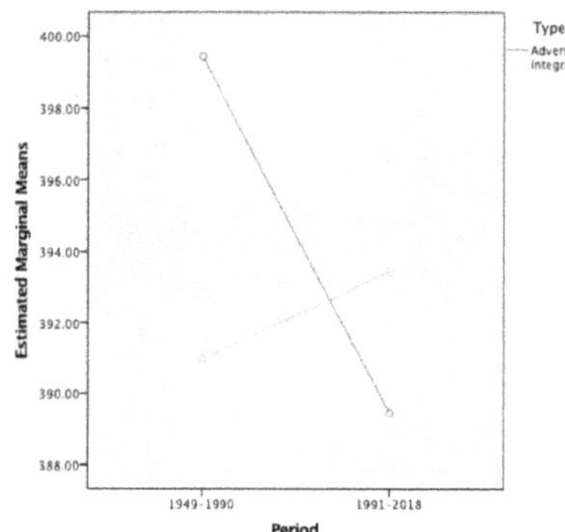
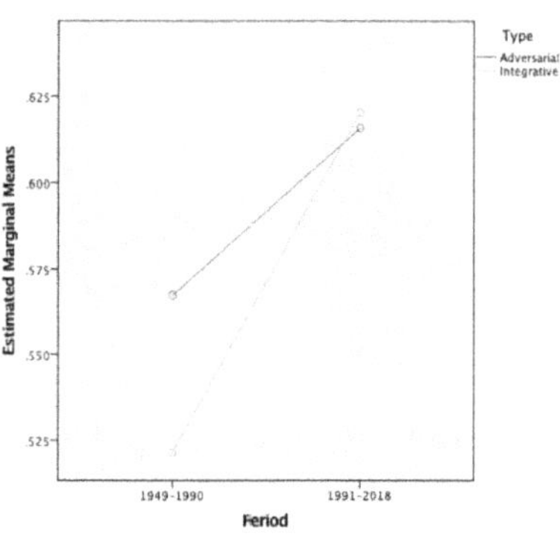

Average number of words within a specific list per sentence (Ovrst GI)

Average number of words within a specific list per sentence (Strong GI)

Average number of words within a specific list per sentence (Quan GI)

Average number of words within a specific list per sentence (Econ 2 GI)

Sentence relevance score standard deviation

Average number of unique verbs per paragraph

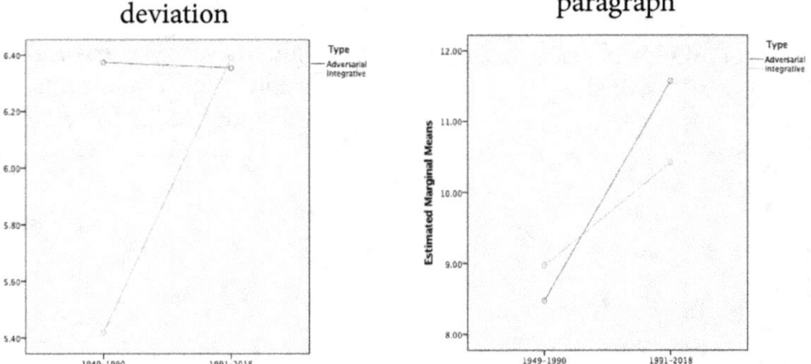

**Fig. 2** Profile plots based on the estimated marginal means of each textual complexity index

The final stage of the process consisted of a stepwise Discriminant Function Analysis (DFA), performed to predict the type and period of a given text based on the underlying writing style properties. The DFA retained five variables as significant predictors:

1. Sentence standard deviation in terms of unique content words;
2. Average number of words within a specific list per sentence (Academ GI);
3. Average word length (characters);
4. Average number of words within a specific list per sentence (Virtue GI);
5. Weighted average start-middle cohesion (Wu-Palmer semantic distance in WordNet).

All remaining variables were removed and considered non-significant predictors. The results prove that the DFA using these five indices significantly differentiated texts, Wilks' $\lambda\lambda$ = .849, $\chi^2$(df = 3) = 29.301, $p < .001$. The DFA correctly allocated 104 (21+21+23+39) of 184 documents from the total set, resulting in an accuracy of 56.50% (the chance level for this analysis is 25%; see figure 3 and Table 4). For the leave-one-out cross-validation (LOOCV), the discriminant analysis allocated 101 (20+20+23+38) of 184 texts for an accuracy of 54.90% (see the confusion matrix reported in Table 4 for detailed results).

| | | Predicted Group Membership | | | |
| --- | --- | --- | --- | --- | --- |
| | Type and Oeriod | Adversarial 1949-1990 | Adversarial 1991-2018 | Integrative 1949-1990 | Integrative 1991-2018 |
| Whole set | Adversarial 1949-1990 | 21 | 5 | 9 | 6 |
| | Adversarial 1991-2018 | 5 | 21 | 4 | 7 |
| | Integrative 1949-1990 | 10 | 4 | 23 | 3 |
| | Integrative 1991-201 | 11 | 10 | 6 | 39 |
| Cross-validated | Adversarial 1949-1990 | 20 | 6 | 9 | 6 |
| | Adversarial 1991-2018 | 4 | 20 | 6 | 7 |
| | Integrative 1949-1990 | 10 | 4 | 23 | 3 |
| | Integrative 1991-2018 | 11 | 11 | 6 | 38 |

**Table 4** Confusion matrix for DFA classifying texts pertaining to different orators based on writing style properties

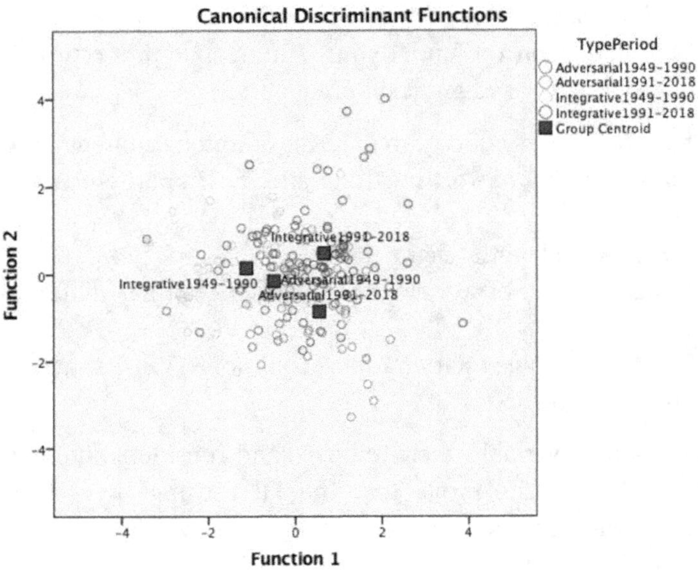


**Fig. 3** Visual representation of the DFA classification

This chapter has offered a quantitative investigation of NATO discourse. Based on the previous chapter's theoretical and practical explanation of corpus selection and sampling techniques, and on the description the method and the instruments applied for the quantitative examination, it has dedicated an extensive portion of the research to the analysis of texts and documents by illustrating, in terms of numbers and statistics, the manner in which manifestations of power have been transferred from institutional practice into discursive ideological representations.

## 3.2. Discursive Patterns of Power Relations

This study has advanced a critical discourse analysis model of the language of power with emphasis on the manner in which the dynamics of power relations are institutionalized through discourse. The institution whose discourse was the object of investigation is the North Atlantic Organization – NATO. Starting from the premise that today's Alliance, composed of nearly thirty members and having expanded to a global reach differs strikingly from the regional security organization of twelve created in 1949, the purpose of the current linguistic investigation was to identify a pattern of power dynamics that has typified NATO throughout its evolution and to confirm the existence of such pattern from a discursive point of view. The most significant goal of the linguistic investigation was to describe, explain, and interpret the relationship between words and actions, with a strong emphasis on the power of language to galvanize military and political will and reify it into action.

Military discourses of power and the social practices associated with them have been traditionally aimed at creating a peaceful, just, and sustainable social order. With this assumed task in mind, the rhetoric associated with NATO ideology can be seen as an effort to utilize language so as to change social reality through the discourses that help constitute it. In order to support this theory, this section deconstructs the dominant discourses of power, identifies the power relations that dominate three different types of discourses – adversarial, integrative, and dominant – and offers an analysis of the language elements that go into the construal of these discursive representations of reality.

Although language is not power, it encodes power. Power is embedded in the ideological workings of language and ideology is invested at all levels of language, be they explicit or implicit, structural or content-related: lexical meanings, syntactic choices, presuppositions, implicatures, coherence, entailment, etc. Talking about the role of language in relation to power, Habermas contends that "language…serves to legitimize relations of organized power" (1977:259). In addition, Fairclough maintains that "the exercise of power is increasingly achieved through ideology, and more particularly through the ideological workings of language" (2001: 2).

This section will investigate the dynamics of power in NATO discourse from the perspective of the relationship between rhetoric and power. In doing so, it focuses on investigating the manner in which language is used as a tool for encoding power and illustrating power dynamics in NATO public discourse. Before starting a detailed analysis of discourse, background research has identified a number of key moments in NATO's evolution, considered relevant for providing a fertile context for the manifestation of power dynamics. Subsequently, this subchapter is dedicated to a critical discourse analysis of the documents considered relevant at certain points during NATO's ideological evolution. Such an approach has proven extremely helpful for locating and interpreting different patterns of discourses of power.

Nevertheless, the following section does not intend to offer a thorough accounting of the political, social, and historical events that occurred between 1949 and 2018. There is already a sizeable industry of scholars, journalists and officials who have produced a myriad of books, monographs, and articles about NATO. However, the role of rhetoric and especially the rhetoric of power seems to have been insufficiently exploited. In order to fill this gap, this section focuses on the declarations about the nature and purpose of NATO, with particular attention to the "in crisis" moments that have generated cooperation and unity or, conversely, imbalances in the power equation, both within the Alliance and between NATO and external actors. Conceptually shaped as ideas, images, notions or plans, these declarations are relevant for an analysis of power dynamics in that they represent the underpinning context against which the relations between NATO members were instrumental in keeping the alliance together or, contrarily, in undermining its coherence.

Working within the broader framework of Wodak's Discourse-Historical Approach, or DHA, which places great emphasis on the importance of historical context, this section traces three specific discourse strands that have been identified in close connection with the type of power they illustrate. Adversarial power relations are exemplified in the discourse of opposition; the integrative or relational power is mostly salient from the discourse of unity; finally, referent, expert and legitimate power manifestations have been collected under the discourse of U.S. predominant power.

The following research questions guided the qualitative analysis:

1. How is internal and external opposition materialized in NATO discourse?
2. What kind of power rhetoric is employed to ensure cooperation both within the Alliance and with external actors?
3. What kind of discourse patterns does the United States use in order to assert its predominant role in NATO?

In other words, the analytical approach focuses on lexicalizations of the concepts of opposition, unity and dominance and the intertextual connections that condense discursive materializations of power dynamics. A summary of the historical, political, and social context that generated the investigated documents is interlocked with a linguistic analysis of the identified discourse strands. As a result, this chapter looks at three patterns of power, embedded in three types of discourses: adversarial – the discourse of opposition, integrative – the discourse of unity, and dominant – the discourse of U.S. predominance.

## 3.2.1. Integrative Power – The Discourse of Unity

Relational or integrative power pivots on the concept of consensus. Decision-making in NATO is, in virtue of the values and organic structure that typify the Alliance, fundamentally based on consensus. It starts from the premise that all allies are equal partners and have equal rights to take decisions that affect one and all at the same time. Nonetheless, consensus is a slower and much more cumbersome way of making decisions than majority voting. In the latter, discussion leads to a vote and the minority is free to decide whether to go along with the decision or leave the organization. Consensus requires unanimity and, therefore, compromise. It has the big advantage that, at the end of the process, everybody agrees and nobody leaves. Its advantage is to produce fewer discussions with more effort.

Inherently, the process of reaching consensus is a manifestation of power dynamics. It involves bargaining, compromise, pressure, cooperation, the understanding that it is important to agree to disagree in order to reach common ground. Although the fundamental premise is that all participants are equal, theory rarely matches reality. Within the Alliance, some members carry more clout than others, through the force of knowledge, expertise, resources, status, or anything else that produces particular respect or deference among the others. For example, the American voice counts more than the others. Moreover, there is a hierarchy among the other allies as well. If the U.S. gains, for instance, the support of the British or the Germans, especially both, that is usually the basis of consensus, though neither Britain nor Germany – the two most influential European powers wholly committed to NATO – could normally stand out alone against consensus for very long.

There are two sorts of consensus within NATO. One is the so-called broad consensus, defined as a commonly endorsed agreement about the desirability and viability of NATO itself. The other type is consensus on specific policies and issues, the sort which is hammered out in part through bilateral contacts between governments, in part through discussions of national representatives in the labyrinth of NATO committees.

Broad consensus is not a matter of unanimity over every dot and comma. It seeks to establish acceptable terms of debate. We have seen that through the 1980s, consensus (both specific and broad) was subject to more challenge than at any other time since NATO's founding. The security debate in that decade was unprecedentedly intense, ranging from intense anti-Sovietism in the period 1981-1985 to a new détente from 1985-1988 and culminating with a radical change of policy brought about by the fall of the Berlin Wall in 1989 and events leading to the dissolution of the Soviet Union in 1991.

The basis of consensus is a series of interlinked assumptions. First, there was the need to deter the perceived threat from the USSR; after the end of the Cold War, the enemy became Russia to this day; in the aftermath of the September 11 attacks, the threat took the fluid and ambiguous form of terrorism. In NATO's early days, the threat was unambiguously defined in terms of invasion and conquest, combined with a parallel political threat of domestic subversion in Western Europe by Moscow-controlled communists. As the sense of threat coming from the USSR's ideological conquest declined and finally disappeared, the military and political strategies focused less on invasion and more on the safeguarding of common values. After 9/11, NATO's role has been widely defined: the Alliance has transformed into a global security institution no longer tasked with ensuring transatlantic defense, but reconfigured so as to play a decisive role in worldwide stability.

It is only logical to assume that resistance to threat requires alliance unity. The relationship between national interests and the interests of NATO is often a tricky one, and when global security is at stake, there is no room for disagreement over how to balance the two. However, many times the national interests had to be balanced against NATO's, with the former often compromised in the name of the latter.

Diplomacy within NATO is largely concerned with finding common ground on specifics within the accepted broader parameters. Those who stand out against consensus are likely to be warned – implicitly or explicitly, publicly or privately – that they are challenging the alliance unity, the American role, the viability of deterrence, and ultimately the values inherent in the concepts of collective defense and cooperative security.

The need for alliance unity remains paramount, as most national leaders, relevant ministers and senior officials have insisted whenever the issue was raised. Words have played an important part in galvanizing the allies around a common objective, but they have not always been powerful enough. There have always been intra-Alliance disputes, unsolved disagreements, governments who accepted the consensus at ministerial meeting and ignored it at home. One illustrative example is the issue of military spending. The period with the most intense such disputes was the 1960s, a period of bickering that led to France's withdrawal from the military structure. The 1990s experienced a period of relative calm, with the allies focusing on defining a new enemy to fill in the vacuum left behind by the dissolution of the Soviet Union. Disagreements reemerged especially against the backdrop of the "war on terror" scenarios, which generated opposition and conflict regarding American and NATO policies outside the traditional boundaries of the Alliance.

## 3.2.1.1. The Internal Multipolar Balance

Transatlantic cooperation is of vital importance for both the Unites States and Europe, and it takes place in a wider variety of arenas. Collaboration can be bilateral, such being the cases when individual European nations offering military contingents to assist the U.S. military effort (for example in Afghanistan, in 2001), or it can be done in the framework of the North Atlantic Treaty Organization. NATO has traditionally been one of the forums that fosters cooperation and promotes consultation among the members of the Alliance and has served the longest as a medium foe exchanging views, reaching compromises and making decisions related to transatlantic and international security. If the scope of alliance cooperation was somewhat confined to the borders of the transatlantic space before the Cold War, when the focus was on dealing with regional challenges, the post-Cold War commitments and programs of the Atlantic Alliance have greatly broadened the latitude of the transatlantic cooperation by taking it to the outer limits of Europe into Central Asia and even to the Chinese border. Regardless of the issues at stake or of the geographical area targeted, the most important linchpin of transatlantic cooperation is the common strategic vision that the Americans and Europeans share regarding Europe's present and future safety and the indivisibility of transatlantic security.

In the aftermath of the Second World War, there was an acute need for the rehabilitation and revitalization of Europe, a task assumed by the United States' postwar policy, as drafted by George Marshall in 1947. "It is logical that the United States should do whatever it is able to do to assist in the return of normal economic health in the world, without which there can be no political stability and no assured peace" he stated in a speech at Harvard in June 1947 (par. 7). The initiative, known as the Marshall Plan, was aimed at appropriating money for the economic assistance of Western Europe, but the real initiative for the restoration of Europe actually came from the Europeans themselves. The role of referent power was assumed by Great Britain through the voice of British Foreign Secretary Ernest Bevin. United by Bevin's initiative, the United Kingdom, France, Belgium, the Netherlands, and Luxembourg signed the Brussels Treaty, on March 17, 1948, with a declared dual purpose: preventing renewed German militarism in Europe and defending Western Europe against the prospect of aggression from the Soviet Union. This treaty is regarded as the first postwar attempt to restore the European balance of power "which had been shattered by the eclipse of Germany, the emergence of a strong Russia and the post-war weakness of Western Europe" (Henderson 1983:ix). At the same time, the initiative was the first example of integrative power relations, a galvanizing mechanism that resulted in the birth of the most important security structure of the modern world.

While 1948 was still a year of long debates about the degree of American involvement in European security, historical events were unfolding in the background. Norway, just as Finland one year before, was compelled to negotiate a pact with the Soviet Union, but, unlike its neighbors, was determined to reject it and was now seeking support from the rest of the Western European countries in case they resisted Soviet threats. This situation entailed both strategic and political considerations: at a strategic level, Russia's moves were considered a threat against the Atlantic states; politically, the efforts to build a western Union were hindered. The global balance of power started to accumulate weight at both ends. Against this background, the need to conclude a regional Atlantic Pact of Mutual Assistance, that would include all countries threatened by the Russian move toward the Atlantic, became even more stringent. In *The Promise of Alliance*, Ian Thomas offers an accurate description of the conditions that laid the conceptual foundation of the North Atlantic Treaty. He concludes that "the gradual coming together and intermingling of strategic, economic, geopolitical, and ideological considerations ultimately prompted policymakers on both sides of the Atlantic to consider the idea of mutual security guarantees" (1997:14).

66

This initiative illustrates the early mechanisms of the power relations that were contouring long before the establishment of the Alliance. It demonstrates the desire of the British, backed up by other European states, to attract and link the United States to the concept of European security, which is an early indication of the expert, referent and legitimate power attributed to the United States in the context of an alliance. America has been historically regarded as a referent power, endowed with the political, economic, and military force to legitimize change, and a country to which other nations have often turned to in search for expertise and endorsement. The soon-to-be-born alliance makes no exception to this framework. Recognized by American participation, the treaty was meant to put an end to the imbalance of power politics in Europe, which was now ushered into a new era that would see no more of the past periodic wars.

The aforementioned concerns related to the security of Europe against the backdrop of emergent threats coming from Russia sparked the initiation of the Washington Talks in early 1948, when the five Brussels Treaty powers, the United States and Canada met for discussions. In *The Birth of NATO*, Nicholas Henderson argues that the purpose of the meeting was "to determine how best to deter the Russians and fortify confidence and reinforce the security of the democratic countries of Western Europe" (1983:40). The fifteen-month negotiations failed to determine the full role of the North American allies within the envisaged treaty, nor did they reach clear consensus on the need for a formalization of a treaty. Nonetheless, at the early stage, the talks were successful in that they represented the first western response to the Soviet threat, later to be embedded in the North Atlantic Treaty. Finally, after more than one year, the initiators of the discussions signed the Treaty in Washington, on April 4, 1949.

From the very beginning, the signed pact was considered extremely valuable from a political, psychological, and military perspective. Having been drafted in consistency with the principles of the U.N., the treaty was, however, an extension of the Charter, in that it was formally founded as a community of interests binding North America and Western Europe. The essence of the agreement was that it represented an instrument of peace stemming from a historical process of political evolution stamped by the principles of democracy, individual liberty and the rule of law. It was a clear statement that the security of Western Europe was inextricably linked to that of North America and that if North Atlantic peace was secured, the same can be done in other areas of the world. In 1949,

Lord Acheson, NATO's first Secretary General, further developed this idea in one of his public statements on the text of the treaty: "To have genuine peace we must constantly work for it. But we must do even more. We must make it clear that armed attack will be met by collective defense, prompt and effective. That is the meaning of the North Atlantic Pact" (384).

In the context of our discussion of power dynamics, this was the initial step taken to galvanize the concepts of Western European countries and the United States into a coherent Alliance. The declaration is an early expression of the main task of the Alliance during its entire existence – "collective defense" – fixed into discourse as well as in practice by the repetitive use of the powerful modal of obligation, used three times in as many sentences.

The conceptual framework under which the treaty was signed in 1949 became effective and materialized into operational coherence in 1950, after the start of the Korean War. NATO would finally receive a tangible challenge, as the invasion was interpreted as the communists' attempt at global domination. Supplemented by the collapse of nationalist China earlier in 1949, the Asian catastrophe posed threats to European security, and it was time for the rhetoric about the power of an alliance to be ironed into action. NATO's first step to actually becoming an organization was taken when the defense ministries of the treaty agreed on a collection of principles framing integrated defense, a strategic initiative that became NATO's First Strategic Concept. The paper plan of defense was forged into an integrated defense force under the control of unified international command.[4] The application of these principles represented the decisive moment that put the "O" in NATO. From this point forward, the defense of Western Europe was no longer upheld by the signatory states of the treaty but by the organization that was born with it.

The North Atlantic Treaty Organization was now a "community of powers" composed of twelve founding states: Belgium, Canada, Denmark, France, Iceland, Italy, Luxembourg, the Netherlands, Norway, Portugal, the United Kingdom, and the United States. This array of nations presupposes the existence of different entities, each with its own perspective and vision regarding the abstract concept of security proposed in the framework of the Treaty. Against this background, one of the initial challenges the

---

[4] At the December 1950 North Atlantic Council meeting in Lisbon, the foreign ministers of member states formally agreed on the notion of a united command and appointed General Dwight Eisenhower as NATO's first supreme commander.

Alliance was confronted with was to maintain an equilibrium of forces and constantly invigorate the relationships between the member countries through increased consultation. One of the many mechanisms through which this goal was achieved placed great importance on the essential role of language to create a common ground for efficient cooperation.

Immediately after its birth, NATO's main objective was to create the actional framework for collective defense. In addition to common policies, agreed upon by the signatory members through an exercise of consensus, the rhetoric of the Alliance was sprinkled with formulations involving the notions of "community", "partnership", "functional cooperation". These discursive expressions were widely used in order to mark the conceptual shift from interdependence to partnership, an ideological journey NATO embarked on for ten years in the period 1956-1966.

In an attempt to create a balanced flow of power that would offer the allies equal opportunities of decision, NATO's conceptual rhetoric now pushed for consultation among member states, especially calling on non-nuclear nations to have a say in the debates surrounding the nuclear key issues of the period (the creation of the multilateral force and of the Atlantic nuclear force). This move was a clear indication of the U.S. acknowledgment of Western Europe's increased economic power and political unity, a change in perception that placed European allies on equal footing with the Americans.

During the mid-1960s until the mid-1970s, the world balance of power seems to have gained more weight on the Eastern side, as U.S. nuclear superiority was replaced by Soviet strategic parity, a move that allowed a less hostile Soviet Union to enter negotiations form a position of strength rather than of fear. Internally, at the level of NATO, allied officials, with Europe in the lead, started to involve the alliance in a policy of détente, which was aimed at improving the relations between the United States and its NATO allies, on the one hand, and the Soviet Union and its Warsaw Treaty Organization allies, on the other. European leaders assumed responsibility and decision power as they became actively engaged in bilateral negotiations.[5]

---

[5] The British started to negotiate a Friendship Treaty with the Soviets; Willy Brandt, the West German foreign minister, was seeking to build diplomatic arrangements with the German Democratic Republic and other Eastern European States; de Gaulle's trip to Moscow in 1966 was a good occasion for the French to negotiate scientific and military cooperation pacts with the Soviet Union; the Belgians established contacts with Poland; Yugoslavia's policy was focused on improved West-East relations.

Against this background, U.S. leaders joined the Europeans in promoting NATO's involvement in détente. The role and contributions of the Alliance in this new configuration of the East-West polarity were framed in a study undertaken by Pierre Harmel, the Belgian Foreign Minister, in what was to be known as NATO's blueprint for détente: the *Harmel Report on the Future Tasks of the Alliance,* adopted at the December 1967 North Atlantic Meeting in Luxembourg. The report outlined the need for political and military solidarity within NATO and the pursuit of more stable relationships with the Eastern adversaries.

A powerful indication of the prescient value of the Harmel doctrine is the fact that the report was referenced six times, on six different occasions during ministerial meetings at the level of the North Atlantic Council (NAC), the Nuclear Planning Group (NPG) and the Defence Planning Committee (DPC) (Brussels, 1-2 Dec 1987; Brussels, 11 Dec 1987; Brussels, 26-27 May 1988; Brussels, 19-20 Apr 1989; Kananaskis, Canada, 9-10 May 1990; Brussels, 17-18 Dec 1992). NATO officials recurrently mentioned the continued validity of the principles contained in the *Harmel Report,* especially in the period immediately before and after the end of the Cold War, when the polarization between the United States, and NATO, by extension, and the Soviet Union was strongly delineated, especially on nuclear issues. The fact that the formulations of the Belgian Foreign Minister remained valid twenty years after the publication of the report are indicative of the pertinent content of the document, as well as of the enduring power of language, effectively used at that time in order to express a doctrine that remained applicable two decades after its first implementation.

The text of the document pivots on the concept of détente which, in that context, was seen as an acknowledgment of bilateralism, putting the strategic unity of the Alliance at risk. Especially important on the backdrop of the French withdrawal from the International Maritime Organization (IMO) and amid an increased independent attitude of the allies, who started to pursue complementary but bilateral détente policies, the *Harmel Report* was acclaimed as providing NATO with a new sense of direction that would serve as a means of pulling together the alliance, in virtue of the integrative power embedded in its doctrine. Taking one step forward from the already agreed upon practice of bilateralism, the report also detected the need to embrace multilateralism, motivated by the conclusion that "certain subjects…by their very nature, require a multilateral solution" (Harmel

70

Report 1967, par. 10-12). This new direction was particularly relevant for Germany, a country whose fate had for too long been decided by others in virtue of their postwar rights (the United States, the United Kingdom, France, and the U.S.S.R.). By embracing multilateralism, NATO opened the door for the influence of other allies in regard to the negotiations on Germany; furthermore, the members of the Alliance were reminded that they all had decision power, a right that came alongside their interests in the discussions over the future of Germany. Within this framework, the smaller allies were able to enter the complex web of negotiations alongside statutory members. This reiterated the importance of cooperation, unity and partnership as basic tenets of the Alliance's strategy and promoted NATO as an organic institution able to permanently adapt to the changing dynamics of power in the international environment.

However, in 1968, the Soviet-led invasion of Czechoslovakia disrupted the equilibrium of forces envisaged by the undergoing détente policy and reminded Western Europe that they were still dependent on the presence of American troops on their territory. Again, NATO's policy and response seemed to be widely influenced by and reliant on the Americans. In order to restore the balance of power and avoid a U.S. negotiating relationship with the Soviets above the heads of the European allies, NATO stepped in and tasked the NAC with monitoring and guiding the process of negotiations. At the 15-16 November 1968 Ministerial Meeting in Brussels, the NAC issued a Final Communiqué regarding the international situation following the Warsaw Pact armed intervention in Czechoslovakia. This was translated as an attempt to eschew the emergence of a superpower condominium that would lead to a superpower agreement on issues of alliance-related significance, disregarding the apprehensions and interests of the European partners. Under NATO's umbrella, members of the Alliance were free to pursue their own versions of détente but, at the same time, were restrained from acting unilaterally. According to the stipulations of the *Harmel Report*, NATO was to be used as "an effective forum and clearing house for the exchange and information and views" on how to best manage détente (par. 10). The notion of consultation was once again activated, and member states felt empowered to express their opinion and participate not only in decision-making but also in the prescribed interventions.

The text of the 1968 NAC Final Communiqué expresses this exact concept. The Alliance condemns the intervention of the Soviet Union, backed by four of its allies in Czechoslovakia, an act interpreted as a violation of the independence principle the people of Czechoslovakia, "like all other peoples", are entitled to (Final Communiqué of the North Atlantic Council 1968, par. 3). The same paragraph reads: "All the members of the Alliance have denounced this use of force which jeopardizes peace and international order and strikes at the principles of the United Nations Charter". The formulation here uses the collective pronoun "all" as a means of sending a shared message of unity and support displayed by all members of the Alliance. Paragraph 12 of the Communiqué reiterates the values the allies hold high and their determination not to remain passive and act in order to ensure their security. "Determined to safeguard the freedom and independence of their countries, they [the members of the Alliance] could not remain indifferent to any development which endangers their security" (par. 12). The importance of collectivity is emphasized by the use of the third person plurality, expressed by the personal pronoun "they" in a subject position, and correlated with its possessive adjectival form, "their" to modify the nouns "country" and "security".

As a characteristic feature of the 1970s, this period witnessed the strength of Europeanism, as the allies from across the Atlantic proved more willing to challenge the authority of their superpower ally. An illustrative example in this vein is the 1973 Yom Kippur War, which opposed the United States and its European allies once again.[6] The U.S. was accused of risking nuclear war without prior consultation, while the Americans criticized their European partners for refusing to protect the stability of the Middle East, which they considered strategically vital.

This crisis resulted in an imbalance of power relations within NATO, heavily polarizing the United States and Western Europe and undermining the very essence of an alliance built around common objectives. At ideological level, NATO's solution was to revitalize allied unity through a new conception, forged into discursive cohesion in the form of a document entitled "NATO Declaration on Atlantic Relations", adopted at the NAC meeting in Ottawa in June 1974. It reaffirmed the basic tenets of NATO's

---

[6] In October 1973, Egyptian and Syrian forces launched a devastating attack on Israel. Kissinger received the White House approval to take critical decisions during this crisis and ordered a $2 billion airlift to Israel using western and southern European air bases. With the exception of West Germany, which soon had a change of heart, the Netherlands, Portugal and the European NATO allies refused to assist the airlift and would not give the U.S. overflight rights. This opposition was soon reinforced by the Soviet Union's involvement on the side of Egypt and Syria, with the Soviets making a bold move and pressing the United States to intervene jointly so as to separate the warring parties. Kissinger's response was to authorize a worldwide U.S nuclear alert, including the American bases in Europe. Despite the deterrent strategy represented by the nuclear alert, the situation finally ebbed when, under U.S. pressure, the Israelis accepted a cease-fire.

indivisibility and security of allies, placed more emphasis on the importance of consultation, noted the emerging U.S.-Soviet parity, and finally aimed at alleviating European concerns regarding a superpower condominium. The document was also the "makeup note" between the Americans and the Europeans, who agreed that nuclear and conventional forces in Europe were "indispensable" and that the presence of American allies on the territory of Europe was deemed as "irreplaceable" (NATO Declaration on Atlantic Relations 1974, par. 5-9). The Europeans also pledged to contribute their own resources to the common defense, and the United Kingdom and France were to maintain their nuclear capabilities and place them in the service of NATO's strategy of deterrence. By acknowledging France and the U.K. as nuclear powers, NATO, and implicitly the U.S., made an important first step toward integrating the French and British in the Alliance from equal positions and recognizing their beneficial contribution, rather than their destabilizing nature, as it had happened before.

The main point of the "NATO Declaration" is illustrated in paragraph 3.

"The members of the Alliance reaffirm that their common defence is one and indivisible. An attack on one or more of them in the area of application of the Treaty shall be considered an attack against them all. The common aim is to prevent any attempt by a foreign power to threaten the independence or integrity of a member of the Alliance. Such an attempt would not only put in jeopardy the security of all members of the Alliance but also threaten the foundations of world peace." (par. 3)

On the whole, the text of the Declaration is populated with numerous references to the common values, aims and ultimately "common destiny" the allies share. A wide array of powerful cognitive verbs is employed so as to demonstrate the commitment and determination of the NATO members to put into action the declarative principles referred to in the document. Present tense constructions such as "are determined", "are convinced", "take the view", "consider", "recognize", "declare", "affirm", "reaffirm", "agree", etc., vouch for the continuity of these tasks and their perpetual significance. The subjects of these cognitive attitudes are always "the Allies", "the member nations", "the member states", "the members of the Alliance", a collectivity of entities that are united by a common identity and, implicitly, by common values.

Culminating in the drafting of the Declaration, in the mid-1970s, the power balance within NATO seems to have been reinstated. The Europeans were now comforted by the thought that the Americans would no longer seek to jeopardize their security by pursuing a unilateral policy of détente with the Soviet Union, while the Americans could depend on a renewed commitment of Western Europe's fair burden share for common defense.

In 1979, NATO made a long-debated decision with numerous implications for the cohesion of the alliance and with various repercussions on the international scene: the alliance's Long-Term Defense Program (LTDP) was extended so as to include nuclear weapons. This initiative was the materialization of NATO's response to the Soviets' deployment of intermediate-range nuclear missiles SS-20. The issue of the Euro-missiles that surrounded the dual-track decision was rather a test for the cohesion of the Alliance than a symbol of unity, as initially intended. Concerns over ownership and control, as well as the timetable for U.S. arms control initiatives (in contrast to the deployment dates that were definite) raised questions about European sovereignty and the unilateral American willingness to commit its allies to nuclear war. The revived rhetoric of peace through strength was imbued with controversial notions and scored the opposite effect: instead of securing peace, it seemed to threaten it. New and powerful nuclear missiles on the territory of Europe were the very antithesis of peace. Strength had indeed a very tragic power if NATO's vision of peace could jeopardize the existence of the peoples it had pledged to protect.

Opposition and adverse reactions notwithstanding, the deployment of new missiles in Europe and the dual-track plan proceeded as planned. By the end of 1983, distribution had started not only in Germany but also in the United Kingdom and France. The result was not so much an issue of practice, but a question of ideology. Due to massive and unexpected pressure coming from public opinion, NATO, an organization that had long benefitted from public support, was now compelled to embrace a new rhetoric: it acknowledged itself as a peace movement, a conceptual shift that went beyond the initially assumed task of seeking to negotiate a Western democratic peace with the Soviets as a means of ending the Cold War.

This new orientation found discursive materialization at the June 1982 NATO Summit in Bonn, where the "Program for Peace in Freedom" was launched in an attempt to compensate for the cleavages in the alliance and reaffirm the ideological commitment of the Alliance to the Washington

Treaty. The program was set forth as part of the text of the Declaration of the Heads of State and Government under paragraph 5 of the document. It is detailed in six other paragraphs (*a* to *f*), all starting with the phrase "our purpose is" followed by a long infinitive that is in fact a pledge to common action: "to prevent war", "to preserve security", "to have a stable balance of forces", "to develop substantial and balanced East-West relations", "to contribute to peaceful progress world-wide", "to ensure economic and social stability". All the action verbs in the text are either expressed in the future or charged with the imperative value of the modal "must" in an attempt to attach importance to the prescribed policy. In all sentences, the agent of the action expressed by the predicates is articulated either in the second person plural, by the collective "we", "all of us", or by a third person reference with the help of the collective noun "the allies". In this example, the language is used not only to prescribe common policy but also to unite the responsible agents under a common practice. Rhetorically, NATO needed to be invested with the notion that the Alliance really stood for peace. As a consequence, the formulation of the program calls NATO "an essential instrument for peace" while attempting to establish the parameters of using NATO's nuclear weapons, restricted to the scenario of a response to an attack.

In the first half of the 1980s, out-of-area issues represented another topic for debate among the members of the Alliance and sparked unequal reactions from the allies. In the wake of its thirty-fifth anniversary, celebrated in Washington on May 29, 1984, American leaders urged NATO to address the issue of Soviet adventurism in the Third World by improving its conventional forces in order to boost the resistance of the nations in that region of the globe. The United States was irritated with the reluctance of their European allies to follow its lead on out-of-area issues and asked for a special effort to redress the situation. At the meeting held in Brussels in May 1985, NATO's foreign and defense ministers declared that "we are concerned that the current disparity between NATO's conventional forces and those of the Warsaw Pact risks an undue reliance on the early use of nuclear forces" (Final Communiqué of the Defence Planning Committee 1985, par. 2). This rhetoric was intended to prod the European leaders to increase conventional forces in Europe so that U.S. forces be freed for use elsewhere. Nonetheless, the European allies were reluctant to reify this discourse into actions, and it was not until the 1990-1991 Gulf War that they agreed to compensatory measures to balance the growing American commitment to Southeast Asia.

In what concerns the standpoint of the most powerful European allies, the reactions were positive but quite diverse. The British were the most willing to countersign the Americans' requests, mainly due to Margaret Thatcher's solidarity with Reagan and against the background of the 1982 Falklands Campaign, where Britain received support from the United States. This attitude exemplifies acknowledgment of the United States' decisional power and Great Britain's willingness to unquestionably follow the American lead, especially since the appeal of the Americans was in line with its own interests. Consequently, Britain reversed its global withdrawal and supported NATO on out-of-area issues, by increasing forces flexibility and defense spending in this direction.

Although it had withdrawn from the IMO in the late 1960s and was therefore not subject to the U.S. calls for compensatory actions in NATO and despite of the fact that it considered out-of-area issues not appropriate for the Alliance's military endeavors, France acted in order to enhance its military capabilities beyond Europe. The decision to coordinate a military response with the United States to the Libyan invasion of Chad in 1983-1984 and the establishment of a Force d'Action Rapide to keep an eye on French interests outside Europe stemmed from the belief that future out-of-area threats were more likely to be generated by regional instability than from Soviet aggression.

The Federal Republic of Germany considered involvement in out-of-area issues quite problematic, partly due to constitutional constraints and partly because they feared that it would increase the tensions on the German border. Nevertheless, the Germans committed to provide financial assistance for U.S. troop-basing costs, a pledge they officialized by signing the 1982 Host Nation Support Agreement.

In order to appease the allies' apprehensions regarding out-of-area issues, the NAC Final Communiqué issued at the December 1984 meeting in Brussels compensates the Washington Treaty's lack of reference to out-of-area issues and legitimizes the obligations and responsibilities of the allies vis-à-vis such concerns. The text of the document underlines the importance of common interests that should form the basis for the willingness of the allies to collectively look beyond NATO's formal range of vision. "Events outside the treaty may affect [the allies'] common interests…

They will engage in timely consultations on such events if it is established that their common interests are involved" (Final Communiqué of the North Atlantic Council 1984, par. 13). The use of a passive construction here leaves room for speculation as of who establishes the need for consultation and under what circumstances. While the agency might have been intentionally left out, the repetition of the phrase "common interests" supports the deduction that the decisional forum for this matter is the Alliance.

The events that typify the decade 1986-1996 had profound implications for the way in which NATO positioned itself immediately before and after the end of the Cold War. By 1990, the Iron Curtain collapsed, Germany was unified, the Soviet Union disintegrated, and the ideological and political confrontation fueled by the Cold War had come to an end.

During the late 1980s, the rhetoric of the Alliance brought nothing new and basically reiterated the same conceptual tenets that had characterized NATO discourse in the last 40 years. With the Americans in the lead, the European allies publicly reaffirmed their belief in the commonly held values of an Atlantic Community. In the early 1990s, the collapse of the Soviet Union brought about new uncertainties and threats, to which NATO responded by forging a set of new strategic and political concepts wrapped around old notions of partnership, which cemented the conceptual framework supporting the Alliance's new objective of consolidating pan-European security into the 21st century.

The signing of the Intermediate-Range Nuclear Forces (referred to as INF) Treaty, between the United States and the Soviet Union in December 1987 came after more than a decade of negotiations and discussions between the two superpowers and was hailed as a NATO triumph.[7] Despite the many obvious advantages it entailed and the mainstream positive attitude of the Allies, the treaty was not unanimously perceived as a NATO achievement. One country strayed away from treating the INF as such. From the very beginning, the French had been reluctant to follow the Harmel doctrine and had never subscribed to the axiom of linking military and political solidarity. The undermining of the treaty and its apparent success was yet another move toward a Gaullist vision

---

[7] The INF Treaty stipulated that all land-based missiles with a range between 500 and 5,500 km will be completely eliminated. The Soviets agreed to eliminate 1,500 warheads while the West would eliminate 350. Under the Treaty, highly intrusive verification and inspection measures were also agreed upon, including monitoring of production facilities and on-site inspections of deployment sites. The Treaty entered into force on June 1, 1988 (DOSB, February 1988, pp. 22-77).

of a European Europe and an attempt to renew French efforts to move away from U.S. leadership, as France called for Western Europe to become directly involved in the issue of collective security if it wished to be taken seriously.

Fearing similar responses from the other NATO allies, backed by the concerns of the European leaders with regard to the emergence of a superpower condominium, NATO appealed once again to rhetoric aimed at binding the allies together under shared values and practices. This initiative took the form of two documents produced on the occasion of the March 1988 Brussels Summit, the first NATO Heads of State and Governments meeting in six years.

The first NAC document, named "Conventional Arms Control: The Way Ahead" contained familiar references to increased alliance cooperation in terms of burden sharing and defense expenditures. The second one, suggestively entitled "A Time for Reaffirmation", was aimed at reiterating the common ideals and objectives of the Alliance as initially drafted by the North Atlantic Treaty almost 40 years before. The text of the declaration restated some of the most essential NATO tenets, among which the indivisibility of security, the political and military strength of the Alliance, which was the basis for East-West negotiations, and the longstanding role of the Alliance as a forum for consultation and cooperation regarding issues related to arms control. In the first paragraph, the document announces that:

"We, the representatives of the sixteen members of the North Atlantic Alliance, have come together to re-emphasise our unity, to assess the current state of East-West relations, to review the opportunities and challenges which lie ahead, and in so doing:

- to reaffirm the common ideals and purposes which are the foundation of our partnership;
- to rededicate ourselves to the principles and provisions of the Washington Treaty of 1949;
- to reassert the vital importance of the Alliance for our security, and the validity of our strategy for peace." (Conventional Arms Control: The Way Ahead 1988, par. 1)

The bulleted "to do" list of activities the sixteen (at that time) allies assumed to engage in during the summit is an indication of a common effort the members of the Alliance embark on in the name of solidarity and cooperation. The possessive pronoun "our" is used four times and is backed up by the reflexive form "ourselves", while the linchpin of the entire discourse is announced with the help of semantically related elements, such as "common, "unity", "together", "partnership".

Furthermore, the document insists on the inextricable relationship between the two pillars of the Alliance, the United States and Europe, and calls for the continuous need for Europe's contribution while asserting its strong position within NATO, as the Alliance cannot be strong if Europe is weak:

"...a free, independent and increasingly united Europe is vital to North America's security. The credibility of Allied defence cannot be maintained without a major European contribution. We therefore welcome recent efforts to reinforce the European pillar of the Alliance, intended to strengthen the transatlantic partnership and Alliance security as a whole." (Declaration of the NATO Heads of State and Government participating in the Meeting of the North Atlantic Council 1988, par. 4)

The core notion stemming from this phrasing is that the security of North America and that of Europe continued to be intricately interconnected, and while a strong and independent Europe was vital for the security of North America, the presence of American troops on European soil was aimed at securing the continent. This particular wording comes as an attempt to alleviate the possible concerns of the allies with regard to the unilateralism that might characterize U.S.-Soviet relations. In order to reinforce the importance of cooperation within NATO and reassure the allies that solidarity will always prevail regardless of the circumstances, President Reagan declared on the occasion that "we will never sacrifice the interests of this partnership in any agreement with the Soviet Union" (1986:4).

Ideologically, the documents of the summit and the values embedded in the texts of the declarations represent a conscious effort of the alliance leaders to recall the enduring traditions and purpose of the alliance. More than aiming to reaffirm, the rhetoric of the 1988 Brussels Summit was meant to reassure. NATO's conceptual canon embedded in the discourse of the meeting was directed at reinforcing the referent power of the Alliance as a whole. The hegemonic tendencies of the United States needed to be softened, and NATO was to be perceived as the entity that promotes unity and cooperation among the members of the organization. Once again, the alliance strengthened its position as the authoritative voice of the West.

The subsequent events, however, came as a challenge to NATO's superiority in Europe. Interestingly enough, they generated a shift in the balance of power that stole the show from the Americans in favor of the Charismatic Soviet leader on the rise, who was seemingly able to lure the Europeans on his side. Paradoxically, it seemed that it was NATO and its role as a harbinger of change that generated the Soviet reforms initiated and implemented by the new rising star, Mikhail Gorbachev. Hailed as a bright and articulated leader in the Western countries where he had made public appearances, the Soviet president and his actions presented a genuine dilemma to the leaders of the alliance. Traditionally, NATO had always been the showcase for the superiority of the West and the only entity that could serve as a powerful counterattraction to the Eastern ideology of communism. With Gorbachev (1988) talking about a "common European home" and about security for all from "the Atlantic to the Urals", it was normal for the allied leaders to feel disturbed by the idea that a common European home did not include a place for the United States. The Americans were most concerned with being excluded form Gorbachev's vision of a new Europe, a worrying sentiment that also populated Bush's speech during the commencement ceremonies at Boston University on May 21, 1989. Referring to the attractiveness of the Soviet leader and his reforms in Europe, the American President warned that there was a "growing complacency throughout the West" (1989:18). Consequently, the U.S. leaders advanced the theme of common values in an effort to remind both their allies and the Soviets that American interests were also at stake in any discussion about the future of Europe.

Accordingly, the May 1989 Brussels Summit was infused with the rhetoric of NATO's image as an entity tasked with safeguarding and fostering common values. Common values implied common interests, and by focusing on the former, the Americans hoped to have a say in shaping the latter. The healing solution for the allies' apprehensions in this period came in the form of the so-called "Design for Cooperation" document, which stated NATO's objective to control the new configuration in the power dynamics and "to establish a new pattern of relations between the countries of East and West, in which ideological and military antagonism will be replaced with co-operation, trust and peaceful competition" (The Brussels Declaration 1989, par. 10).

Quite a comprehensive document, the text of the Brussels Declaration is composed of eleven separate parts that are nonetheless framed as a continuous discourse. The first two paragraphs proudly salute NATO's achievements over "40 Years of Success", in an exercise of historical reiteration of the stability and cooperation NATO had represented over time. "These are the fruits of a partnership based on enduring common values and interests, and on unity of purpose", reads one of the opening statements of the document. The text continues with an itinerant ideological journey acknowledging "A Time for Change", whose "Global Challenges" dictate the strategies the Alliance needs to employ in "Shaping the Future", among which "Maintaining our Defence", taking "Initiatives on Arms Control", and "Overcoming the Divisions of Europe" are the most important steps "Towards an Enhanced Partnership". NATO even proposes its own "Design for Co-operation" and rounds up the essential takeaways of the document in the section entitled "The Future of the Alliance", which also represents an invitation to an extended framework of cooperation: "The Alliance will continue to serve as the cornerstone of our security, peace and freedom. Secure on this foundation, we will reach out to those who are willing to join us in shaping a more stable and peaceful international environment in the service of our societies" (The Brussels Declaration 1989, par. 37).

The document sought to re-establish the internal unity of the alliance as a prerequisite for the opening of new East-West relations, in the context of the recent challenges and changes that transcend the resources of both Europe and North America. In an attempt to bind the United States and Europe under the conceptual umbrella of common security, the final declaration of the summit reiterated the importance of transatlantic relationships while promoting, at the same time, a European security identity, which was essential, as one senior U.S. policymaker observed, so as to maintain an "essential balance in Europe" (Eagleburger 1989:40). In the wake of the Summit declarations, the United States seemed to have secured their place in a NATO that had finally rejected Gorbachev's idea of a common Europe as being too narrow. The Alliance regained the initiative and established itself as an agent of change, capable to adapt to the multifaceted challenges of the Cold War. The reiteration of the founding principles from which NATO originated was a common acquiescence of the power of the Alliance and a validation of its conceptual history.

NATO's victory in the ideological Cold War was complete in 1989, the moment that marked the weakening and even the collapse of the East European communist governments. In November that year, the Berlin Wall fell, and in December, a U.S.-Soviet meeting in Malta announced that the era of the Cold War had (declaratively) ended. Against this background, the relations of power in Europe and in the alliance acquired new dynamics that inherently generated the adaptation of both NATO's rhetoric and practice.

Under the already promoted rhetoric of common values, the freshly reunified Germany was provided with an easy passage into NATO. West Germany had been a NATO member since 1955. In 1990, the Two-plus-Four Talks succeeded in lessening French and British concerns, and the two countries, under American pressure, overcame their fears about a resurgent Germany and finally fully agreed to an immediate German membership in NATO.[8] The way to Germany's integration had been paved in 1989, when Chancellor Helmut Kohl gave a speech to the Bundestag on 28 November, noting that

"The development of inter-German relations remains embedded in the pan-European process, that is, within the framework of East-West relations. The future architecture of Germany must fit into the future architecture of Europe as a whole. In this regard, the West has served as a pacesetter with its conception of a lasting and just European order of peace." (103)

In his speech, Kohl set the stage for the establishment of a federation that would seek close cooperation with the European institutions. After reunification, Germany reemerged as one of the continent's leading powers, but the initial positioning of the country was still subordinated to the goals of continental security, as expressed in NATO's policies.

Coupled with the total collapse of the Soviet Union in December 1991 and other events that changed the scene of international relations (the end of the Gulf War, the dissolve of the Warsaw Pact, the start of the Yugoslavian wars), the emergence of Germany as a powerful NATO member required a fundamental strategic review to further consolidate NATO's role in the new Europe and its relation to other European security organizations. Amidst these changes, the Americans insisted that the role

---

[8] In February 1990, the Four Powers (The United States, United Kingdom, France and the USSR), in ax exercise of postwar rights over Germany, endorsed the unification of the GDR and FRG. Under the Two-plus-Four formula, the two Germanys decided on the process of reunification and, together with the four states, agreed to maintain external ties with the rest of Europe.

of post-Cold War NATO was crucial to transatlantic security, as well as to the United States' own leading power in the world.

The adaptation started with NATO's first post-Cold War Summit, held in London in May 1990 and was finalized at the Rome Summit, sixteen months later. In Rome, President Bush reasserted the important role NATO had played in winning the Cold War by promoting Western-inspired conceptions and reinforced the relevance of the organization in the new era: "The Alliance has been more successful than any of us dared to dream. It was designed to defend our freedom, but in fact it triumphed over totalitarianism. What we have built is not some military pact but a community of values and trust – unique in history, perpetual and vital for the new order" (1991:7).

The Rome Summit in November 1991 completed the conceptual work initiated in London and produced three documents by which the future strategy of the Alliance was fixed in discourse: the "New Strategic Concept", the "Declaration on Peace and Cooperation" and a "Communiqué on the Developments in the Soviet Union". It is important to note here that before the Cold War, the Strategic Concepts were classified documents dealing with military strategy. After 1991, they have been conceived as instruments of public diplomacy and distributed for public consumption, for the purpose of defining a legitimate and politically acceptable role for NATO, perceived as a reference point in a continuously changing world. Although these documents proved important for the new strategic direction the allies agreed on as an exercise of consensus and cooperation, they are considered more illustrative in the context of the external bipolar balance and have been analyzed in the following section of the paper, which is dedicated to examining the dynamics of cooperation between NATO and its former adversaries.

In the period preceding the April 1999 Washington Summit celebrating the Alliance's fiftieth anniversary, NATO engaged in an open consideration of its new strategic concept. Against the background of an increasingly unified Europe – the upcoming summit was the first enlargement summit of the post-Cold War era with Poland, Hungary and the Czech Republic having joined the Alliance just days before the summit – there was a tendency to define NATO in a new way that would allow the expansion of the traditional venues for national influence.

Adopted on April 24, 1999, the New Strategic Concept was an attempt to bridge the gap between the old NATO's "essential and enduring purpose", as outlined in the Washington Treaty and the requirements of the new "environment of continuing change" (The Alliance's Strategic Concept 1999, par. 12). The new concept was based on the 1991 one but differed from it in that it did not seek to renovate the Alliance's strategic thinking but to reflect evolutionary change. In July 1997, the NATO heads of state and government who gathered in Madrid had expressed their intention to "examine" the old Strategic Concept. The verb itself points to a level of restructuring that goes beyond revision.

Part I of the new Strategic Concept outlines the "Purpose and Tasks of the Alliance" that supplements the objectives stated of the Washington Treaty with a several "fundamental security tasks" adapted to the new security environment. Of the four security tasks, three are also expressed the 1991 Strategic Concept: "to provide an indispensable foundation for a stable Euro-Atlantic security environment"; "to provide an essential transatlantic forum for consultation"; "to defend and deter against any threat of aggression to allies" (par. 20). The fourth, however, was a new addition. It mentioned the need to enhance "the security and stability of the Euro-Atlantic area", a task that was double-fold and implied crisis management strategies and actively promoted partnership. Critical debates over the formulation of this fourth task split the allies in two camps: those who wanted a vaguer formulation that would reinforce collective defense but not overlap with the first fundamental task, and those who argued that crisis management and partnership are two different concepts and should therefore fan out as two separate tasks. The discussions ended in the adoption of a compromise, wrapping up the two notions in a single point, confusingly restating the topic of the first fundamental task. The compromise indicates that the new strategic concept heavily relied on the idea of collective security, which remained an ideal jointly pursued by all NATO allies.

The terrorist attacks on the United States on September 11, 2001 radically changed NATO's security priorities. On the day following the attacks, the (then) nineteen allied countries declared that they "stand ready to provide the assistance that may be required as a consequence of these acts of barbarism" (Statement by the North Atlantic Council, 2001 para. 4). The attacks put on the first pages of the Alliance's agenda the exact strategic perspectives discussed and adopted in the 1999 Strategic Concept. Terrorism acquired the dimension of a "fundamental security task", given the fact that the attacks came from abroad and were directed on the territory of an ally. The events were instrumental in shaping NATO's future strategic vision, forcing the Alliance to adopt a new doctrine that would renew the power and purpose of transatlantic cooperation.

This change was ironed into rhetoric during the "transformation summits" in Prague in November 2002 and in Istanbul, in June 2004. It was generated by the need to make the organization function effectively while dealing with new challenges, although there were voices arguing that this string of transformation summits was rather indicative of symbolic activity and of the political paralysis stemming from the clash of American and European worldviews. Very well illustrated by the extent of political disagreement in relation to the war in Iraq, the tensions between the U.S. and its European allies almost fractured NATO's critical infrastructure. Although both parties agreed on the fact that the status quo was under attack and committed to defend it, the disagreements came from the manner in which this could be achieved. Unity was at stake, but the developments in recent decades proved that the concept no longer had the same meaning it used to have during the Cold War. At the beginning of the 21st century, unity entailed a new dimension, that of flexible cooperation, which required the activation of different power dynamics.

A legitimate reason for the exercise of integrative power, the terrorist attacks on September 11th created an opportunity for NATO to invoke its identity as the key security institution of the Western community, appealing to its fundamental principles of liberal democratic norms and values in an attempt to ward off the challenges brought about by the "war on terror". Reinforcing the strong bond existing between the United States and Europe in this context, NATO Secretary General George Robertson's rhetoric in early 2002 united the world under one notion, previously emphasized by *Le Monde* on September 12th: "We are all Americans".

"September 11th was an enormous tragedy. But it revealed many truths. That the bond between the United States and Europe is as strong as ever… That NATO is and will continue to be the essential pillar of Euro-Atlantic security and cooperation between the two sides of the Atlantic. So ignore the merchants of doom. September 11th was not a blow to NATO. It was further proof of its enduring value." (par. 48-49)

Incited by the "We are all Americans" trope, the free world automatically empathized. The reactions spurred by the terrorist acts of September 11 were also an indication that the human race is more likely to reunite in sorrow and pain than in any other type of shared experience. Paradoxically enough, despite the disagreements over the merits of resorting to military action in the name of combating terrorism and its "sponsor states" (in this case Iraq), and contrary to the different interpretations of and the various responses to the new "war on terror", NATO members continued to work together and even reached a consensus in identifying, if not the means to fight it, at least the conceptual definition terrorism, assessed as the key source of threat in the Euro-Atlantic world. This agreement was discursively reified at the NAC June 2003 meeting in Madrid, where the Alliance confirmed its commitment to the war on terrorism, understood as the main threat to international security:

"Terrorism continues to pose a great threat to alliance populations, forces and territory, as well as to international peace and security. It also poses a threat to the development and functioning of democratic institutions, the territorial integrity of states, and to peaceful relations between them… We are implementing a military concept for defense against terrorism, improving civil preparedness, and working closely with our Partner countries in this area… To fight terrorism effectively, our response must be multi-faceted and comprehensive." (Final Communiqué of the Ministerial Meeting of the North Atlantic Council 2003, par. 11)

The extent of the threat is acknowledged by the discursive unification of "alliance populations, forces and territories", a formulation that encompasses civilians and military alike, as well as their homeland, later rephrased in the reference to "the territorial integrity of states". The multifold response involves new approaches that might go beyond the initial purview of the Alliance, and such rhetoric is used here to set the stage for the coming changes that have reformed NATO's traditional strategies.

In response to the threat of terrorism, NATO leaders have endorsed a series of measures and initiatives so as to restructure the manner in which the Alliance had traditionally responded to security challenges. In the aftermath of September 11, the allies worked together to implement a series of policies aimed at enhancing their collective ability to monitor and act against individuals and groups with alleged links to organized crime and terrorist organizations. The implemented policies enabled the Alliance to assume tasks that had been traditionally attributed to domestic law enforcement agencies, thereby blurring the line between inside and outside areas of responsibility. One such example of cooperation in this direction is the agreement reached by the allies during the 2004 Istanbul

Summit, where the "Policy on Combating Trafficking in Human Beings" was adopted. Describing human trafficking as a "serious abuse of human rights" and a "modern day slave trade" (par. 1), the allies committed to ratify and accept the U.N. Convention against Transnational Organized Crime, to exchange information and cooperate with the EU and other international bodies in order to ensure maximum efficiency of the new policy, and to identify and punish all those responsible for organized crime.

Amid the developments on the international scene, there seemed to be a growing recognition of the fact that the United States and Europe need each other's support to effectively cope with the new challenges. In late 2005, NATO foreign ministers meeting in Brussels formally promoted an "enhanced political dialogue" within NATO, which would transform the Alliance into "an essential forum for security consultation between Europe and North America and an effective instrument for Allies to provide peace and stability, now and into the future" (Final Communiqué of the Ministerial Meeting of North Atlantic Council 2005, par. 18).

As noted so far, one of the most important characteristics of the Alliance is its ability to adapt to changing circumstances while preserving unity and solidarity as the most cherished pillars of its enduring role as a security institution. Adaptation and flexibility to an ever-changing security environment are best illustrated in the frequency with which the Alliance changes its doctrine and how efficiently that responds to the dynamics of the international scene. The one before the last time NATO adapted its strategic concept was in 1999. This took several months of detailed negotiations between the – then – 16 countries of the Alliance. After the Strasbourg/Kehl Summit on 3-4 April 2009, held on the occasion of the Alliance's 60th anniversary, the leaders of the NATO countries asked the Secretary General to develop a new strategic concept, in close consultation with all allies, and to present his proposals at the following summit, to be held in Lisbon between November 19 and 20, 2010. The "Declaration on Alliance Security" agreed on in France announced NATO's desire to renovate the Alliance by addressing today's threats and anticipating tomorrow's risks.

The document adopted in Portugal, entitled "Active Engagement, Modern Defence", was designed as the Alliance's roadmap for the following ten years. It re-emphasizes the notion that Euro-Atlantic security is fundamentally based on common defense and cooperative security. The document generously describes a growing Alliance that will be ready to protect its members from modern threats. Against the backdrop of an ever-changing security environment, NATO's essential mission will be to ensure that "the Alliance remains an unparalleled community of freedom, peace, security and shared values" (Strategic Concept for the Defence and Security of the Members of the North Atlantic Security Organization adopted by heads of State and Government in Lisbon 2010, par. 3).

The last paragraph of the document, entitled "An Alliance for the 21st Century", recaps the most important values that bind together the twenty-eight (as of 2010) member countries into "the globe's most successful political-military Alliance":

"We, the political leaders of NATO, are determined to continue renewal of our Alliance so that it is fit for purpose in addressing the 21st Century security challenges. We are firmly committed to preserve its effectiveness as the globe's most successful political-military Alliance. Our Alliance thrives as a source of hope because it is based on common values of individual liberty, democracy, human rights and the rule of law, and because our common essential and enduring purpose is to safeguard the freedom and security of its members. These values and objectives are universal and perpetual, and we are determined to defend them through unity, solidarity, strength and resolve." (par. 38)

The same semantic universe that has populated all NATO discourses so far is recreated by the already recognizable concepts of "unity", "solidarity", "strength", "freedom", "security", "liberty", "democracy", most of which are modified by strong adjectives such as "essential", "enduring", "universal", "perpetual".

The Lisbon Summit represents another waypoint in the Alliance's evolution from a security institution dedicated to East-West deterrence and defense to one re-adapted to cope with the trials of an increasingly fluid and ambiguous environment. The initial focus of the Lisbon Summit was to answer the question raised by the end of the traditional Cold War bipolarity: what is the purpose and function of an alliance initially designed, in the oft-quoted words of Lord Ismay, NATO's first Secretary General, "to keep the Russians out, the Americans in and the Germans down". The latest new concept was drafted, discussed and adopted against the backdrop of a changing international political order in the world, which repositioned NATO on the scene of a new global power configuration. As a result of this unsteady environment, the world political order emerged as increasingly

88

complex and uncertain, generating a shifting and re-shifting of the global constellation of power.

In the aftermath of the end of the Cold War, NATO needed to address a multiplicity of new missions and tasks, which have broadened the Alliance's agenda but, at the same time, raised doubts about its strategic rationale. The increasingly complex and ambiguous strategic landscape in which NATO operates has diluted the solidarity that NATO enjoyed during the Cold War. As a result, consensus-building and decision-making have become even more strenuous processes. Against this background, the summit in Lisbon represented a way of redefining the Alliance's role in the fluctuating international order of the 21ˢᵗ century.

The New Strategic Concept "Active Engagement, Modern Defence", and the talks in Lisbon were typified by two key international events: the shifting global balance of power and the global recession. As the world was transitioning from a unipolar to a multipolar order, we experienced "the decline of the West and the rise of the Rest". The development of the BRIC countries (Brazil, Russia, India and China) has imposed a new configuration of international diplomacy and has affected the power balance. As Fareed Zakaria noted, this new world was "defined and directed from many places and by many people" (2009:5), adding more elements on the international scene.

In NATO's own words, the security environment of the present is "dangerous, unpredictable, and fluid" (Brussels Summit Declaration 2018, par. 2). The years leading up to the most recent summit of the Alliance, held in 2019 in July, in Brussels, are typified by "enduring challenges and threats from all strategic directions; from state and non-state actors; from military forces; and from terrorist, cyber, and hybrid attacks" (par. 2). In this context, all summit documents produced between 2010 and 2018 call for close cooperation in defense, reaffirm the Alliance's fundamental tasks and values and place extreme emphasis on unity, solidarity, and cohesion.

The final paragraph of the Chicago 2012 summit document, entitled "Summit Declaration on Defence Capabilities: Toward NATO Forces 2020" starts with the following sentence: "NATO's greatest strength is its unity" (par. 1). This sentence may contain a hint of propaganda, reminding of advertisement slogans and set phrases, but such formulations, fairly abundantly present across all military discourses promoting unity and cooperation, have proven quite efficient in galvanizing collective action whose shared motivation empowers the organization and offers it the most needed impetus to face diverse challenges successfully.

The following summit, held in Wales two years later, opens with a statement of reaffirmation of common Alliance values and the need for their integration within the broader framework of European defense, starting from the premise that "A stronger European defence will contribute to a stronger NATO" (The Wales Declaration on the Transatlantic Bond 2014, par. 6).

> "The North Atlantic Alliance binds North America and Europe in the defence of our common security, prosperity and values. It guarantees the security of its members through collective defence. It strengthens security in Europe, and projects stability further afield through crisis management and cooperative security with its unique set of partnerships. Our commitment to defend freedom, individual liberty, human rights, democracy and the rule of law makes our community unique." (par. 1)

In 2016, at the Warsaw summit, the allies restated the importance of the core set of common values, which, in the formulation of the first paragraph of the "Warsaw Declaration on Transatlantic Security", are traced back to the founding principles stipulated in the UN Charter.

> "We stand together, and act together, to ensure the defence of our territory and populations, and of our common values. United by our enduring transatlantic bond, and our commitment to democracy, individual liberty, human rights and the rule of law, NATO will continue to strive for peace, security and stability in the whole of the Euro-Atlantic area, in accordance with the principles of the UN Charter." (Warsaw Declaration on Transatlantic Security 2016, par. 1)

The sense of unity and partnership as well as the shared belief in common values is communicated by the repetition of almost identically formulated concepts, enumerated as nouns pertaining to the same lexical category "peace", "security", "stability", for the notion of what collective defense aims at, and "freedom", "individual liberty", "human rights", "democracy" and "the rule of law" as examples of commonly shared principles.

The most up-to-date documents, issued in the aftermath of the most recent NATO summit in Brussels, held between July 10th-11th 2019, are reflections of the Alliance's unaltered ideology that pivots on the importance of collective defense, crisis management, and collective security. The introductory paragraphs of the two most essential texts produced in 2018, "The Brussels Declaration on Transatlantic Security and Solidarity" and "The Brussels Summit Declaration" mirror each other in terms of key concepts and formulations encapsulating the ever-relevant ideological landmarks of the seventy-year-old Alliance. Both texts define NATO, outline its role and mission and reiterate the Alliance's unbroken belief in unity and solidarity.

Example 1:

"NATO guarantees the security of our territory and populations, our freedom, and the values we share – including democracy, individual liberty, human rights and the rule of law. Our Alliance embodies the enduring and unbreakable transatlantic bond between Europe and North America to stand together against threats and challenges from any direction. This includes the bedrock commitment to collective defence set out in Article 5 of the Washington Treaty. NATO will continue to strive for peace, security and stability in the whole of the Euro-Atlantic area, in accordance with the purposes and principles of the UN Charter." (The Brussels Declaration on Transatlantic Security and Solidarity 2018, par.1)

Example 2:

"NATO will continue to strive for peace, security, and stability in the whole of the Euro-Atlantic area. We are united in our commitment to the Washington Treaty, the purposes and principles of the Charter of the United Nations (UN), and the vital transatlantic bond. We are determined to protect and defend our indivisible security, our freedom, and our common values, including individual liberty, human rights, democracy, and the rule of law. NATO remains the foundation for strong collective defence and the essential transatlantic forum for security consultations and decisions among Allies.

The Alliance will continue to pursue a 360-degree approach to security and to fulfil effectively all three core tasks as set out in the Strategic Concept: collective defence, crisis management, and cooperative security. NATO is a defensive Alliance. NATO's greatest responsibility is to protect and defend our territory and our populations against attack. Any attack against one Ally will be regarded as an attack against us all, as set out in Article 5 of the

Washington Treaty. We will continue to stand together and act together, on the basis of solidarity, shared purpose, and fair burden-sharing. "(The Brussels Summit Declaration 2018, par.1)

The syntax is straightforward and unpretentious, condensing core notions in simple sentences whose subject is almost invariably the entity of the North Atlantic Organization, reflected in the use of the pronoun "we" or in collective nouns such as "NATO" or "the Alliance". Present posture and future actions are expressed by using the exact same formulations as in almost all previously analyzed discourses: "we are determined", "we are united", "we will continue", communicating a resolute attitude and shared beliefs that have remained unaltered throughout the Alliance's seventy-year history. Basic components of ideology (self-identity, activities, goals, values, and norms) are synthetized in these opening paragraphs, which, as in all other summit documents so far, are emblematic for what the organization represents and for what it intends to transmit.

### 3.2.2.2. The External Bipolar Balance

Framing the external bipolar balance in the context of power dynamics starts form the premise that NATO, on the one hand, and its adversaries, on the other, have traditionally been the two weighs at each end of a dual weighing scale. Since its creation in 1949, NATO was geared toward counteracting the menace embodied by the Soviet Union, and the communist system of beliefs represented a great threat to the security of Western Europe in the aftermath of World War II. Although NATO's initial goal was to forge a consistent transatlantic response to the Soviet threat, during its ideological evolution the Alliance has undergone a series of conceptual changes that were required in order to adapt its initial purview to the power dynamics on the international scene.

One of the most illustrative examples of integrative power in the context of the external power balance resides in the bipolarity that opposes NATO, on the one hand, and the USSR on the other, at least until the moment of the Soviet Union's dissolution. While the first two decades after its foundation were dedicated to strengthening American and Western European cooperation, with most of the strategy and doctrine of the Alliance pivoting around the concept of partnership, the period starting in the mid-1960s is characterized by the so-called "policy of détente". *Détente*, a word borrowed from French rhetoric that referred to a relaxation of tension between the superpowers in the East-West confrontation, characterized the strategic conceptions of the Alliance, whose leaders eschewed the previous belligerent attitude in favor of speeches that praised a "peaceful coexistence", tried to build a new "era of negotiations" and promoted a long-lasting "structure of peace". This conceptual shift was a response to "the modifications in the once monolithic Soviet bloc" (Humphrey 1967:681). The changes mentioned by U.S. Vice President Hubert Humphrey in his 1967 address to the NAC occurred amid the dynamics of the new factors characterizing the international environment of that period: the development of U.S.-Soviet nuclear parity, the disintegration of the Communist bloc, and the rise of a gradually cohesive and vocal Western Europe.

The Cold War was characterized by edgy relations between the United States and the Soviet Union, with the two superpowers constantly struggling to resolve their outstanding issues in terms of nuclear armament. Against this background, the strategic arms limitations talks (SALT) initiated by Lyndon Johnson in January 1967, and continued by Richard Nixon until 1972 could be regarded as an attempt of cooperation between the United States and the Soviet Union.[9] In the context of the investigation of NATO discourse, the research has returned a number of textual references to the SALT initiatives, especially during the Ministerial Meetings held between 1969 and 1981. The topical thread that incorporates the concept of détente is populated with formulations that welcome the agreement to achieve nuclear parity. Two Final Communiqués, one of the Defence Planning Committee and the other of the North Atlantic Council, issued in May 1979, with a two-week difference, and on two different occasions, contain an identical formulation:

Example 1:

"Ministers welcomed the agreement reached between the United States and the Soviet Union in the Strategic Arms Limitation-Talks. They agreed that an *equitable* limitation of the nuclear weapons capabilities of the Soviet Union and the United States will make an important contribution to East-West relations and security." (Final Communiqué of the Defence Planning Committee, Brussels 1979, par. 5)

Example 2:

---

[9] While abolition of nuclear weapons was considered impossible, the initiation of strategic arms limitation talks was aimed at stopping the development of both offensive and defensive strategic systems and at stabilizing the tense U.S.-Soviet relations.

"Ministers welcomed the agreement reached between the United States and the Soviet Union in the Strategic Arms Limitation-Talks. They agreed that a balanced limitation of the nuclear weapons capabilities of the Soviet Union and the United States will make an important contribution to East-West relations and security." (Final Communiqué of the North Atlantic Council, the Hague 1979, par. 5)

The only difference, operated for the sake of variation alone, resides in a single instance of semantic flexibility, as the adjective "equitable" in the first document was replaced with a total synonym, "balanced", in the second text (not italicized in the original quotation).

Both discourses emphasize the reaction of the allies to the agreement, and the reference to an emotional attitude embedded in the word "satisfaction", used almost awkwardly in the second communiqué, testifies for the sense of fulfillment the agreement sparked at the time. Anticipation is also expressed in the predicative construction of the second sentence.

"Ministers expressed their satisfaction with the past record of close and full exchanges within the Alliance on issues arising from these talks and confirmed the importance of continuing these exchanges. They looked forward to the opportunity to study in depth the official SALT II text once the treaty is signed." (Final Communiqué of the North Atlantic Council, the Hague 1979, par. 5)

Subsequent Final Communiqués hail the triumph of the Alliance, which had made remarkable efforts to convince the Soviets to adhere to these treaties.

"Allied efforts to persuade the Soviet Union to change its policy from one of intervention in the affairs of other states to one of respect for their sovereignty serve the general interest of the international community. The Allies will keep open channels of communication and be ready to respond positively to concrete steps by the Soviet Union to cease aggressive activities and to restore the basis for constructive East-West relations." (Final Communiqué of North Atlantic Council, Brussels 1980, par. 4)

The text used here as an example is one of many indications of the integrative power embedded in NATO's discourse of unity. The takeaway from this paragraph is that in virtue of their relational power, the Alliance members, united by a common goal, succeeded in operating structural

94

modifications at the level of international policy, swaying the longstanding enemy – the Soviet Union – to even reconsider its strategies. A strong verb is used here to reflect the depth of the cognitive changes achieved in the name of global security. Openness to cooperation is announced, and a positive answer is promised, but such a perspective entails a condition which, although not explicitly framed in the text, is embedded in the formulation that rejects aggressiveness in favor of peace, under certain circumstances, implying "concrete steps by the Soviet Union to cease aggressive activities".

At the Paris meeting of the NAC in June 1983, the allies sum up the steps they had taken as part of their strategy of external cooperation and call upon the Soviets to respect their part of the deal. The opening paragraphs of the Final Communiqué of the NAC inform that

> "… the countries of the Alliance They have put forward a broad set of arms control and disarmament initiatives on:
> - strategic arms reductions (START)
> - intermediate range nuclear forces (INF)
> - Mutual and Balanced Force Reductions (MBFR)
> - a Conference on Confidence- and Security-Building Measures and Disarmament in Europe (CDE)
> - a total ban on chemical weapons.
>
> They call upon the Soviet Union to demonstrate by its deeds an equal resolution to achieve concrete results in these negotiations." (Final Communiqué of North Atlantic Council, Paris 1983, par. 3-5)

The agreements concluded with the Soviets during this period were perceived to have brought an important contribution to the stability of East-West relations. As a matter of fact, this theme is a constant topical thread that typifies a series of approximately twenty NATO official documents between 1964 and 1989. The identified texts are general references to the development of East-West relations (Final Communiqués of the North Atlantic Council: Paris, 15-17 December 1964; Paris, 15-16 December 1965; Luxembourg, 13-14 June 1967; Brussels, 11-12 December 1974; Brussels, 11-12 December 1975; Brussels, 9-10 December 1976; Brussels, 7-8 December 1978; Paris, 9-10 June 1983; Brussels, 13 December 1984); welcome the progress and efforts to improve East-West relations (Final Communiqués of the North Atlantic Council: Bonn, 30-31 May 1972;

Brussels, 13 December 1979; Brussels, 8-9 December 1983); emphasize the need for East-West relations to be stable, constructive, more cooperative and improved (Final Communiqués of the Defence Planning Committee: Brussels, 16-17 May 1984; Brussels, 28-29 November 1989) or advocate for stronger basis to create better East-West relations (Final Communiqué of the Defence Planning Committee: Brussels, 3 December 1985).

One of the key documents that discursively reified the concept of cooperation between NATO and its counterbalance, the Soviet Union, is the "Washington Statement on East-West Relations", issued by the Foreign Ministers at the North Atlantic Council Meeting. Held in Washington D.C., on May 31, 1984, the ministerial meeting produced a text that undertook "an appraisal of East-West relations with a view to achieving a more constructive East-West dialogue" (Washington Statement on East-West Relations 1984, par. 1). The stated purpose of the document, basically encompassing all the stipulations of the documents issued before and after, is "to maintain adequate military strength and political solidarity, to pursue a more stable relationship between the countries of East and West through dialogue and cooperation, to alleviate sources of tension and to create a propitious climate for expanded cooperation" (par. 2). The last paragraph of the Washington Document invites to cooperation ("united", "to join in") in the name of peace and stability and reaffirms the openness of the Alliance to any initiative that brings about a mutually beneficial relationship between the parts.

> "Peace and stability require a united effort: the Allies look to the Soviet Union and the other Warsaw Pact countries to join in an endeavor which would be of benefit to the world at large. The Allies are prepared to do their part and are ready to examine any reasonable proposal. A long-term, constructive and realistic relationship can then be brought about." (par. 21)

As illustrated by the analysis conducted so far, during the late 1980s, the rhetoric of the Alliance brought nothing new and basically reiterated the same conceptual tenets that had characterized NATO discourse in the last 40 years. With the Americans in the lead, European allies publicly reaffirmed their belief in the commonly held values of an Atlantic Community. In the early 1990s, the collapse of the Soviet Union brought about new uncertainties and threats, to which NATO responded by forging a set of new strategic and political concepts wrapped around old notions of partnership, which cemented the conceptual framework supporting the Alliance's new objective of consolidating pan-European security into the 21st century.

When Gorbachev resumed arms control negotiations with the West, began to withdraw from the Third World, and eased constraints on his Warsaw Pact allies in Eastern Europe, the stage for the end of the Cold War was set. With the United States characteristically in the lead, NATO publicly took credit for these changes. The forty years of alliance solidarity in the face of fluctuating Soviet maneuvers were recalled as to account for the improved relations in the East-West confrontation. In December 1985, NAC declared that the Alliance's policy of peace through strength, backed up by the dual-track approach, "demonstrate the validity of our policy" (Final Communiqué of the North Atlantic Council 1985, par. 1).

The October 1986 Summit held in Reykjavik, where Reagan and Gorbachev came enticingly close to reaching an agreement on reducing strategic nuclear forces opened prospects for encouraging advances in East-West relations. The discussions about the possibility to completely eliminate ballistic missiles and to reduce intermediate nuclear forces, as well as to verify and limit nuclear testing revealed great potential for a superpower cooperation on arms control. Despite their apparent support for these new arrangements, West Europeans were not pleased with the Americans and the Soviets striking deals over their heads. Moreover, the allies feared the emergence of a superpower condominium that could agree on a possible denuclearization of Europe, ultimately threatening regional and national security. In reaction, the American leaders presented the Reykjavik Summit as a meeting where the decisions taken were in the best interest of the alliance as a whole and in congruence with NATO's previous policies. In a speech given to the officers of the Department of State and the Arms Control and Disarmament Agency on October 14, 1986, Reagan declared that "We went to the Iceland meeting in a position of strength. The Soviets knew that we had the support, not only of a strong America but a united NATO alliance ..." and that "... it was this strength and unity that brought the Soviets to the bargaining table" (Reagan 1986:20). With this formulation, the integrative power operating within the Alliance is also acknowledged as the main mechanism for cooperation outside NATO, especially with the Soviet Union.

The INF Treaty, signed between the United States and the Soviet Union in December 1987, was perceived by the allies as a confirmation of their

Cold War strategies, axiomatically enunciated by the 1967 *Harmel Report*, which had called on negotiations with the Soviets based on military strength and political solidarity. "This is an alliance treaty", U.S. Secretary of State George P. Schultz argued during a news conference at NATO headquarters in 1988, highlighting the fact that it "has proceeded very much from the tradition, philosophy and concept of the Harmel Report" (1988:13). For NATO's conceptions, it was a success that opened the door to a new era of international relations. It reasserted the notion of peace through strength that NATO had steadily pursued for the last 20 years and validated NATO's central role in improving East-West relations. The Alliance's conceptions gained legitimacy, and NATO confirmed its importance as a forum for negotiations and exchange of ideas between the Western countries and the nations of the Warsaw Pact. By sticking firmly to the basic principles of the Harmel Report and by using public discourse to win the hearts and minds of the people – the ever-pursued goal of any ideology – NATO extended its purview beyond the limits of a military alliance: it became an entity that promoted good in the world. This new tendency of triumphalism was increasingly pronounced as Soviet control weakened in Eastern Europe and eventually at home.

The reunification of Germany in 1990 and the demise of the Warsaw Pact in 1991 rendered the Alliance's previous strategic concept of flexible response obsolete. As a consequence, a new Strategic Concept was needed in order to address the dynamics of relations in a context in which the enemy threatening NATO's eastern frontier had disappeared. The concept of flexible response was dismissed in favor of a new force posture based on smaller, more mobile forces that had a lower level of readiness.

The "New Strategic Concept" was issued at the 1991 Summit in Rome. The document announced the four core security functions of the Alliance, all of which were meant to reassert NATO's part for the security of Europe, its dimension as a forum for consultation, its continuous goal of acting as a shield against any threat of aggression and its role in preserving the power balance in Europe (The Alliance's New Strategic Concept 1991, par. 21). With this new strategic orientation, NATO restated its central role in post-Cold War security and reiterated its referent, expert and legitimate power, the most essential pillars underlying the authority of the Alliance on the international scene.

The second document produced on the occasion of the 1991 Rome Summit, "Rome Declaration on Peace and Security" further consolidated

NATO's authoritative power by extending the principles of cooperation and consultation so as to include former adversaries:

> "... in a world where the values which we uphold are shared even more widely, we gladly seize the opportunity to adapt our defenses accordingly; to cooperate and consult with our new partners; to help consolidate a now undivided continent of Europe; and to make our alliance's contribution to a new age of confidence, stability and peace." (par. 20)

This statement contains an important indication in terms of how NATO changed the perception of its former adversaries. Backed up by the conviction that "our own security is inseparably linked to that of all other states in Europe", this formulation announced an essential extension of NATO's power of influence beyond the initial geographical borders existing at the moment of its conception.

The two documents represented a departure from the forty-two years of conceptual formulations focused on countering the Soviet threat. Instead, they reflected NATO's new tasks in the post-Cold War era, in which an existential threat was no longer the hub of the alliance. In the context of new security challenges in a changing world, NATO made it clear that there were no longer geographical and political limitations to its claims of expertise, especially since the end of the Cold War eroded the former distinction between in- and out-of-area issues.

During the last decade of the 20th century, NATO's response to the different challenges of the security configuration marked a turn point in its ideological evolution. The Alliance assumed new roles in the geopolitical arena and opened, more than ever before, to external cooperation, especially with countries that had been traditionally considered "adversaries". David Yost considers that the phrase "cooperation with former adversaries" refers to "the magnitude of the more ambitious and demanding of the Alliance's new roles" (1998:91). Indeed, in the aftermath of the Cold War, NATO has repeatedly expressed a commitment to bring its contribution to building a more peaceful political order in Europe as a whole. In order to achieve this goal, the Alliance has set up a number of institutions through which to mitigate cooperation on security issues between NATO and former adversaries or other non-NATO countries. Among these institutions, the North Atlantic Cooperation Council, replaced by the Euro-Atlantic Partnership Council in May 1997, the Partnership for Peace, and the NATO-Russia Permanent Joint Council are the most notable. The cooperation was cemented through a series of authoritative declarations, underlining NATO's self-assigned role as an "agent of change" throughout Europe.

NATO's ambition to contribute to long-lasting peaceful diplomatic ties in Europe was initially expressed in the *Harmel Report*: "The ultimate political purpose of the Alliance is to achieve a just and lasting peaceful order in Europe, accompanied by appropriate security guarantees" (par. 8). At NATO's July 1990 London Summit, the first one held after the downfall of the communist governments in Eastern Europe in 1989, the allies expressed their resolve to maintain the peace and invested in NATO's ability to construct a Europe "whole and free". In the words of the London Declaration, this vision is made possible through cooperation, unity and the promotion of shared values, all of which are the pillars of integrative power.

> "We need to keep standing together, to extend the long peace we have enjoyed these past four decades. Yet our alliance must be even more an agent of change. It can help build the structures of a more united continent, supporting security and stability with the strength of our shared faith in democracy, the rights of the individual and the peaceful resolution of disputes." (London Declaration on a Transformed North Atlantic Alliance 1990, par. 1-2).

Furthermore, in London, NATO announced that it would embark on a mission aimed at reaching out "to the countries of the East that were our former adversaries in the Cold War and extend to them the hand of friendship" (par. 6). In practical terms, this translated into military contacts between NATO and the Warsaw Pact states and a joint declaration in which the two parties affirmed that they were "no longer adversaries".

These ideas were reiterated in the 1991 Strategic Concept, which uses a similar formulation to recall that "the Alliance has worked since its inception for the establishment of a just and lasting peaceful order in Europe" (The Alliance's New Strategic Concept 1991, par. 16). While the *Harmel Report* makes an initial reference to this goal, it remains unexplored by the document in terms of the specific means of achieving it and was rather considered a generally assumed task of the Alliance. However, the 1991 strategic document adds an important aspect: that the vision of a peaceful Europe shall be achieved by pursuing "the development of cooperative structures of security for a Europe whole and free" (par. 19). The formulation of the Strategic Concept emphasizes that one of the Alliance's fundamental tasks is "to provide one of the indispensable foundations for a stable security environment in Europe, based on the growth of democratic institutions and commitment to the peaceful resolution of disputes, in which no country would be able to intimidate or coerce any European nation or to impose hegemony through threat or use of force" (par. 21).

This vision was extended five years later, during the Ministerial Meeting held in Brussels, on December 10, 1996. On the occasion, the North Atlantic Council advocated the construction of "cooperative European security structures which extend to countries throughout the whole Europe without excluding anyone or creating diving lines" (Final Communiqué of the Ministerial Meeting of the North Atlantic Council 1996, par. 4). With these tasks on its agenda, NATO assumed the role of unifying nations throughout Europe through the display of relational power in both discourse and practice.

This galvanizing exercise was also supported by U.S. policy. In February 1997, U.S. Secretary of State Madeleine Albright remarked that it was time for the new NATO to do the same things for the east that it had done for the west after World War II. In the politician's own words "the fundamental role of our policy is to build, for the very first time, a peaceful, democratic and undivided transatlantic community" (Albright 1997a:22). The assumed task of the Alliance was to extend eastward – toward Central Europe and the states of the former USSR – and to offer the Eastern part of the continent the peace and prosperity that Western Europe had benefited from in the last fifty years.

Adopted in Paris in May 1997, the NATO-Russia Founding Act encompasses a greater vision, with goals for extended collective security in the Euro-Atlantic region.

> "NATO and Russia, based on an enduring political commitment undertaken at the highest political level, will build together a lasting and inclusive peace in the Euro-Atlantic area on the principles of democracy and cooperative security... Proceeding from the principle that the security off all states in the Euro-Atlantic community is indivisible, NATO and Russia will work together to contribute to the establishment in Europe of a common and comprehensive security based on the allegiance to shared values, commitments and norms

of behavior in the interest of all states…NATO and Russia will seek the widest possible cooperation among participating States of the OSCE with the aim of creating in Europe a common space of security and stability, without dividing lines or spheres of influence limiting the sovereignty of any state." (Founding Act on Mutual Relations, Cooperation and Security between the North Atlantic Treaty Organization and the Russian Federation 1997:2-3).

The language of the illustrated documents is extremely straightforward and repetitive, with great emphasis laid on the words "security" and "stability" throughout the formulations. The syntactic linchpin of the cooperation between NATO and Russia is the usage of the prospective tense employed as to direct the future actions of the two actors toward a common practice to be equally assumed by both. "Democracy", "indivisibility" and "shared values", norms and attitudes are abstract concepts that populate the discourse with the aim of ideologically strengthening the exercise of cooperation. In the text of the document, augmentative markers such as "wider" and "comprehensive" underline the importance and the extent of cooperation, which is to be achieved through all means. The key concept to be identified in the last three mentioned examples is, without any doubt, that of "indivisibility". Cooperation is efficient and conceptually valid as long as it does not affect the sovereignty of any state and given that it functions on the principle of an "undivided community", without creating "diving lines".

Such a goal is achievable through the creation of institutions and partnership programs that function under a set of pre-established rules and base practice on commonly agreed values and norms. The North Atlantic Cooperation Council and the Partnership for Peace represent the Alliance's initial efforts to institutionalize cooperative relations with the former adversaries and other non-NATO countries in the Euro-Atlantic region. Starting from the premise that discourse is the linguistic locus of institutional expression and communication, it is relevant in this context to briefly mention the institutions established for and tasked with promoting the Alliance's cooperation activities and to analyze their activities and rhetoric in so far as it serves the purpose of illustrating their contribution to the exercise of relational power.[10]

---

[10] A paper on expressions of relational power in NATO discourse from the perspective of the Alliance's mechanisms of cooperation with former adversaries was presented at the International Conference "Knowledge-Based Organization, organized by "Nicolae Bălcescu" Land Forces Academy on June 26,

*The North Atlantic Cooperation Council*

The North Atlantic Cooperation Council (henceforth referred to as NAAC) was the Alliance's initial attempt to outstrip military and diplomatic contacts with the states of the Warsaw Pact (formally disbanded in 1991) and to develop, as stated in the Rome Declaration, "a more institutional relationship of consultation and cooperation on political and security issues" with Bulgaria, Czechoslovakia, Estonia, Hungary, Latvia, Lithuania, Poland, Romania and the Soviet Union (Rome Declaration on Peace and Cooperation 1991, par. 11). The foreign ministers of all the former Warsaw Pact states were invited to encounter their NATO counterparts in December 1991, a date that marked the first meeting of the NAAC.

With the accent placed on "cooperation" and "consultation", one of the aspects discussed at the first NACC meeting was that its members would reconvene annually at the foreign minister level and every other month at ambassadorial level, with further meetings depending on the circumstances. Under the auspices of different NATO committees, the NACC members would meet regularly to discuss security-related issues such as "defense planning, conceptual approaches to arms control, democratic concepts of civil-military relations, civil-military coordination of air traffic management, and the conversion of defense production to civilian purposes" (North Atlantic Cooperation Council Statement on Dialogue, Partnership and Cooperation 1991, par. 4).

NACC activities consisted of meetings – seminars, workshops, colloquiums, conferences, etc. It was composed of sixteen NATO countries and twenty-two other states, all "former adversaries". It encompassed all the members of the Warsaw Pact, including the successor states of the Soviet Union, as well as Slovakia and the Czech Republic. Some other states, such as Austria, Finland, Slovenia, Sweden, and Switzerland were given observer status in NACC.

Given that the Alliance is an intergovernmental organization, national views may sometimes be divergent and consequently need to be reconciled. However, the NACC was relatively uncontroversial. With the exception of France, which initially opposed the creation of the Council, given the fact that French defense ministers had not participated in meetings with their NATO counterparts since France's withdrawal from the integrated command structure in 1966, all the other members seem to have found

2018. The paper entitled *Expressions of Relational Power in NATO Discourse: Cooperation with Former Adversaries* was published in Vol. 24/2 of the Conference, pp. 282-287.

common ground when discussing topics related to peacekeeping, arms control, scientific research and environmental cooperation, and the transformation of defense industries. With the subsequent development of the Partnership for Peace (PfP), NACC was replaced in May 1997 by the Euro-Atlantic Partnership Council (EAPC), a wider organization including all PfP and NACC participants.

*Partnership for Peace*

In January 1994, at the Summit held in Brussels, NATO announced its intention to "launch an immediate and practical program that will transform the relationship between NATO and participating states" (The Brussels Summit Declaration 1994, par. 18). It was a new program intended to go beyond cooperation and dialogue and aimed at forging a real partnership – the Partnership for Peace. The declaration continues "We invite the other states participating in the NAAC, and other OSCE countries able and willing to contribute to this program, to join us in this Partnership" (par. 18). The invitation clearly bridges the gap between "the other states" and "us", and although the text of the document does not explicitly mention it, the two adjectives used to characterize the potential members of this program are indicative of the requirements the Alliance is targeting: the candidates must be "able", in terms of capabilities and "willing" in so far as their commitment to the values of the Alliance goes. The document states the goal of the partnership, which aims to "expand and intensify political cooperation throughout Europe, increase stability, diminish threats to peace and build strengthened relationships by promoting the spirit of practical cooperation and commitment to democratic principles that underpin our Alliance" (par. 19). The enumeration of predicates expressed by strong present tense action verbs illustrates the array of ambitious tasks envisaged by the PfP. Furthermore, the "by" phrase is used so as to indicate the manner in which these activities must be performed, thus tying the institutional practice to the ideology promoted by NATO.

The example of the Partnership for Peace program and the rhetoric associated with the Framework Document are illustrative of the referent and expert dimensions of power assumed by NATO in this context. The Alliance has been the sponsor or senior partner in PfP in that it was NATO that established the purview of the program, including the list of activities available for inclusion in the program. The major powers in the

104

Alliance acted as points of reference for the smaller powers in Europe, who are perceived as valuable partners but not yet ready to become full members. The document refers to the member states of the North Atlantic Alliance and to other States, all of which are "resolved to deepen their political and military ties and to contribute further to the strengthening of security within the Euro-Atlantic area" (Partnership for Peace: Framework Document issued by the Heads of State and Government participating in the Meeting of the North Atlantic Council 1994, par. 1).

The next logical question to be asked is in what manner the scope of PfP integrates within the broader framework of the Alliance. The language used to define the purposes of this partnership resembles closely, as if copied, to the formulation in Article 4 of the North Atlantic Treaty: "NATO will consult with any active participant in the Partnership if that partner perceives a direct threat to its territorial integrity, political independence or security" (The Brussels Summit Declaration 1994, par. 19.). The text of Article 4 of the North Atlantic Treaty reads "The Parties will consult together whenever, in the opinion of any of them, the territorial integrity, political independence or security of any of the Parties is threatened". The key words that are identical in both documents are "territorial integrity", "political independence" and "security", representing three of the major ideological pillars on which the Alliance was initially built. A further step taken toward the consolidation of the values inherent in NATO's ideology and their alignment with the goals of the program consists in the agenda of the PfP, which included the promotion of standardization, especially in what regards the operational language used by the Alliance. To this aim, more than eight hundred NATO standardization documents were transferred to the Partners, containing references to concepts of operation, standard operating procedures, and military doctrine.

## NATO-Russia Founding Act

Developing a positive relationship with Russia remains one of the most essential challenges for NATO in its new dimension as an alliance promoting constructive cooperation with former adversaries. In December 1996, at the ministerial meeting held in Brussels, the North Atlantic Council restated its "commitment to a strong, stable, and enduring security partnership between NATO and Russia" (Final Communiqué of the Ministerial Meeting of the North Atlantic Council 1996, par. 10).

This was the expression of the hope that European security was entering a new, more promising phase. U.S. officials reiterated the importance of establishing strong connections with Russia and sought to build new frameworks of dialogue that would promote the strategic goal of reversing Russia's perception of NATO being a threat. Walter Slocombe, the then under-secretary of defense for policy noted "Such steps are useful, not only because they facilitate NATO-Russian cooperation on military matters, but because, we believe, the more Russia and the Russian military is involved in active cooperation with NATO, the more they see of what NATO really is and really does, the more they will see that NATO is no threat to them" (qtd. in Yost 1998:141).

The steps Slocombe referenced became reified as the NATO-Russia Founding Act (NRFA), signed in Paris, on May 27, 1997. From the Americans' perspective, this document was aimed at abating Russian hypernationalistic criticism of enlargement and at discouraging self-imposed Russian isolation. In April 1997, while anticipating the contents of the Act, U.S. secretary of defense William Cohen announced that

> "As our negotiations with Russia continue, we will adhere closely to five principles. Russia will not be allowed to:
> - Delay enlargement;
> - Veto NATO internal decisions;
> - Exclude any country from membership, now and in the future;
> - Subordinate NATO to any other institution; or
> - Impose second-class membership on any new member. (par. 12)"

Building a cooperative relationship between Russia and NATO has been an essential endeavor of the Alliance and a prerequisite for peaceful order in the Euro-Atlantic region. In addition to the PfP, other Alliance-based security structures (the NATO-Russia Council and the NATO-Ukraine Commission) have encouraged reconciliation processes regarding borders and minorities and have functioned as concrete instruments for constructive cooperation. Both the United States and European allies regard good relations with Russia as a precondition for stability in Europe. NATO conducts important bilateral relations with Moscow.

Issues outside the European theater have been largely responsible for enhancing the relationship between Russia and the transatlantic allies. Matters of countering terrorism and weapons proliferation were at the heart of the decision to upgrade NATO's relationship with Russia to the level of the NATO-Russia Council. The three documents produced on the occasion of the first NATO-Russia Summit held in Rome on May 28, 2002 ("NATO-Russia Relations: A New Quality", the "NATO-Russia Council Statement", and the "Decision Sheet of the Meeting of the NATO-Russia Council at the level of Heads of State and Government") jointly express the belief that NATO member states and the Russian Federation are ready to begin a new chapter in their relations, focusing on improving their ability to cooperate in areas of common interest and to work together against common threats and security risks. Russia was given a stronger voice in relation to WMD non-proliferation, missile defense, counter-terrorism, and crisis management. However, the new body does not give Russia a veto power or a vote in NATO enlargement discussions, and one NATO member can terminate a discussion if it chooses to do so. The second paragraph of the "NATO-Russia Relations:A New Quality" document clearly states the extent of cooperation between the two entities. It is relevant to note that the verbs that operationalize the tasks assumed in the framework of this forum are expressed in the future, a double indication of the long-term cooperation and of the willingness expresses by the modality embedded in this tense.

> "In the framework of the NATO-Russia Council, NATO member states and Russia will work as equal partners in areas of common interest. The NATO-Russia Council will provide a mechanism for consultation, consensus-building, cooperation, joint decision, and joint action for the member states of NATO and Russia on a wide spectrum of security issues in the Euro-Atlantic region." (NATO-Russia Relations: A New Quality 2002, par. 2)

The language of the other documents issued on the numerous occasions of the NATO-Russia Council meetings demonstrate that, after September 11, NATO members and Russia entered a joint enterprise to meet common threats to an extent unparalleled since the end of World War II. A key word search has revealed more than fifty documents that were produced between 1995 and 2013, on the occasion of the yearly meetings of the NATO-Russia Permanent Joint Council, replaced by the NATO-Russia Council after the 2002 bilateral summit.

In 2004, for instance, the Council issued a joint "Action Plan on Terrorism", superseded by a second similar document in 2011, at the

NATO-Russia Council meeting in Berlin. In an identical opening formulation, both documents reiterate the shared goal of NATO and Russia to fight terrorism in all its forms and join efforts to support of the commonly agreed upon policies.

> "The NATO-Russia Council categorically rejects terrorism in all its manifestations. It reconfirms that terrorist acts pose a direct challenge to common security, to shared democratic values and to basic human rights and freedoms. NRC nations agree that there is no cause that can justify such acts, and call for unity of action in the international community in addressing this insidious threat. They will do everything in their power to fight all forms of terrorism, acting in conformity with the UN Charter, international human rights and humanitarian law, as well as other existing commitments. They stand united in support of the relevant UN Security Council Resolutions, as well as the UN Global Counter-Terrorism Strategy." (NATO-Russia Council Action Plan on Terrorism 2004, par. 1 & 2011, par. 3)

The determination that permeates the actions is illustrated in language by the use of the adverb "categorically", later supported by the absolute predicative phrase "will do everything in their power". Even more so, the choice of the verb "stand" in lieu of "be/are" in the phrase "stand united" indicates the resilience of the actors to carry out their task despite potential difficulties.

Many documents that were generated after the NATO-Russia Council meetings are not public. However, an analysis of the statements issued by the Chairman in the aftermath of the proceedings has revealed that the topics tackled a variety of current international security issues, in the context of enhancing practical and operational military cooperation. Also, in the words of the Council's Chairman Statement from June 14, 2007, "Ministers reiterated the NRC's value as a forum for constructive dialogue on issues where there is agreement and for building clarity and understanding where there is disagreement" (Meeting of the NATO-Russia Council Chairman's Statement 2007, par. 5). The use of the verb itself encourages the generalization that reference to cooperation and constructive dialogue was a recurrent topic of the NATO-Russia meetings.

More recently, President Vladimir Putin's speech on different occasions was sprinkled with references to the Russian values being rooted in European values, while asserting Russia's prevailing policy of seeking more cooperation and a larger role in Europe. He was also the first Russian leader to visit NATO on October 3, 2001, a signal that the discourse of relational power was strong enough to generate action.

The 2001 bilateral summit in the United States opened the door to a better relationship between the two countries and with the rest of Europe. A year later, after the Prague Summit, President Bush traveled to Moscow to meet Putin and inform him of the NATO decision to include seven new members, all former Soviet allies, or, in the case of the Baltic States, former parts of the Soviet Union itself. In 2001, describing the United States' relations with Russia within NATO's framework, President Bush declared that "we share a vision of a European Atlantic community whole, free and at peace ... Russia should be a part of this Europe. We will work together with NATO and NATO members to build new avenues of cooperation and consultation between Russia and NATO" (2001, par. 6-7).

Nonetheless, subsequent developments have proven that the NRC and other mechanisms of cooperation between NATO and Russia were not effective in mitigating the emerging disagreements, as the meetings were interrupted after the 2014 Russian invasion of Crimea, and the Council dissolved.

## NATO-Ukraine

NATO has always been careful to pay special attention to former adversaries, and, in addition to Russia, Ukraine is another important country for the configuration of the security environment in Eastern Europe. On June 3, 1996, during the Meeting of the Ministers of Foreign Affairs in Berlin, the North Atlantic Council called for "stronger ties of cooperation with all Partner countries, including the further enhancement of our relationship with Ukraine" (Final Communiqué of the Ministerial Meeting of the North Atlantic Council June 1996, par. 2). Six months later, at the Ministerial Meeting held in Brussels on December 10, the Alliance expressed interest in "expanding and strengthening cooperative relations with all Partners, including building a ...distinctive relationship with Ukraine" (Final Communiqué of the Meeting of the North Atlantic Council in Defence Ministers Session, Brussels, 10-11 December 1996, par. 2). The December 1996 NAC Final Communiqué continues to assert the significance of strong ties between NATO and Ukraine, whose "strong, enduring relationship with NATO is an important aspect of the emerging European security architecture" (par. 50). The Alliance emphasized its commitment to pursue cooperation with Ukraine and formalize an effective NATO-Ukraine partnership at the future Summit in July 1997. The Alliance also demonstrated openness to Ukraine's proposal of cooperation, which were reified in the promised document, issued at the July 1997 NATO Summit in Madrid, in the form of the NATO-Ukraine Charter. The text specifies that the NAC and Ukraine will meet as the NATO-Ukraine Commission no less than twice a year. Furthermore, the Charter pivots on the shared view that NATO enlargement "is directed at enhancing the stability of Europe, and the security of all countries in Europe without recreating dividing lines" (Charter on a Distinctive Partnership between the North Atlantic Treaty Organization and Ukraine 1997, par. 12).

The special, or, in the formulation of the documents, "distinctive" relation with Ukraine is a manifestation of integrative power that discursively hinges on shared values of "security" and "stability" and is defined by repetitive adjectives belonging to the same lexical field and that populate all three mentioned documents: "strong", "enduring", "enhanced".

Cooperation between NATO and Ukraine is also viewed in practical terms, as the most important issues of common concern are, as revealed in the Charter, "armaments" and "military training". The text of the document reiterates the ideological pledge NATO extends to all allies and partners, which demonstrates the Alliance's commitment to consider and treat Ukraine as an important member of the security configuration NATO envisages in Europe. The Charter also notes that

> "NATO allies will continue to support Ukrainian sovereignty and independence, territorial integrity, democratic development, economic prosperity and its status as a non-nuclear weapon state, and the principle of inviolability of its frontiers, as key factors of stability and security in Central and Eastern Europe and in the continent as a whole." (Charter on a Distinctive Partnership between the North Atlantic Treaty Organization and Ukraine 1997, par. 58)

Anchoring these statements to the geopolitical reality of the period presupposes considering the existence of Russia as a key player in the context. The formulations in the Charter as well as those in the preceding documents express NATO's interest in discouraging a recreation of a

110

Russian empire by keeping Ukraine sovereign and autonomous. They are also indicative for NATO's, and more specifically the United States' and other major allies' strong commitment to make cooperation an important security mechanism in Europe, in an attempt to advert and prevent a possible Russian control over Ukraine.

The Russian invasion and annexation of Crimea in 2014 demonstrated that NATO was right in insisting to create a framework for formal cooperation with Ukraine, but the non-member status of the country prevented the Alliance from intervening in the crisis. Nonetheless, through the cooperation mechanism it created for such situations, the NATO-Ukraine Commission, the Alliance was able to have an indirect strategic say in the developments. The 2014 "Statement by NATO Defence Ministers on Ukraine" reiterates the importance of the cooperation between NATO and Ukraine and expresses the Alliance's standpoint vis-à-vis Ukraine's actions and its involvement:

> "NATO and Ukraine have a distinctive partnership, embodied in the NATO-Ukraine Commission. Through that partnership framework, NATO stands ready to continue to engage with Ukraine and assist with the implementation of reforms. Defence reform and military cooperation remain key priorities. We commend the Ukrainian armed forces for not intervening in the political crisis." (par. 2)

NATO's support for Ukraine's sovereignty and independence is repeated with almost identical words in a number of four documents issued in 2014 and 2015, during the Alliance's Ministerial Meetings.

Example 1:

> "A sovereign, independent and stable Ukraine, firmly committed to democracy and the rule of law, is key to Euro-Atlantic security. Consistent with the Charter on a Distinctive Partnership between NATO and Ukraine, NATO Allies will continue to support Ukrainian sovereignty and independence, territorial integrity, democratic development, and the principle of inviolability of frontiers, as key factors of stability and security in Central and Eastern Europe and on the continent as a whole." (Statement by NATO Defence Ministers on Ukraine 2014, par. 3)

Example 2:

> "An independent, sovereign and stable Ukraine, firmly committed to democracy and the rule of law, is key to Euro-Atlantic security. Allies firmly support Ukraine's sovereignty and territorial integrity." (Statement of the NATO-Ukraine Commission 2014, par. 10)

Example 3:

> "We reaffirm that an independent, sovereign and stable Ukraine, firmly committed to democracy and the rule of law, is key to security in the Euro-Atlantic area, of which – as stated in the Charter on a Distinctive Partnership – Ukraine is an inseparable part. The Alliance continues its full support for Ukraine's sovereignty, independence and territorial integrity within its internationally ecognized borders." (Joint Statement of the NATO-Ukraine Commission 2014, par.7)

Example 4:

> "Recalling earlier statements of the NATO-Ukraine Commission, we reiterate that an independent, sovereign and stable Ukraine, firmly committed to democracy and the rule of law, is key to Euro-Atlantic security." (Joint Statement of the NATO-Ukraine Commission 2015, par. 9)

In all four illustrations, Ukraine is defined by the same three adjectives "independent", "sovereign", and "stable". The fact that they are constantly used without any semantic or structural modification testifies to their importance for NATO and reflects the Alliance's vision in terms of the characteristics any state actor on the international scene should have for peace and stability to be a palpable reality. In virtue of these features, Ukraine is considered to be a "key" element for Euro-Atlantic security. The repetition of this sentence is indicative of the equal position NATO places itself on in relation to Ukraine, although not an Alliance member, and of the broader perspective the North Atlantic Organization has in terms of how comprehensibly international security is defined and of the fact that it also depends on cooperation with other non-NATO countries.

It has been a long-stated goal of Ukraine to become a NATO member. However, despite Kyiv's alternating manifestations of interest in NATO membership, Ukrainian ascension to the Alliance is still unmaterialized, mainly because of a general Western hesitancy to provoke Russia on such a sensitive issue. One step has been nonetheless taken, as NATO has recently granted Ukraine the status of "aspirant country", which allows for a more comprehensive involvement in the MAP as a key preparation mechanism for membership. In July 2017, NATO Secretary General Jens Stoltenberg and Ukrainian President Poroshenko met in Kyiv to celebrate the twentieth anniversary of the signing of the distinctive partnership document between NATO and Ukraine, a meeting that also reaffirmed the Alliance's support for Ukraine. The text of the 2018 "Brussels Summit Declaration" mentions the relationship between NATO and Ukraine and briefly reminds Ukraine's desire to become an Alliance member. While commended for its progress in compliance with NATO requirements, Ukraine is also reminded that it still has a long way until all prerequisites are met.

> "An independent, sovereign and stable Ukraine, firmly committed to democracy and the rule of law is key for Euro-Atlantic security. We stand firm in our support for Ukraine's right to decide its own future and foreign policy course free from outside interference. In light of Ukraine's restated aspirations for NATO membership, we stand by our decisions taken at the Bucharest Summit and subsequent Summits. The success of wide-ranging reforms, including combatting corruption and promoting an inclusive electoral process, based on democratic values, respect for human rights, minorities and the rule of law, will be crucial in laying the groundwork for a prosperous and peaceful Ukraine firmly anchored among European democracies committed to common values.
>
> We welcome significant reform progress already made … NATO will consider this in view of the decisions taken at the Wales and the Warsaw Summits. We will continue to work with Ukraine, a longstanding partner of the Alliance, based on the principles and values enshrined in the Charter on a Distinctive Partnership between NATO and Ukraine." (Brussels Summit Declaration 2018, par. 66)

In a 2018 article discussing the prospect of Ukraine's membership in NATO, political analyst Taras Kuzio presents pro and con arguments to the issue and concludes that Poroshenko could be the president to take Ukraine into NATO, given the significant security reforms happening in the country and also the elite and public pro-NATO orientation. The author remains an optimist that Ukraine will soon join NATO as a fully-fledged member, which, in his estimation, will significantly contribute to the European security environment.

*NATO – Mediterranean Dialogue*

Among other strategic directions it offered, the Istanbul Summit in 2004 was also focused on enhancing NATO's existing partnerships and extending the partnership model to the Middle East. A symbol that NATO used for the Istanbul Summit was "bridge building". Indeed, in NATO's Secretary General Jaap de Hoop Scheffer's words, the June Summit's announced main goal was to build bridges to the Mediterranean and the Middle East, by strengthening the Mediterranean Dialogue and reaching out to the wider region that some have called the Greater Middle East: "The Istanbul Summit will help us deliver. It will provide us with many new tools to help us project stability: enhanced Partnerships, notably with our Partners in the Caucasus and Central Asia; a deepening of our Mediterranean Dialogue and a new offer of cooperation to countries from the wider region of the Middle East" (2004:para. 12).

In Istanbul, the Americans sought to engage the Allies in projecting stability beyond the Euro-Atlantic area, ranging from the Central Asian and Caucasus states, and finally extending to the Middle East. These states, traditionally viewed as bordering the Euro-Atlantic area, became an area of interest after the Alliance's involvement in Afghanistan. The U.S.-initiated "war on terror" had provided an opportunity for greater NATO influence in the region, in part because the physical presence of American and other international armed forces in the area had an important symbolic effect in emphasizing the links between Central Asia and the West after a decade of fragile contacts. The interests were not, however, limited to NATO's needs in Afghanistan. The new geostrategic environment, comprising a mix of rising and declining regional powers, required NATO's ability to extend its power to the east and to the south. Security, democracy, and economic prosperity were among the Alliance's objectives for the Caucasus and Central Asia; furthermore, the region was perceived as a bridge to the Middle East.

References to the importance of the Mediterranean Dialogue are abundant throughout the long text of the Final Communiqué issued at the Istanbul 2004 Summit. Paragraph 68 of the document reads

"From its inception in 1994, NATO's Mediterranean Dialogue has greatly contributed to building confidence and cooperation between the Alliance and its Mediterranean partners. In the current security environment, there are greater opportunities for effective cooperation

114

with Mediterranean Dialogue partners. Following our decision at Prague to upgrade the Mediterranean Dialogue, we are today inviting our Mediterranean partners to establish a more ambitious and expanded partnership, guided by the principle of joint ownership and taking into consideration their particular interests and needs. The overall aim of this partnership will be to contribute towards regional security and stability through stronger practical cooperation, including by enhancing the existing political dialogue, achieving interoperability, developing defence reform and contributing to the fight against terrorism." (Istanbul Summit Communiqué 2004, par. 68)

The paragraph takes a brief journey into the history of the program and defines its importance in the context of the current configuration of the security environment, which requires "a more expanded and ambitious partnership" and "stronger practical cooperation". The concept of joint ownership leaves room for a certain degree of autonomy for the Mediterranean Dialogue partner countries, which are encouraged to consider "their particular interests and needs" while securing regional stability. From the perspective of integrative power and its manifestation through language, the discourse in imbued with references to cooperation and mutual pursuance of common objectives.

In terms of military and political strategic directions, the Istanbul Summit occasioned the launch of the Istanbul Cooperation Initiative (ICI), an initiative directed at promoting security cooperation between NATO and the states of the Greater Middle East. The Bush's administration agenda for this summit must be understood as part of a long-term U.S. effort to broaden NATO's focus beyond Europe. According to this vision, NATO' evolving role in the Middle East was subsequently focused on providing the linchpin between Middle Eastern and transatlantic security. With these new engagements, NATO was no longer a static, Euro-centric organization.

These shiftings in the tectonic plates of the global power balance impacted the Alliance's ideological evolution on several levels. First of all, NATO strove to build more cooperative relations with the Soviet Union and, after the end of the Cold War, with Russia. After 1991, working side by side with former adversaries was a pivotal mechanism in the Alliance's exercise of integrative power in the context of the external bipolar balance of powers. Against this backdrop, NATO's discourse became more oriented toward fostering and encouraging expanded cooperation with Russia, Ukraine and former Warsaw Pact states.

The second noteworthy effect of the shifting global balance of power was the realization of the fact that NATO countries are becoming more and more vulnerable to security threats generated from beyond the Euro-Atlantic area. The 2010 Strategic Concept explains: "Instability or conflict beyond NATO's borders can directly threaten Alliance security, including by fostering extremism, terrorism and transnational illegal activities such as trafficking in arms, narcotics and people" (Strategic Concept for the Defense and Security of the Members of the North Atlantic Treaty Organization 2010, par. 13).

Furthermore, the MENA region became the geographical hub for NATO's concerns regarding regional conflicts, failed states, terrorism, and nuclear proliferation. Consequently, NATO's strategic discourse repeatedly emphasized the importance of the Alliance's efforts to secure cooperation with its partners in the Gulf area. Most of the rhetoric was centered on NATO's willingness to receive new members in the ICI. The shift of focus on the MENA region accounts for a wider geostrategic reorientation of the Cold War East-West axis to a new North-South one.

In the context of these new strategies, the "out-of-area" protracted issue reemerged during the Lisbon Summit, whose discourse highlighted the importance of extended partnership between NATO and other actors, while placing the importance of the Alliance's single global role in the background. This theme has been identified as being a central thread running throughout all the documents that illustrate NATO's use of integrative power. In the framework of global security challenges, the Alliance has kept a truly efficient balancing act in its relationing with other non-NATO countries, an exercise that stemmed from the imperative that the Alliance be anchored in a wider security system. By pursuing the goal of developing a series of new partnerships with the other countries, NATO cemented its role as a security institution that "continues to be effective in a changing world, against new threats with new capabilities and new partners" (Preface of the Strategic Concept for the Defense and Security of the Members of the North Atlantic Treaty Organization 2010).

## 3.2.2 Adversarial Power Relations – The Discourse of Opposition

Traditionally, the North Atlantic Treaty Organization was forged on the basis of the "dumbbell concept" that assumed the existence of equal forces at both end of the power spectrum: the United States and Western Europe. Nevertheless, as with any organic structure, characterized by dynamism and continuous change, the alliance's fragile balance of power has been repeatedly challenged, with either of the two "weights" struggling to assume decisional and actional power amid the developments that typified the international scene since NATO's inception.

Despite the rhetoric of equality and sovereignty, internally NATO remains an alliance of unequals. Inequality among NATO members is the root cause of many of the tensions and disagreements that have marked the development of the Alliance over seven decades.

The most prevalent imbalance lies between the U.S. and the rest of the allies, mostly due to the fact that American capabilities and commitments are the foundation upon which western states have traditionally based their security and plans. The presence of U.S. troops in Europe, the nuclear umbrella the United States offers, the American dominance of the seas around the European continent, and its strategic forces are the predicate of European defense thinking.

U.S.'s commitment to Europe is the main part of its global apparatus of power and security. It started with the Marshall Plan and the formation of NATO in 1949, as a materialization of the American international policies. The creation of an entity called Western Europe and the economic restoration of its nations were regional elements of a global process that has been under constant evolution, culminating with the enlargement of the Alliance toward the eastern European countries and its involvement in out-of-area issues, as a means of cementing the promise of security and stability in the world.

Historically, American policy has been more than the traditional confrontation with the former USSR. The cataclysm of World War II marked the end of the European age of history, the end of great empires, especially the French and the British, but also the Belgian, Dutch and Italian. In the context of the war-inflicted disasters, the former European powers – most of them almost totally destroyed by the defeat, turned to the U.S. for survival. In virtue of their inability of playing a truly global role, they were also incapable of competing for world power. Americans seized the opportunity and were there to seal the vacuum left by the emerging demise of the European empires.

As a transatlantic alliance, aimed at unifying both common values and strategic interests under the same umbrella, NATO has experienced disparities between the visions of the world on the two sides of the Atlantic. These discrepancies have produced intra-NATO tensions and have resulted in different perspectives on major issues, such as détente, the vision of the Soviet-terrorism as being the fundamental cause of world tensions, or the American-led Alliance's interest and involvement in operations outside NATO's area.

In the early days of NATO, the problems caused by disparity were more unpretentious than unshared values and perspectives. It was simply jealousy. America's ascension toward the status of world power in the aftermath of World War II, although dressed up in the language of defending freedom against the Soviet threat, was resented by the former European great powers. Britain and France particularly found the fall from greatness hard to accept and experienced even more difficulties in reconciling with the new realities of American power and their own enfeeblement.

## 3.2.2.1 The Internal Multipolar Balance

The issues of opposition discussed here are relevant to the present investigation of power dynamics from the standpoint of the belief that the manifestation of power is clearer and better expressed in conflicting contexts. While NATO official documents are not infused with contradictory discourses – especially in virtue of the consensus that needs to be reached at the level of the Alliance before anything becomes official and is made public – it would be extremely pertinent to take a peek behind the curtains and investigate the political rhetoric that accompanies the decision-making processes regarding various incompatible issues. The arguments on which military representatives as well as key statesmen constructed their discourses on different occasions have been gathered as secondary sources to be analyzed with the aim of providing a more comprehensive image of the social and cognitive dimensions of power. The dynamics that characterize decision-making processes have a critical impact on the future strategic directions of the Alliance.

118

In NATO, the mutual reliance the transatlantic partners have on each other is, in addition to representing the bedrock of cooperation, a source of conflict and tension. The Alliance has experienced a fair share of "crises" during its evolution. The issues varied and included debates around concepts such as deterrence or interdependence, nuclear issues, out-of-area issues, the need and validity of the European Security and Defense Policy, the process of enlargement, or even the possibility of Russia's membership in NATO.

From the very first moments of its implementation, the concept of an American-led plan for the defense of Western Europe was a legitimate source for the manifestation of adversarial power. The initiative was quickly challenged by the introduction of a parallel plan for collective European defense, stemming from the views of French Defense Minister René Pleven, who had called for the creation of a European Army, integrating national units. In May 1952, France, Italy, West Germany, and the Benelux countries signed the European Defense Community (EDC) Treaty. Although the newly established force was to be closely tied to the newly emerged NATO, as the EDC would work within the framework of and reinforce the North Atlantic Organization, the Americans felt their supremacy and interests were challenged. In order to secure the founding concepts of the Treaty, they felt the need to emphasize the notion of structured defense, with Dean Acheson, the then U.S. Secretary of State insisting in 1953 that West European unity can only exist at the center of an Atlantic Community. The official warned that, without this hierarchy, there will be "disunity and weakness throughout the Atlantic community" (1953:7). This was actually an attempt of the Americans to safelock their hierarchical power and make sure that the Treaty's collective defense conceptions are not undermined by individual powers (although re-collected in another form, but away from the U.S. scrutinizing eye).

The role and position of the EDC having been established within the strategic and operational framework of NATO, the treaty was still pending the ratification of France in 1953. The country's resistance to ratify the document was the lack of agreement on the protocols interpreting the treaty and the fear that a continental conception of European security that excludes the United Kingdom from the equation might leave France vulnerable in the face of potential dominance from a revived Germany. The French ultimately chose not to ratify the treaty, which was dismissed by the National Assembly in August 1954.

The political and military implications of the stance France took in this situation are multifold and do not represent the purpose of this discussion. Suffice it to say, for the context of power dynamics analysis, that it represented an act of independent national action and a warning for those who argued that alliance unity must be maintained at all costs. The French demonstrated they can resist (American) pressure and asserted their power within the Alliance. Ideologically, the French defeat of the EDC set the stage for future conflicts in the evolution of NATO, as other European nations will also challenge the status quo of the U.S. power and ultimately one of the basic tenets underlying the creation of NATO – that no nation could go alone.

### The concept of interdependence

The allies made use of their adversarial power on more than one occasion. When, at the beginning of the 1960s, the Kennedy administration reiterated the concept of interdependence to characterize the relations between the United States and its European allies in the context of NATO, the latter group manifested various adverse reactions. In his 2002 *Kennedy, Macmillan and the Cold War: The Irony of Interdependence*, Nigel Ashton uses a truck and trailer metaphor to describe the concept of interdependence as illustrated by the relationship between the Americans and NATO. The trailer (NATO) would only move if pulled by the truck (the United States), which actually translates as a "more effective central, and hence, American control" (16). Behind the veiled rhetoric of interdependence used by the U.S. policymakers hid the reality that the balance of power was unequal. "… for one party was one of partnership and equality and for the other one of patron and client" (223).

From France's position, Kennedy's rhetoric, which promoted the concept of a Grand Design envisioning closer links between the United States and a united Western Europe, was countered by de Gaulle's vision of a French-led "European Europe". The implementation of this vision was never seen through and was received by West Germany and other European leaders as an attempt to replace American with French hegemony. A clash of power relations was subsequently sparked by de Gaulle's decision to withdraw from NATO's integrated command, followed by the request that NATO forces leave French soil, which resulted in the move of NATO headquarters from Fontainebleau to Brussels in 1967. As a consequence, many allied leaders wondered if France's decision might trigger an irreversible chain of events climaxing with the United States withdrawing from Europe.

The 1956 Suez Crisis was a key event that fueled U.S.-European tensions at the level of NATO.[11] While the Anglo-French response called for a military intervention against Egypt in cooperation with the Israeli forces, the Americans feared that such action would tilt Nasser toward the Soviets. Moreover, they undermined British economy by deciding to sell a significant amount of the U.S. pound sterling holdings. To end the conflict, the British, the French and the Israelis agreed on a ceasefire, but NATO's unity had already been dented by the disagreements in terms of how to best manage the situation. In *The Western Alliance: European-American Relations since 1945*, Alfred Grosser argues that for the Europeans, the Suez Crisis represented "a spectacular humiliation of Great Britain and France by their American partner" (1980:98).

Germany was a stout supporter of the U.S.-induced status quo and of the multilateralism and partnership policies of that period. The only exception was the use of nuclear weapons, as Germany questioned the issue of their control, which mistakenly induced the United States' belief that the Germans were developing a taste for nuclear weapons and that this might attract them on the side of France. Other than that, both Adenauer and his follower, Erhard, placed Germany at the forefront of the Alliance, pushing for integration and cohesion as a means of preserving national independence and power of decision in international matters.

The United Kingdom also aimed at obtaining political influence, a goal that prompted its leaders to endorse the American-generated strategies. The essence of British policy in relation to NATO, which was based not on the appearance of independence but on the reality of dependence, is illustrated by the Nassau Agreement, which won Britain a role of junior partner of the United States in NATO.[12]

*Nuclear issues*

In the 1980s, nuclear weapons emerged as the most controversial issue in NATO. This issue functioned as a surrogate for other questions –

---

[11] In May 1956, Egyptian President Nasser announced that Egypt would nationalize the Suez Canal, a decision that sparked antagonistic reactions within the alliance.

[12] The Nassau Agreement, negotiated between U.S. President John F. Kennedy and the Prime Minister of the United Kingdom, Harold Macmillan was concluded on December 21, 1962. Its applicationput an end to the Skybolt crisis and activated the UK Polaris program.

especially about U.S. leadership of the Alliance – as well as being a crucial issue in its own right. It sparked peace movements in Western Europe (especially in the Federal Republic of Germany and the Netherlands) and their force affected NATO's decisions at the time. On this occasion, the Alliance learned a valuable lesson about how to frame major decisions and handle public controversy.

The problem had emerged earlier, in the 1960s, when U.S. policy advocated the number reduction of tactical nuclear weapons (TNW), a suggestion that was met with reluctance by the European allies. The main argument lay in the view that the fundamental task of NATO was deterrence, not defense, and rather than act after a war had started, it would be better to prevent it from happening. In the first decade of the 1960s, pressure that arose partly from French policies and partly from a desire to prevent the FRG being tempted to become an independent nuclear weapons state, led the U.S. administration to promote the idea of a multilateral force – a transnational, NATO nuclear force. Agreement on this was never forthcoming and the administration itself was divided by it. The issue sputtered on for several years before being finally killed off.

In the same period, the U.S. administration was pushing for a different adjustment in NATO's nuclear strategy, placing greater emphasis on conventional forces. This raised fears in Europe that America would go cold on the nuclear guarantee, even though the change in strategy did not involve a reduction in TNW. The Eisenhower/Dulles strategy of massive retaliation was widely criticized because its emphasis on nuclear retaliation to aggression both lacked credibility and reduced the flexibility of US forces.

The response of the Kennedy administration, which took office in 1961 and which continued under Johnson after Kennedy's assassination, was to seek renewed utility in conventional forces. This emphasis involved moving away from NATO's "tripwire" concept in Europe in which conventional forces were intended to do a little more than put up token resistance.

In 1967, in one of the many institutional adjustments NATO made in the wake of the French rebellion – including the setting up of the Nuclear Planning Group (NPG) in 1966 to give European allies the sense if not the reality of participating in forming NATO's strategy – a new doctrine was adopted. Known as "flexible response" and embodied in a strategic document entitled MC14/3, the new approach attempted to balance the US desire for flexibility with the Western European governments' desire for the U.S. nuclear guarantee. The response relied heavily on U.S. strategic retaliation – nuclear bombardment of the USSR – to the Soviet threat. TNW remained a link between conventional and nuclear war. Compared to the earlier doctrine, the flexible response laid more stress on conventional forces and on the possibility of limiting the war even after it had gone nuclear. It continued to assert NATO's inclination to use nuclear force first but placed this in the context of a graduated response that would be appropriate to the degree and form of aggression. Nonetheless, the strategy of flexible response could not fully reconcile the United States' and Western European allies' preferences – the former seeking flexibility and the latter virtual automaticity – but its formula was ambiguous enough to satisfy, if not please, all parties.

In the same vein, the adoption in 1979 of the Long-Term Defense Plan, extended to include nuclear weapons, was yet another test for the cohesion of the Alliance. The dual-track approach was unique in that it was the first time a U.S. nuclear program had been made dependent on a prior allied commitment to deployment. It meant that before the United States would agree to produce new missiles, the allies had to agree to deploy them. Moreover, it also sparked a wide array of reactions both inside the Alliance and between NATO leaders and public opinion in their countries. Politically, this decision became a symbol of the European elite's support for NATO. In the words of Helmut Kohl, this decision was "synonymous with the survival of democratic Europe, the preservation of the Atlantic Alliance and the continuation of relations on an equal basis with the Soviet Union" (1983:8) and represented, as British Secretary of State for Defense Francis Pym put it, "a reaffirmation of American commitment to Europe" (qtd. in *Hansard* col. 1542).

Political will needed practical back up, and it was essential that the implementation of this plan be followed through, or otherwise it would represent a Soviet victory and the loss of prestige for NATO's leaders in relation to their constituents. But, contrary to the apparently supportive political trend, the implementation phase generated further controversy. The first track, which referred to deployment, was indeed a multilateral decision, shared between the allies. The second track, which envisaged arms control, was to take the form of bilateral negotiations between the United States and the Soviet Union. It meant that, although the European allies had control over the deployment, they would be shut out from the negotiations while facing harsh parliamentary and public opposition. The issue of control over the dual-track confronted French and British leaders with a special dilemma, in that they hoped to be able to influence future intermediate range nuclear forces (INF) negotiations while not renouncing to their own nuclear forces during negotiations. French Prime Minister Pierre Mauroy declared: "When a balance of forces had been struck between the two superpowers at the lowest possible level, when the two no longer have the means to destroy each other several times over – then it will be the time to talk about all the nuclear forces in the world. Until such time, France will stay away from the negotiations" (1983:23).

Here, opposition is embedded in the diplomatic language. Although no refusal or denial of the strategy is explicitly formulated, the hypothesis Mauroy constructs clearly specifies that France does not agree with the strategic control specified in the dual-track. The hint of "unless" is used here to build an improbable scenario, whose unlikeliness will justify France's lack of involvement in the issue.

In 1983, as quoted by NATO Review, Margaret Thatcher uttered an almost identical formulation. By displaying such an adversarial attitude, the two European countries reinforced their position as nuclear powers and situated themselves away from the strategic decisions taken by the United States, challenging American leadership once again. This power dynamics resulted in European public opinion blaming the Americans – and, ironically, not the Soviets – for the increased likelihood of nuclear war in Europe.

In an attempt to restore the balance of power, certify the legitimacy of the decisions taken by NATO and endorse the American vision of defense and security to meet strength with strength, West German Chancellor Helmut Schmidt assured the American and the Soviet parts that the German people did not share the other European's opinion and even reprimanded the members of the Bundestag who opposed the deployment of nuclear missiles in Europe, accusing them of acting "as if existing Soviet SS-20 missiles directed at targets in Germany and elsewhere were less dangerous than American missiles that are not even here yet" (1982:7 ). Both Schmidt and his follower, Helmut Kohl, viewed NATO as a means of a unified and independent Germany and considered that endorsing the dual-track decision would be beneficial for the country, and failure to do so would result in undermining the Federal Republic's position as a dependable ally and destroy NATO as an alliance.

## Out-of-area issues

After 1996, the United States sought to redirect the Alliance's attention toward new sorts of threats, based on their recent experiences with the newly emerging surge of terrorist attacks.13 In December 1998, at the NATO foreign ministers' meeting, U.S. Secretary of State Madeleine Albright argued that NATO needed a further transformation. In particular, as remarked in the text of the press statement issued after the meeting, the Alliance needed to be better prepared "to address appropriately and effectively the challenges of the proliferation of NBC weapons and their means of delivery." (Final Communiqué of the North Atlantic Council 1998, par. 14). As a consequence, NATO needed to expand the flexibility of its geographical borders, while enlarging its areas of operations and explicitly including and addressing nonconventional threats in its documents.

Nonetheless, the issue of geographical scope was not a comfortable topic and sparked a dispute between the U.S. and its European allies. The Americans made their point based on Article 4 in the Washington Treaty, which, in their interpretation, allows for going-out-of-area options; the allies were disinclined to issue a policy on this subject and insisted that they would rather take decisions only if and when circumstances demanded them. In an October 1988 report on the new NATO, U.S. Senator Roth maintained his (and the U.S. government's) line of thought according to which asymmetric or nonconventional terrorist threats, either independently organized or state-supported, demand careful planning. Consequently, NATO's defense and deterrence strategies require the military authorities "to plan and practice operations far from NATO territory and in a wide range of geographical and climatic conditions" (Roth 1988:22). Roth concluded that even when isolated international terrorist acts affect only one Ally, this is actually part of a broader terrorist phenomenon that threatens the entire Alliance, and NATO allies should neither suggest that NATO missions will assume a "global" character nor put artificial geographical borders on such limits.

Due to the reluctance of the allies, NATO was not drawn into the U.S.-proposed "flexible" framework. It would have meant a break up from the security management strategies that had supported the notion of cooperative security throughout the 1990s. Instead, a compromise was

---

13 The terrorist attacks on the World Trade Center, New York, in February 1993; the bombing of the U.S. compound, Khobar Towers in Saudi Arabia, in July 1996; bomb explosions outside the U.S. embassies in Kenya and Tanzania in August 1998.

finally reached, in that both parties agreed that collective defense needed to become flexible, and that NATO required adapted military tools that would successfully address with the entire spectrum of threats. It was against the background of this debate that the two core concepts – crisis management and partnership – were introduced in the text of the 1999 Strategic Concept. Moreover, the U.S. concerns of the risks and challenges ahead and the need to respond to them were worded as follows:

> "Any armed attack on the territory of the Allies, from whatever direction, would be covered in Articles 5 and 6 of the Washington Treaty. However, Alliance security must also take account of the global context. Alliance security interests can be affected by other risks of a wider nature, including acts of terrorism, sabotage and organized crime, and by the disruption of the flow of vital resources." (The Alliance's Strategic Concept 1999, par. 24)

With the introduction of the word "global" in the text of the document, the United States obtained an enlargement of the Alliance's operational boundaries, stretching the Euro-Atlantic area of operations to include North Africa, the Middle East, and the Caucasus. It resulted in geographical and operational flexibility, without trying, in Albright's own words, "to get NATO to go global" (1998, par. 21).

The allied governments were not interested in issues that went beyond Europe. France and Great Britain, for example, had been engaged in the Balkans since 1992, which demonstrated the two allies' common concern for the revitalization of European security cooperation. In the St. Malo Declaration of December 1998, the two powers called for a "E.U. capacity for autonomous action" in cases "the Alliance as a whole is not engaged" (Rutten 8). Germany also pursued a policy that would facilitate cooperation between NATO and other European security institutions. The new Social Democratic German government insisted on NATO's maintaining a first-strike nuclear capability – as stipulated in the 1991 Strategic Concept and therefore up for the 1998-1999 revision – but the Americans strongly refused to consider it. Finally, the Germans gave up, but the debate revealed the fact that Germany considered that the security challenges in Europe hinged on securing stability more than on the management of threats.

The dynamics of reactions and interactions resulted in a compromise that espoused regional crisis management with the new threats outside

126

Europe. The fourth Strategic Concept, drafted in 1999, stipulating the need for a strategic balance in Europe was replaced with the notion of collective defense, while security needed to be extended beyond the traditionally recognized borders of the Alliance. In 1998, David Yost argued that a rejection of strategic balancing could generate a multiplicity of commitments brought about by collective security thinking. His forecast was materialized by the stipulations of the new Strategic Concept drafted one year later, which was indicative of the fact that the United States was drawing the Alliance toward a flexible approach to security management in addressing divergent and serious risks outside Europe.

## The European Security and Defense Policy (ESDP)

At the end of the 1990s, the fluid security environment and NATO's desire for more flexible alignment caused a split between the allies, opposing the proposition for an enlarged Atlantic framework with a more restricted European crisis management policy. The challenge for NATO was to define the extent of its involvement in crisis management – a task assumed by the European Security and Defense Initiative (ESDI). At the Washington Summit in April 1999, a consensus was finally reached. NATO acknowledged "the resolve of the European Union to have the capacity for autonomous action so that it can take decisions and approve military action where the Alliance as a whole is not engaged" (An Alliance for the 21st Century, Washington Summit Communiqué 1999, par. 9). This prerequisite of EU action was discursively framed by the EU at the Cologne European Summit, in June 1999, when the Union assumed "the capacity for autonomous action, backed up by credible military forces, the means to decide to use them, and a readiness to do so, in order to respond to international crises without prejudice to actions by NATO" (European Council Summit 1999, par. 1, annex III). The Americans did not delay in protesting this wording. In October 1999, at a conference on the future of NATO, Deputy Secretary of State Strobe Talbot talked about the possibility of how "European countries can improve Europe's capacity to act by enhancing capabilities without duplicating NATO" (1999, par. 17). As a consequence, during the Helsinki Summit the following December, the EU agreed that action can be initiated only if NATO "as a whole is not engaged". In 1998, the British announced their decision to sponsor an

ESDP initiative. Prime Minister Tony Blair backed it up with the following argument:

> "The initiative I launched last autumn on European defence is aimed at giving greater credibility to Europe's Common Foreign and Security Policy. Far from weakening NATO this is an essential component to the Transatlantic Alliance. We Europeans should not expect the United States to have to play a part in every disorder in our back yard…Europe's military capabilities at this stage are modest. Too modest…But let me assure you of this: European defence is not about new institutional fixes. It is about new capabilities, both military and diplomatic." (1999:19)

Blair basically appealed to European nations to improve their military capabilities and did not expect any help from the United States during crises the Americans have no interest in. He even created a rift of polarized entities between "we Europeans" and the United States, in an illustrative framing of opposition, both conceptual and linguistic. Nevertheless, diplomacy stepped in to eschew the sense of adversity, and Blair's speech acknowledges the integration of the new defense initiative within the framework of NATO.

As far as the allies were concerned, the view on ESDP was intricate: the Americans uttered their suspicions; the French transformed it in a political goal; the British perceived it as a way of strengthening NATO. The issue of the Americans' involvement in regional crisis management paved the path for European operations, either independent or NATO assisted. The issued sparked contradictory attitudes: Britain trusted that improving European capabilities would attract the United States and thus revitalize transatlantic relations; France was hoping that NATO would slowly disengage and leave a number of security functions to the EU. To this aim, France was pushing for the creation of defense planning and command options in Europe, while the British and the Americans still wanted them anchored in NATO.

## NATO enlargement

The enlargement debate began in late 1993, a few months before the 1994 Brussels Summit. The decision taken at the summit on the issue of enlargement was to

> "…reaffirm that the Alliance, as provided for in Article 10 of the Washington Treaty, remains open to the membership of other

European states in a position to further the principles of the Treaty and to contribute to the security of the North Atlantic area. We expect and would welcome NATO expansion that would reach to democratic states to our East, as part of an evolutionary process, taking into account political and security developments in the whole of Europe." (The Brussel Summit Declaration 1994, par. 12)

On the same occasion, the allies highlighted the importance of the PfP program, as an essential mechanism in the process of NATO's expansion. It was yet another example of relational power outside the traditional membership of the Alliance that was intended to galvanize the efforts of smaller powers and redirect them toward NATO's goal.

The enlargement process started with NATO tackling the issues of "how" and "why" before discussing "who" and "when". At the December 1994 meeting of NATO foreign ministers, the NAC "decided to initiate a process of examination inside the Alliance to determine how NATO will enlarge, the principles to guide this process and the implications of membership" (Final Communiqué issued at the Ministerial Meeting of the North Atlantic Council 1994, par. 9).

The answers to the two questions concerning the manner and the reason for expansion were set out in the "Study on NATO Enlargement", issued in September 1995. The documents lay out seven rationales for the enlargement of the Alliance, among which the prevailing concepts are "cooperation", "consultation", "consensus building", "common defense", "shared democratic values", "European and international security", "Trans-Atlantic partnership" (Study on NATO Enlargement 1995, par. 3). All these goals are completely in line with the doctrine the Alliance has put forward on numerous occasions, which makes the framework for NATO's expansion be based on the very essence of the Alliance's role as an international security organization.

As for the "who" and "when", these two issues were addressed in a formal manner at the July 1997 NATO summit in Madrid. On that occasion, the allies invited three countries – the Czech Republic, Hungary, and Poland to begin talks and sign protocols of ascension in December of the same year, while complete membership was to become effective in April 1999.

Although the decisions for the first steps of the enlargement process to begin had been officially taken by allies' consensus, the road to agreement was not smooth. The issue sparked numerous debates among allies, with

Germany and the United States being the two NATO powers where extensive discussions on these topics took place. However, the discussion received a certain amount of attention in France and Britain as well.

Against this backdrop, the U.S. debate is the most important, since the credibility of the Alliance commitment depends, to a great extent, on the Americans. Cons of NATO enlargement were pioneered by former Under Secretary of defense Fred Iklé, who was among the first to express an opinion regarding the potential negative impact of enlargement on NATO's military posture: "Far from solving an alleged crisis, expanding NATO now would fatally weaken it. The Atlantic Alliance must not become a chain letter – some Ponzi scheme that escapes bankruptcy only by signing up new members" (1995:A21). Senator James Inhofe (R-Oklahoma) continued: "This is just the beginning of more and more countries. After the first three recruits, I don't see where there's an end to it" (qtd. in Schmitt, "Senate Reject Bid" A14). Senator John Warner (R-Virginia) expressed similar concerns about a dilution of the Alliance's cohesion and effectiveness, given the number of applicants for membership.

> "We don't know what NATO is going to look like after we go from 16 to 28 nations.
> I look upon a proliferation of problems of unknown origins and unknown descriptions" (qtd. in Schmitt 1998a:A14).

The three examples are illustration of the use of negative language, expressed by either a disaster-announcing adverb or by negative predicative constructions hinting at the American officials' lack of insight regarding the future of the Alliance in the aftermath of the enlargement. The last example is a prophetic caveat about the uncontrolled propagation of complications hard to contain due to their unforeseen nature.

George Kennan's warnings the year before, imbued with semantically-related references to a gloomy outcome ("error", "inflame", "adverse effect", "unforeseeable", "improbable") stemmed from ideological concerns regarding U.S.-Russian relations and a resurrection of the Cold War era friends and foes dilemmas in the East-West geostrategic arena:

> "Expanding NATO would be the most fateful error of American policy in the entire post-cold-war era. Such a decision may be expected to inflame the nationalistic, anti-Western and militaristic tendencies in Russian opinion; to have an adverse effect on the development

of Russian democracy; to restore the atmosphere of the cold war to East-West relations, and to impel Russian foreign policy in directions decidedly not to our liking…Why, with all the hopeful possibilities engendered by the end of the cold war, should East-West relations become centered on the question of who would be allied with whom and, by implication, against whom in some fanciful, totally unforeseeable and most improbable future military conflict?" (1997:A23)

Other senators, among which Paul Wellstone (D-Minnesota) later reiterated Kennan's qualms. "What worries me the most is that NATO expansion needlessly risks poisoning Russia's relationship with the United States and increase the odds that Russian ultranationalists will gain power in the post-Yeltsin era" (qtd. in Schmitt 1997b:A14).

The pro arguments were mostly focused on issues such as Russian neo-imperialism, coercion, aggression, and advocated the rationale of NATO enlargement based on the need to curtail potential power competitions in Central Europe. In the words of Peter Rodman, "The only potential great-power security problem in Central Europe is the lengthening shadow of Russian strength, and NATO still has the job of counter-balancing it" (1994:A27). In 1997, while the U.S. was debating on NATO enlargement, Senator Jesse Helms (R-North Carolina) reiterated the idea that "a central strategic rationale for expanding NATO must be to hedge against the possible return of a nationalist or imperialist Russia" (1998:4). Retired U.S. Army General William Odom underscores the argument that only NATO, as an international security institution, has the power and ability to provide a reliable framework for "democratization, free-market prosperity, and constructive solutions to border and minority issues" (1997:C3). Even more so, in his opinion, NATO needs to step in and get proactively involved in Central Europe, so as to forestall the emergence of competitive diplomacy involving powers such as Russia, Germany, France, and Britain. In other words, the Americans will make sure that their European allies will not act unilaterally in Central Europe, but under a NATO mandate, while working together (among themselves and with other countries they intend to co-opt) to contain and isolate the threat coming from the Russians. Odom's caveat empowers NATO as the only actor capable of circumventing such an outcome: "Central Europe will again become the scene of some, if not all, of the perverse dynamics of the interwar period unless NATO enlarges to preempt them" (C3). Richard Holbrooke, one of

Clinton administration officials, explicitly advanced the belief that NATO expansion is an obligatory step for geopolitical or balance of power reasons. Holbrooke's arguments build-up on Odom's view that NATO enlargement will preserve stability and prevent German-Russian rivalries in Central Europe.

> "For Germany and Russia, the two large nations on the flanks of central Europe, insecurity has historically been a major contributor to aggressive behavior… The West must expand to central Europe as fast as possible in fact as well as in spirit… Stability in central Europe is essential to general European security, and is still far from assured. (1995:41)

Secretary of State Madeleine Albright's discourse does not make specific reference to the rivalry between Russia and Germany but addresses the issue of NATO enlargement in more general terms. In a speech prepared before the Senate Foreign Relations Committee, in 1997, Albright expressed the belief that the risk of the Alliance's failure to enlarge "could cause confidence to crumble in central Europe, leading to a search for security by other means, including costly arms buildup and competition among neighbors" 1997c:15).

In Germany, the talks on NATO enlargement mostly mirrored the debates in the United States. The arguments were not only political but also ideological in nature, encompassing the need to project stability eastwards, the desire to not allow Russia a veto over NATO's security arrangements, the commitment to Western values and responsibilities of promoting and fostering democracy in Europe. The con positions also referred to the risk that the enlargement could provoke nationalist reactions in Russia, paralyze Alliance decision-making and import new instabilities in NATO in the form of minority and border disputes.

Germany has been seen as the strongest enlargement proponent of the European allies, an attitude spearheaded by Defense Minister Volker Rühe, who believed that extensive membership would cultivate democracy in Eastern Europe. Three aspects of the German discussions on the issue of enlargement deserve attention here. First and foremost, of all the allies, Germany has exerted the most powerful cultural and economic influence in Central and Eastern Europe. Secondly, Germany feels morally and politically responsible for the destiny of Eastern European

132

countries. Lastly, from a geopolitical perspective, Germany has had a greater geographic exposure to potential trouble from the former Soviet empire. In April 1996, Rühe argued that NATO's expansion to the East is an essential German objective, especially given the geographical location of the country. In his view, NATO's moving eastward will remove Germany from the position of being the Alliance's front line: "A situation in which Germany's eastern border is the border between stability and instability in Europe is not sustainable in the long run. Germany's eastern border cannot be the eastern border of the European Union and NATO. Either we export stability or we import instability." (1993:7-8)

However, since these arguments were inconsistent with the official Alliance rhetoric, asserting that there will be "no diving lines" in the new Europe, they were later removed from public policy statements.

In March 1998, the Bundestag approved enlargement to the Czech Republic, Poland, and Hungary by an overwhelming majority (554 in favor, 37 against and 30 abstaining). In the German parliament, most of the Green members abstained or voted against, on the grounds that enlargement would affect relations with Russia and endanger stability in Europe. Despite their reaction, the opposition in Germany was fable and did not transform the issue of NATO enlargement into a controversy in the country. It was widely agreed that this movement will serve Germany's interests, politically, strategically, and morally.

In contrast to the extended debates in Germany and the U.S., France did not make an issue out of NATO's prospects of enlargement. However, the general attitude was toward rejection, with a number of French officials expressing reservations on the matter as early as the end of 1993. In the then Foreign Minister, Alain Jupé's assessment, NATO expansion might dilute the Alliance, create new dividing lines, and cause fears in Russia, offering Moscow a pretext to transform the Commonwealth of Independent States into a rival institution. François Léotard, the French defense minister at the time, reiterated de Gaulle's Europe-centric vision of security and publicly expressed the general view that NATO is a means through which the United States extends protection to Europeans. In his opinion, European security issues should be addressed to European institutions: "To knock at NATO's door is to knock at America's door and ask for the American guarantee. That is understandable, but it is not our conception. We want the request for security to be directed to the countries of Europe. Hence our proposal for association with the WEU" (qtd. in Boniface 1997:38).

After the principle of enlargement was approved at the 1994 Brussels Summit, the official French position shifted to express worries that the process might advance too rapidly, and this haste might weaken the Alliance and give the excluded countries the impression that they had been encircled. Once Jacques Chirac became president in May 1995, the French refrained from expressing doubts in public and declared that they see the enlargement "in a very positive spirit", as the French foreign minister Hervé de Charette mentioned a press conference after a North Atlantic Council meeting the same year (1995:38).

The con arguments in public discussions warn about the danger of Russia building up on arms and advocate for a stronger security treaty between Russia and NATO that must come before any enlargement prospects. In the words of former French prime minister, Michel Rocard, "a serious and binding security treaty between the Atlantic Alliance and Russia must precede any enlargement of NATO" (1997:94).

The French attitude regarding the issue of enlargement testifies for at least three aspects. First, it is indicative of a widespread feeling of detachment about NATO matters that has been fueled ever since 1966, when France withdrew from NATO's integrated military structure. At the time of the enlargement debates, France's agenda was oriented toward other issues, such as its efforts to build a European security and defense identity. It was a matter that affected France's status in the Alliance more than the eastward expansion. Although rarely expressed in public, the fear that the enlargement might conflict with the pursuit of ESDI was the main fuel that propelled the French opposition to the matter.

Secondly, the general perception was that NATO enlargement represents an extension of the area over which the United States wants to extend its control. Continuing the traditional French-U.S. acrimony, President François Mitterrand equated the enlargement of the Alliance as an attempt of the Americans to "extend their influence in Eastern Europe, at low cost and to the detriment of the countries of western Europe, which, moreover, are bearing the burden of most of the economic aid to these countries" (qtd. in Boniface 1997:36).

Last, in order to display an exercise of power greater than that of the U.S. or of other European allies, France championed a larger first round of enlargement. The particular support offered to Romania was, in the words of a British scholar, an attempt to demonstrate that "France will rejoin NATO on its own terms", and that it seeks to "actively influence European security arrangements" (Eyal 1997:708). Supporting Romania's ascension to NATO might be interpreted as an exercise of decisional power cast within the Alliance, and, indirectly, on smaller powers that might benefit from France's official endorsement.

The French were fervent supporters of Romania's inclusion in the Alliance for a number of substantive reasons. First, they thought that separating Romania and Hungary would be unwise, given the large Hungarian minority in Romania and the prospect that Hungary might join the European Union before Romania. Secondly, Romania's presence in the Alliance might help stabilize the Balkan/Danube region and provide a good "north/south" balance in the area. Romania was also perceived from the point of view of its cultural heritage and links to the French history and tradition. It was believed that it might act as a counterweight to Anglo-Saxon and Germanic influence and methods and to the predominant use of English in the Alliance. Lastly, it might play an essential role in compensating for the German satellites in NATO.

Finally, and despite the debate surrounding the topic, the French Senate approved the ratification of the protocols for Alliance membership for Poland, Hungary, and the Czech Republic in May 1998, and the National Assembly gave its ratification the following month. However, discussions did not go smoothly in the National Assembly, with most of the debate being centered on questions concerning U.S. influence in NATO, the establishment of the ESDI and France's own status in the Alliance.

In spite of all the national disputes that took place in some NATO countries on the issue of enlargement, the Alliance continued its strategic development on the grounds on the expressed belief that "the ascension of new members will...help to consolidate the security and stability in the entire Euro-Atlantic area" (Final Communiqué of the Meeting of the North Atlantic Council in Defence Ministers Session 1996, par. 36).

As seen by the Eastern European countries, the enlargement of NATO was nothing short of a golden opportunity. They were clearly seeking NATO membership especially because Russia was perceived as a threat to their security and because they feared that Russia might attempt to rebuild a tsarist-like empire including the former Soviet satellite states. Having new members from this part of the world in the Alliance would help balance Russia's power potential in the region. Against this background, it is natural to conclude that NATO enlargement is consistent with the Alliance's aims of promoting a wider process of security cooperation in Europe. In the NAC communiqué, issued after the ministerial meeting held in Berlin in June 1996, the Allies reaffirm their determination NATO's enlargement "should not create dividing lines in Europe or isolate any country ... The enlargement of the Alliance is consistent with a wider process of cooperation and integration already under way in today's Europe" (Final Communiqué of the Ministerial Meeting of the North Atlantic Council 1996, par. 54).

*Russian membership in NATO*

Russia's potential membership in NATO has been a public source of disunion among the allies. The Alliance's September 1995 study on enlargement did not imply that Russia could become a member and implicitly suggested that NATO and Russia would remain distinct entities. The text reads "NATO-Russia relations should reflect Russia's significance in European security and be based on reciprocity, mutual respect and confidence, no 'surprise' decisions by either side which could affect the interests of the other" (Study on NATO Enlargement 1995, par. 27). The concept of bringing the entire Euro-Atlantic community under the umbrella of a common security culture does not indicate that Russia could be excluded from NATO membership. Moreover, in referring to "Central and Eastern Europe" as an undefined region, NATO secretary-general Javier Solana maintained that "we must not draw a line across Europe, dividing it into winners and losers. In the new security architecture, there will only be winners. We have made it clear that our door is and will remain open" (1997, par. 4). The secretary-general's address hints to NATO's desire of integrating countries in the region in the new security configuration and offering them "one of the best means of moving forward and sharing in the future peace and prosperity we in the West are aiming for" (par. 4). Although the discourse is clearly constructed around the "we" – "they" polarization, by opposing the current status of the Central and Eastern European countries to the promise of "peace" and "prosperity" the West embodies, the real gauge of this speech is the fact that the open-door policy embraced by NATO does not specifically exclude Russia from the post-enlargement security architecture of the area. Although Russia is not referred to as a possible NATO member, the text of the address advocates

136

"a strong and united NATO, working in a close and productive partnership with Russia" (par. 4).

European politicians and analysts, however, posited that the bedrock security function of the Alliance remains collective defense, which, according to the formulation in the 1991 Strategic Concept, includes maintaining "the strategic balance within Europe" (The Alliance's New Strategic Concept 1991, par. 21). The phrasing itself was chosen as a more politically palatable phrase to replace the concept of "power balance", which implies that Russia's power must be balanced. The underlying concept of this rhetoric is the belief of the European allies that Russia must be managed from a position that does not allow its integration in the Alliance. In May 1997, German Defense Minister Volker Rühe argued: "it goes without saying that the new strategic partnership between NATO and Russia can only be based on cooperation and not on integration" (par. 15). This statement comes three years after the September 1994 German-American conference held shortly after the withdrawal of the last Russian occupation troops from Germany, when Rühe had argued that

> "Russia just doesn't qualify for various reasons to be integrated into the [NATO] structure, even if they [the Russians] work economic miracle ... Our policy must be absolutely clear, that not all countries in Central and Eastern Europe are candidates for integration... Russia cannot be integrated, neither into the European Union nor into NATO." (qtd. in Shanker 1994:2)

The German Defense Minister was categorical in rejecting Russia's integration in the Alliance, an attitude transparent from his frequent use of negatives "doesn't", "cannot", "not", "neither...nor". By phrasing a collective policy attached to the possessive "our", Rühe assumed the role of NATO's messenger in framing an "absolutely clear" rule that, according to his choice of words, should not even be challenged.

The doubts about extending NATO membership to Russia were not limited to the European allies of the moment. Other prospective NATO members shared the concerns and acknowledged Russia's status as a superpower that might be difficult to manage in a NATO context. In 1997, Vaclav Havel, the president of the Czech Republic stated: "An enlarged NATO should consider Russia not an enemy, but a partner... But Russia is nonetheless a Eurasian superpower, so influential that it is hard to imagine it could become an intrinsic part of NATO without flooding the alliance with the busy agenda of Russian interests" (A21).

Nonetheless, the Americans stepped in and, even if their opinion did not sway the Allies' stance on Russia's membership in NATO, it is interesting and worth investigating from a discursive perspective. They were the power to champion the idea of holding open the possibility or Russia's joining the Alliance. The then U.S. secretary of defense William Perry's opinion was at variance with Rühe's position. He stated that the United States "is not prepared to close the door on that issue" (qtd. in Shanker 1994:2). Furthermore, in March 1997, President Clinton restated the American support for

> "… a European union that is expanding, and still tied…to the United States and Canada … not only economically and politically but also in terms of our security alliance, but [that] also has a special relationship with Russia and [that] does not rule out even Russian membership in a common security alliance." (A11)

Although declaratively unifying, the phrase "common security alliance" suggests vagueness. A "special relationship with Russia" does not imply that Russia is seen as a potential member of the Alliance but does hint to the U.S. openness to the principle of Russian membership. In his public statements, Deputy Secretary of State Talbott employed formulations implying that NATO membership could be feasible for the states of the former USSR, which might thus feel motivated to take a number of steps in order to become eligible for membership. With regard to Russia, Talbott suggests that the Russia that might someday enter NATO should be a fully democratic one, at peace with its neighbors and with itself. He salutes the evolution of Russia and of other Eastern European states toward democracy and peace and encourages the Allies to take Russia's potential membership into account for the future, due to the fact that "the extraordinary transformations that have taken place both in Russia and throughout Europe over the past decade should make us reluctant to exclude possibilities for the future – and ambitions in pursuing them" (1995:27).

If Russia were to be explicitly excluded – and this is where the power of language should intervene, as no plain statements were made neither against nor in favor of such a prospect – then many Russians would probably see NATO's purpose as ultimately one of expanding the western zone of influence while confining Russia to a much smaller sphere of influence, which Moscow would perceive as humiliation. Future developments (the Russian invasion and annexation of Crimea in 2014, the more recent Russian threat in the Baltics, Russia's nuclear weapons build-up) have shown that the sense of alienation experienced in the Kremlin prompted the Russians to engage in a sharp confrontation with NATO.

On the other hand, inviting Russia to become a NATO member would translate in draining the Alliance of its collective defense ingredient and turning it into a second OSCE, at least in the eyes of the Western Allies. The strongest argument against Russia's membership remains its Eurasian geopolitical configuration, given that Russia pursues policies along Asian, Central Asian, and Middle Eastern borders that are not in line with NATO objectives. In summing up all arguments against Russia's membership in NATO, Henry Kissinger sharply concludes: "Russian membership would dilute the Alliance to the point of irrelevance" (1997:A15).

By and large, the entire discourse against Russia's potential membership in NATO is constructed on notions that fuel the existence of a clear polarization between the United States and its European allies on one hand, and Russia, on the other. Such an ideological divide encourages the concept of power balance, whose existence and dynamics continue to remain the Alliance's raison d'être.

## 3.2.2.2 The External Bipolar Balance

Since its birth in 1949, NATO was endowed with the ideological power of counteracting the menace the Soviet Union and the communist system of beliefs represented for the security of Western Europe in the aftermath of World War II. Although its initial purview was to forge a consistent transatlantic response to the Soviet threat, during its ideological evolution NATO has undergone a series of conceptual changes that accounted for the relevance and endurance of the alliance throughout its almost seventy-year history. These strategic reorientations have been adopted so as to renovate the Alliance's ideology not only during its internal development, but also in its relations with external state or non-state actors on the international scene.

Ever since the initiation of the Washington talks in 1948, the consensus reached by the participating powers (the Brussel Treaty powers,[14] the United States, and Canada) acknowledged the importance of the Soviet threat. This was the first formalized indication that the Soviet Union will be counterbalanced from a position of equality by what was to become the North Atlantic Treaty Organization the following year. The Korean War, which broke in June 1950, activated the conceptual framework of the Treaty. The invasion and the Soviets' involvement were seen as the communists' attempt at global domination, which offered NATO a concrete occasion to act upon the principles expressed in the rhetoric of the founding document.

This section deconstructs and interprets the discourse strand of adversarial power in the framework of the external bipolar balance from multiple perspectives. First of all, the analysis exploits the strained relations between NATO and the USSR in the context of nuclear issues and the topic of the Soviet invasion of Afghanistan. After the dissolution of the Soviet monolith, the most noteworthy opponent of the Alliance remained Russia. Two issues were considered important from this standpoint: the issue of enlargement, which proved fertile for an analysis of the discourse that illustrates Russia's opposing views to NATO's expansion to the East and the tense relations between the Alliance and Russia in the aftermath of the Crimean crisis, a pivotal event that dissolved most of the NATO-Russia cooperation agreements. The final part of the analysis is dedicated to NATO's role in the "war of terror" and the salient discursive elements that typify the public documents dealing with this concept. Terrorism was given special attention in this investigation because it occupies a large amount of NATO's strategic preoccupation in the last decade and a half. The issue of terrorism is crucial for the current understanding of the power dynamics that characterize the relations between NATO allies and also between NATO and its adversaries. In NATO's Secretary General Jens Stoltenberg's words,

"Terrorism affects every NATO ally. It is a long-term threat to our values, freedom and way of life. And the alliance is ready to do more to counter this threat. The unique bond between Europe and North America

---

[14] The Brussels Treaty (1948) was an agreement signed by Britain, France, Belgium, the Netherlands, and Luxembourg, with the aim of creating a collective defense alliance. One of the main objectives of the treaty was to attract the United States' involvement in the security of Western Europe, by demonstrating close cooperation between Western European states.

has delivered unprecedented peace for almost seven decades, and NATO's role in the fight against terrorism is an important chapter in that story." (2017, par. 15)

## NATO vs. USSR – Nuclear issues

Following the USSR's first detonation of its first nuclear device in August 1949, President Truman asked for a study of U.S. nuclear policy and capability by a joint team from the Defense and State Departments. Dean Acheson, the then Secretary of State, turned the report into a full-scale review of Soviet policy in its totality and of the U.S.'s possibilities to resist and reverse it. The document, entitled the National Security Memorandum 68, or NSC-68, officially known as "A Report to the National Security Council by the Executive Secretary on the United States Objectives and Programs for National Security", was written by Paul Nitze, the head of the Policy Planning Staff at the State Department.

The document was as much about policy details as it was about ideology. Its tone was highly polemical, eschewing the finer points and concentrating on the broad brushstrokes. It called for a major increase in military spending and reaffirmed America's commitment to a world role. In an exercise of power opposition, the study characterized the U.S. as utilizing mush less power than it possessed, while the USSR was seen as having less potential but a greater ability to use it. It described the Soviet leaders' "fundamental design" as "the complete subversion or forcible destruction of the machinery of government and structure of society in the countries of the non-Soviet world" (A Report to the National Security Council by the Executive Secretary on the United States Objectives and Programs for National Security 54). The entire document is infused with language more suitable for public debates than for internal, highly classified policy documents. Describing the policies of the Soviets, the document goes on "The concentration camp is the prototype of the society [which the USSR's] policies are designed to achieve" (60).

NSC-68 marked a reinterpretation of the doctrine of containment formulated by Nitze's predecessor, George Kennan. It was a doctrine that the U.S. policy was tending toward, but for which it lacked formal expression and ratification. The document was the ideal opportunity to officially adhere to and implement that policy, while stating that "every consideration of devotion to our fundamental values and to our security demands that we seek to achieve them by the strategy of cold war" (57). Having dismissed the other options, including that of hot war, surrender or isolation, the document defines the aims of containment as

> "... by all means short of war to block further expansion of Soviet power, expose the falsities of Soviet pretensions, induce a retraction of the Kremlin's control and influence and, in general, so foster the seeds of destruction within the Soviet system that the Kremlin is brought at least to the point of modifying its behavior to conform to generally accepted international standards." (68)

The text of the document is a relevant manifestation of adversarial discourse, being permeated with formulations that carry negative connotations ("to block", "expose falsities", "retraction", "destruction") aimed at vilifying the opposing Soviet attitude and behavior. The main idea is that Soviet power, semantically reiterated by the use of two synonyms ("control and influence"), needs to be stopped and forced into withdrawal. The example here is an illustration of prescriptive discourse, by which the Alliance calls on the Soviets, considered outside the range of international standards, to conform to generally endorsed behavior.

NSC-68 was completed in March 1950 and formally approved by the National Security Council the following month. Acheson reiterated many of the important aspects of the documents to the NATO foreign ministers, but the ideological appeal did not echo well with the Western European allies. Although the British and French diplomats were ready to pay the various prices of getting U.S. economic aid and strategic protection, they remained reluctant to be told what to think by their American counterparts.

All in all, NSC-68 remained polemical in nature and was only used internally, in order to galvanize the American administration to consider the Soviet threat legitimate and take further political and military measures against it. The document was declassified in the 1970s.

NATO's decision to include nuclear weapons in its Long-Term Defense Plan, in 1979 was the Alliance's strategic modality of responding to the challenges represented by the Soviet deployment of SS-20 intermediate-range nuclear missiles. The dual-track plan, adopted by the NAC in December 1979 in Brussels, was received with hostility both inside and outside the Alliance. It raised questions about European sovereignty and drew an alarm signal regarding the Americans' unilateralism, who appeared willing to commit their allies to nuclear war.

142

In this context, American and European leaders alike made extensive efforts to obtain public and legislative support for the deployment of new missiles in Europe. They largely advocated the importance of deterrence in this context as the only way to preserve security and freedom. From their end, the Soviets were conducting an aggressive propaganda aimed at fueling the Europeans' fears of a nuclear war and at depicting NATO and the United States as warmongers.

The polarization of powers that was generated by this event was illustrated by the rhetoric of the occasion. In order to reverse the tide of antinuclear and anti-American sentiment that was growing in Europe, NATO embarked on a public relations program that was centered on the notion that the Alliance really stood for peace, a notion whose advancement would soon take an official form at the 1982 Bonn Summit. This endeavor was extensively backed up by Ronald Reagan, who took office after Jimmy Carter in January 1981, and who started a vehement campaign reinforced by the rhetoric of peace through strength. Reagan blamed Carter's initiative of withdrawing America from global leadership and held the latter's moralistic and humanistic policies accountable for the shift in the balance of power that allowed the Soviets to catch up with the United States in terms of nuclear parity. Furthermore, in order to substantiate and legitimize the U.S. nuclear build-up, Reagan promoted a powerful anticommunist rhetoric that described the Soviet Union as an "evil empire" and the Soviets as malicious agents in the modern world. Communism, he said, was but "a sad, bizarre chapter in human history whose last pages are even now being written" (1983:10). The Soviets were portrayed as an implacable and untrustworthy foe who understood only force. And it was by American and allied (NATO) force that their threat must be met. The purpose of such language was two-fold: it was aimed at vilifying the Soviet adversary while reasserting American prestige and global leadership. In this context, the dual-track approach was a resolute demonstration of collective will among the allies, united, again, in face of a common enemy.

However, this strong anti-Soviet language was rejected from the discursive formulations adopted by NATO discourses in the early 1980s. The NAC Final Communiqués of June 26, 1980, May 5, 1981 and December 10, 1982 show the European allies' reluctance to intensify the war of words and do not carry the vehemence or the moralism associated with Reagan's speech. The only European leader whose New Right convictions and similar anticommunist rhetoric matched the U.S. President's was Margaret Thatcher, who called the Soviet Union "a modern version of the early tyrannies of history" (qtd. in Jenkins 1987:288). The other European allies, who were still hoping to hang on the benefits of détente, were less outspoken against the Soviets. They adopted a status quo approach, wishing "to maintain what has been achieved" (10), as Schmidt remarked in March 1980, or chose to avoid confrontation, as stated in a Franco-German communiqué the previous month (Joint Statement on Franco-German Consultations 1980).

## NATO vs. USSR – Soviet invasion of Afghanistan

One of the most illustrative oppositions that NATO launched against the USSR happened in the context of the Soviet invasion of Afghanistan, in late December 1979. Immediately after, NATO documents promptly expressed the allies' concerns with these developments that pose threats to the foundations of global security and stability. Between 1980 and 1988, twenty different documents refer to the situation in Afghanistan and condemn the Soviet military occupation. The document issued after the 1980 NAC meeting in Ankara reads:

> "In reviewing the international situation, Ministers noted with concern that the past six months have been overshadowed by developments which challenge the foundations of stability in the world. The rules which govern relations between states are defined in the United Nations Charter: the violations of these rules have led to tensions which are prejudicial to the understanding and trust which ought to govern relations between states. Ministers underlined the opposition of their Governments to threat or use of force and they reaffirmed their commitment to the peaceful settlement of international disputes." (Final Communiqué of the North Atlantic Council 1980, par. 2)

Disagreement with the Soviets' move is embedded in the formulation of the text through the strong language used to depict the military intervention: "violation of trust", "threat" and "use of force". Opposition is explicitly stated as the ministers address this issue in a very concerned manner. "Ministers expressed their deep concern at the continued occupation of Afghanistan by Soviet armed forces" (par. 3). The document continues to emphasize the gravity of the situation, which they label as a "threat" intended to overturn the power balance in the world:

144

"Ministers noted that the Soviet occupation of Afghanistan carried with it very serious implications for the general strategic situation. By using its own military forces directly to impose its will, this time on a non-aligned country, the Soviet government has clearly demonstrated its readiness to exploit opportunities to shift the balance of forces in its favour. It has thus given rise to grave concerns about its future intentions and is threatening the security of a region which is vital for world peace and stability." (par. 4)

The "resolute, constant and concerted response" the following paragraph makes reference to is an illustration of the allies' determination to counteract the Soviet power. The subjunctive clause introduced by the "it is" adjectival construction unequivocally articulates the confrontational stance taken by the Alliance: "It is vital that the Soviet government should be left in no doubt as to the extremely grave view which the Allies take of this situation which jeopardizes world peace" (par. 5).

Messages become stronger when they depend on the total rejection of an envisaged development. From this perspective, solid opposition is embedded in the use of negative and absolute formulations: "no question", "only...if": "Ministers reaffirmed that there could be no question of accepting a fait accompli resulting from the use of force ... The recent announcement that some Soviet troops are being withdrawn from Afghanistan would only be of interest if it were the beginning of a total withdrawal" (par. 5).

The condemnation continues in subsequent NATO documents, issued in the following years of the Soviet occupation of Afghanistan. The commonality resides in the similar formulation of disagreement, reiterating the identification of the military move as a "violation": "The Soviet invasion and occupation of Afghanistan is a particularly flagrant example of violation of the principles of restraint and responsibility in international affairs" (Final Communiqué of the North Atlantic Council 1981, par. 3). The Soviets are compelled to cease hostilities, in an extremely direct and powerful formulation: "Soviet forces must be withdrawn" (para 3).

The lexical analysis of the NAC or DPC communiqués issued during the ten years of the Soviet invasion of Afghanistan reveals a striking plethora of references to "threat" and "use of force". The offensive is seen as a "violation" and "flagrant defiance" of human rights, and the Soviet Union is called upon "to end its unacceptable military occupation of Afghanistan".

After the demise of the Soviet Union, the most powerful remaining heir of the communist block was Russia. The Alliance's goal of building a peaceful political order in Europe hinges, to a great extent, on forging durable cooperative relations with Russia. This issue can be explored from two perspectives: Russia's response to the PFP program and the issue of NATO enlargement, processes that at some point prompted the Russians to judge them as contrary to their interests. Far from acknowledging Russia's actional power in actually blocking the Alliance's expansion, I argue that these two aspects are worth investigating from the perspective of the discourse that illustrates Russia's ideological opposition and the arguments that justify it.

By signing the PfP Framework Document in June 1994, Russia consented to develop a cooperative relationship with the Alliance, inside and outside the stipulations of the document. Nonetheless, Russia's involvement in the program has been limited, with Russians taking a rather passive stance and involving only in programs dealing with civil-emergency planning. Russia's passivity has been accounted to a variety of reasons: financial limitations, the country's disbelief of NATO, its unwillingness to offer support and legitimacy to a NATO-centered network, and a desire to show discontent with the Alliance's ambitions of expansion. In an attempt to reconcile Russia's distrust and adversity, NATO formulated an extended welcome and invitation for participation and partnership in the Final Communiqué of the NAC, issued on December 10, 1996: "We welcome Russia's participation in Partnership for Peace and encourage it to take full advantage of the opportunities which the Partnership offers" (Final Communiqué of the Ministerial Meeting of the North Atlantic Council 1996, par. 41). Despite the open call to integrate and benefit to the fullest from the advantages of the partnership, many Russian viewed this discourse as empty words and continued to show suspicion of it. Vladimir Lukin, chairman of the International Affairs Committee of the State Duma, aptly summarizes his countrymen's position, arguing that reality cannot be altered by the use of "phantoms" such as the Partnership for Peace. He also explains that the Russians view the program as a "formula to defer the East European countries' affiliation to NATO" (1995:22), in which case the Partnership is welcomed. Nonetheless, he illustrates the other side of the coin: "If the intention is to anesthetize Russia for the

146

period that its Eastern neighbors are being dragged into NATO, Russia's refusal to undergo such anesthesia should be clearly and definitely stated" (22). Two important attitudes are salient in Lukin's discourse. On the one hand, the popular belief is that the Eastern countries are "dragged into" the Alliance, a lexical choice that suggests the fact that these countries have no self-interest and desire to be part of NATO, and that the Alliance forces enlargement on them. Second of all, Lukin prescribes behavior and response to Russia's being anesthetized by such move and even reinforces the prescriptive modal with two powerful adverbs that add to the strong undeniable character of the reaction.

With NATO embarked on a journey of transformation into an entity that increasingly devotes itself to pan-European collective security purposes, U.S. officials tried to persuade Russians that NATO does not expand to the detriment to their country's interests in the region. However, the effort has fallen short of being successful, as many Russian politicians, officials and commentators maintained the view that NATO enlargement is contrary to Russia's security interests, even if not a near-term military threat.

Rather than seeing NATO enlargement as a positive process of exporting stability in the general interest of all countries in the Euro-Atlantic area, of which Russia is definitely part of, many Russian officials and experts professed the view that NATO' expansion in the region is an attempt to broaden the Alliance's sphere of influence. They considered NATO's rhetoric to be contradictory, given NATO's dual policy. On the one hand, the Alliance pursues a relationship of partnership and cooperation with Russia; on the other hand, NATO engages in collective defense commitments with nations that have openly manifested distrust and antipathy toward Russia. The standard Russian prescription calls for "expanding the role of the OSCE as the basis for a new pan-European security system" (Angelakis 1997:1) and "the transformation of NATO from a military Alliance into a peacekeeping/making organization" (Lieven 1995:97) that would function as a secondary tool to the OSCE.

Some Russian analysts even considered NATO enlargement an evidence of the United States' assertiveness and power, blaming the Americans for exploiting Russia's weakness to enforce a U.S.-designed security order in Europe. The growing interests of the Alliance are seen as an expansion of a U.S.-directed sphere of influence, in violation of the western commitments supposedly made in 1990, when the reunited Germany remained in NATO.

Many Russians asserted that there was an agreement with the Western powers that, as Lukin puts it, "the unification of Germany was conditional on the non-expansion of NATO to the east" (1995:22). This belief was also uttered by Russian President Boris Yeltsin in 1993, when he argued that the 1990 treaty on German reunification includes "stipulations banning the deployment of foreign troops in the eastern federal Laender of the Federal republic of Germany" and that "the spirit of these stipulations ruled out any possibility of a NATO expansion eastwards" (6). These references can also be tracked back to an "unwritten gentlemen's agreement" between Washington and Moscow, according to which "NATO would not enlarge beyond the admission of the territory of the former East Germany into the united Germany" (Hoagland 1996:A21).

Russians who believe that such a bargain was made are convinced that NATO enlargement is a betrayal and an exploitation of Russia's weakness. However, the western Europeans have a counterargument. In the words of Eyal, "Helmut Kohl did not formally promise anything about NATO's future intentions. But at the same time, there is no doubt that the main thrust of the German-Soviet discussions – and, indeed, the discussions between the United States and the Soviet Union at the time – was precisely in the direction of reassuring Moscow that its 'loss' in central Europe would not be translated into a Western 'gain'" (1997:699). Moreover, European observers have pointed out that the insistence of many Russians that such an arrangement was indeed concluded, although informally, implies that the latter in fact support great power sphere of influence arrangements, to the detriment of national self-determination and the rights of states to freely choose whether to seek membership in specific alliances or other security arrangements.

Lukin's view that NATO enlargement reflects continuous distrust of Russia and that it contradicts the Alliance's declared interests in setting up all-European security structures remains the most articulated perspective.

"We want all-European security. But if we are refused room there, we will have to worry about our own security… Not the best option, but it is the minimum necessary if the best option proves impossible… We are told: You do not have the right of veto over NATO decisions. Legally speaking, this is perfectly true. Politically speaking…an attempt is being made to kick Russia like a puppy out of the door of a room where questions of all-European security for the strategic future are being discussed. This kind of kick can trip you up yourself." (1995:23)

Lukin's metaphor is a sugar-coated stylistic twist that actually hides the frustration that Russia is not welcomed in the civilized democratic community of the European powers, grouped under the repeated indefinite collective pronoun "all", used here to illustrate the "us" versus "them" ideological polarization. By acknowledging Russia's somehow isolated position on the scene of international security, Lukin also admits that Russia's security matters will have to be dealt with by Russia itself, outside an alliance framework of which it is obviously "kicked out like a puppy". And with this, Lukin reinforces the Kantian prophetic vision that power struggles are something eternal, regardless of the nations' internal political systems.

There have been some sensitive issues associated with the stipulations of the NRFA, but the text of the document is formulated in such a manner as to appease such apprehensions. First and foremost, the Russians feared that the enlargement could result in the deployment of NATO nuclear weapons on the territory of the new Allies. In a prepared statement before the Senate Committee on Armed Services, Secretary of Defense William Cohen recalled the Alliance's collective defense commitment, reiterated in the December 1996 document: "In the context of an agreed NATO-Russia Charter, NATO will reaffirm its December 1996 statement that it has no plan, no intention and no reason to station nuclear weapons on the territory of the new members" (1997, par. 13). The "three no's" were supplemented by a fourth one included in the text of the NRFA, which mentions the fact that the allies see no need "to change any aspect of NATO's nuclear posture or nuclear policy – and do not foresee any need to do so" (Founding Act on Mutual Relations, Cooperation and Security between NATO and the Russian Federation 1997, par. 60). The attempts of the Russians to hinder the establishment of military infrastructure assets on the soil of the new allies were not successful. NATO found a way to honor its collective defense commitments and at the same time respect international agreements. This balancing act was clearly worded in paragraph 70 of the NATO-Russia Founding Act:

"NATO reiterates that in the current and foreseeable security environment the Alliance will carry out its collective defense and other missions by ensuring the necessary interoperability, integration, and capability for reinforcement rather than by additional permanent stationing of substantial combat forces. Accordingly, it will have to rely on adequate infrastructure commensurate with the above tasks. In this context, reinforcement may take place, when necessary, in the event of defense against a threat of aggression and missions in support of peace consistent with the United Nations Charter and the OSCE governing principles, as well as for exercises consistent with the adapted CFE Treaty, the provisions of the Vienna Document 1994 and mutually agreed transparency measures."

A second sensitive issue was related to the possibility that Russia's might exert a certain influence over the Alliance's decision-making through various consultative bodies. At the March 1997 U.S.-Russian Summit in Helsinki, President Boris Yeltsin proposed using the consensus method as a decision-making mechanism in the NATO-Russia Council. The method of consensus is the way in which decisions are made among NATO countries. Fearing that Russian initiatives of this kind might give an unrealistic measure of Russia's decisional power, U.S. officials felt the need to clarify the limitations of the scope of the proposed NATO-Russia council. In his address, Secretary Cohen explained that

> "The NATO-Russia joint Council will not replace the NAC, or give Russia a voice in NATO's own decisions… Russia will not participate in the NAC, the Military Committee, or subordinate NATO bodies like the Nuclear Planning Group, the Defense Planning process or in the High-Level Task Force which sets Alliance arms control policy…" (1997, par. 13)

Although excluded from NATO's decisional forums – otherwise rightfully, since it is not a NATO member, but a partner – Russia will cooperate with NATO in separate bodies that will provide mechanisms for consultation, when possible. The purpose of this clarification was to ensure collaboration while not allowing NATO-Russia arrangements "compromise the Alliance's ability to plan effectively, prepare carefully and act decisively in military matters", regardless of Russia's position (Founding Act on Mutual Relations, Cooperation and Security between NATO and the Russian Federation 1997, par. 14).

As far as the mechanisms of consultation were concerned, the NRFA stipulated that NATO-Russia Permanent Joint Council would meet twice a year at the level of foreign and defense ministers and chiefs of national military staffs, and monthly at the level of military representatives and ambassadors to the NAC.

Russia's role in shaping the European security environment creates a dilemma for NATO, mainly stemming from the uncertainty about how to deal with Russian sensitivity and gain Russian cooperation. In the last decades, the United States has been inclined to treat Russia as a fellow super power and as a virtual equal. However, this form of respect proved to be risky, generating false assessments about Russia's power and potential, and eventually resulting in ill-decisions in the Kremlin. Recent developments have validated these apprehensions, and Russia's invasion and subsequent annexation of the Crimean Peninsula in 2014 prompted NATO's countries to unanimously cease cooperation with the Russian Federation as of April 1, 2014.

In addition to expressing their views about NATO expansion representing direct threats to their own country, many Russians observers have also articulated opinions concerning the future status of former Soviet republics as members of the Alliance. In 1997, Russian President Boris Yeltsin admitted that he was pursuing a bilateral agreement with the United States that no former Soviet republic can ever join the Transatlantic Alliance. This proposed agreement was an obvious concern for the Baltic States in particular, who feared that, if left outside NATO's protective umbrella, they were in danger of being re-annexed by Russian nationalists. In March 1997, Ukrainian foreign minister Gennadiy Udovenko declared that his country's strategic objective was to join the Atlantic Alliance, because of concerns about its "unpredictable neighbor" (qtd. in Shihab 1997:2). In May 1997, after having agreed with the Alliance on the terms of the NATO-Russia Founding Act, Yeltsin said that the agreement could be placed into question if NATO accepted any former Soviet republics as a member. However, the Founding Act specifies that NATO and Russia will show respect for "… sovereignty, independence and territorial integrity of all states and their inherent right to choose the means to ensure their own security, the inviolability of borders and people's right of self-determination as enshrined in the Helsinki Final Act and other OSCE documents" (Founding Act on Mutual Relations, Cooperation and Security between NATO and the Russian Federation 1997, par. 15).

It is unquestionably difficult for the United States or for NATO as an organization to explicitly agree with Russia to exclude all former Soviet states from future Alliance membership. Such an arrangement would definitely be an artifact of the Yalta arrangement, in which big powers determine the fate of smaller powers. Furthermore, Article 10 of the Washington Treaty stipulates that the Allies may "invite any other European state in a position to further the principles of this Treaty and to contribute to the security of the North Atlantic area to accede to this Treaty". Under this principle, NATO invited Estonia, Latvia and Lithuania to join the Alliance at the 2002 Prague Summit, and the three Baltic States became full-fledged NATO members in 2004, along with Bulgaria, Romania, Slovakia and Slovenia.

However, long before this became a reality, Russia showed its willingness to even occupy the Baltic republics before they became NATO members, out of the conviction that, in Anton Surikov's words, "nobody intends to fight with Russia for the Baltic countries", partly due to the fact that Russia's nuclear forces are "one of the few convincing arguments for the West" (1996:5). This rhetoric asserting Russia's power was supplemented by Lukin, who warned that a "morally crushed, but heavily armed Russia" will retaliate: "If the blind egoism of the shortsighted politicians to the west of our borders prevails, we will resort to the means we still have in our hands. These are means of some kind of desperation, but effective nonetheless" (1995:23). Reference is undoubtedly made to Russia's nuclear power, somehow diminished in the context of this declaration by the reference to its use representing a means of "desperation", which only indicates that such measures would be taken impulsively and not really cold-bloodedly, in a reasonable framework. However, the front conditional indicates a possibility, rather than an assumed reality. The position of the author is extended to the general attitude characterizing all the actors he includes in the collectivization of the verb forms, expressed by the usage of the plural pronoun subject "we". The passage of time has demonstrated that, fortunately, Russia did not see this menace through, although subsequent developments have prompted analysts and observers to still fear a Russian invasion of the Baltic States, especially in the light of the Crimean annexation in 2014.

Although Ukraine gained independence in 1991, after the disintegration of the Soviet Union, Russia has continued to perceive the ex-Soviet country as part of its sphere of influence. According to some analysts, "Russia seems to apply a policy of continuation of the Brezhnev Doctrine on limited sovereignty, which dictates that the sovereignty of Ukraine cannot be larger than that of the Warsaw Pact prior to the demise of the Soviet sphere of influence" (Chifu et al. 2009:181). Several statements made by Russian leaders generate the conclusion that Ukraine's status as a NATO member would jeopardize Russia's national security interests.

President Vladimir Putin's decision to invade Crimea in February 2014 was internationally perceived as an unacceptable violation of Ukraine's territorial integrity and an attack to its sovereignty. As early as April 2014, the Foreign Ministers of the NATO-Ukraine Commission, who met in Brussels, on April 1, issued a statement jointly condemning "Russia's illegal military intervention in Ukraine, and Russia's violation of Ukraine's sovereignty and territorial integrity" (Statement of the NATO-Ukraine Commission 2014, par.1). They were publicly and harshly critical of Russia's annexation which they labeled as "illegal and illegitimate". This was the first of many subsequent examples of adversarial discourse NATO employed to express its strong disagreement with Russia's intervention, by utilizing powerful negative adjectives ("illegal", "illegitimate", "aggressive") and by urging Russia to take a series of measures to defuse the conflict it unlawfully sparked.

> "We call on Russia to de-escalate by reducing its troops in Crimea to pre-crisis levels and withdrawing them to their bases; to reduce its military activities along the Ukrainian border; to reverse the illegal and illegitimate "annexation" of Crimea; to refrain from any further interference and aggressive actions in Ukraine; to respect the rights of the Ukrainian population including the Crimean Tatars; and to fulfil its international obligations and to abide by international law." (par. 2)

NATO's straightforward message is condensed in an enumeration of infinitives describing the actions Russia is expected to take and anchoring the opposing attitude in a prescriptive type of discourse by which the Alliance asserts its power.

The same adversarial discourse is continued in December 2014, in another document, entitled "Joint Statement of the NATO-Ukraine Commission", in which the Alliance reiterates its strong disapproval with Russia's "continued and deliberate destabilization of eastern Ukraine", the military build-up in Crimea and its intentions to "exacerbate tensions" (Joint Statement of the NATO-Ukraine Commission 2014, par. 2). The text of the document is filled with powerful negative words, employed so as to depict a damaging image of the Russians, by adversely describing their activities: "condemn", "breach", "violate", "undermine", and by assigning harmful adjectives "worsening", "illegal", "illegitimate" to their stated course of action.

If in the 2014 documents, NATO formulated prescribed behavior with the introductory "we call on Russia to…", the 2015 "Joint Statement of the NATO-Ukraine Commission" issued after the Ministerial Meeting held in May, in Antalya, Turkey, not only changed the opening phrase to the stronger "we urge Russia to…" but also repeatedly formulated the Alliance's profound worries related to the worsening of the situation, Russia's statements regarding the possibility to station nuclear weapons and delivery systems in Crimea and the military build-up concentrated in the Black Sea area.

> "We are deeply concerned about the worsening human rights situation on the peninsula. We urge Russia to respect the rights and freedoms of the entire local population, including the native Crimean Tatars and other members of local communities, and to allow for international monitoring of the human rights situation in Crimea. We condemn Russia's ongoing and wide-ranging military build-up in Crimea, and are concerned by Russia's efforts and stated plans for further military build-up in the Black Sea region, which will potentially have further implications for the stability of the region. We are also deeply concerned by statements of the Russian leadership with regard to possible future stationing of nuclear weapons and their delivery systems in Crimea, which would be destabilizing." (Joint Statement of the NATO-Ukraine Commission 2015, par. 3)

In all documents issued in the aftermath of the Crimean crisis, NATO makes it clear that it does not recognize "Russia's illegal and illegitimate self-declared annexation of Crimea", nor does it intend to do so in the future. The discourse of the post-2014 Summits (Wales, 2014; Warsaw, 2016; Brussels, 2018) is also infused with references to the Crimean situation, described as a "pivotal moment in Euro-Atlantic security", which has "fundamentally challenged our vision of a Europe whole, free, and at peace" (Wales Summit Declaration para. 1). The document issued in Wales dedicates eight substantial paragraphs to clarifying NATO's position with regard to Russia and its aggressive actions against Ukraine. Paragraphs 18 to 21 reiterate the same concerns and apprehensions expressed in previous texts, while paragraphs 22 and 23 diplomatically declare "NATO's decision to suspend all practical civilian and military cooperation between NATO and Russia", given Russia's breach of international agreements and its policy, no longer in line with "common security concerns and interests" (Wales Summit Declaration 2014, par. 22). Furthermore, while announcing a peaceful and nonthreatening attitude toward Russia, NATO takes a solid unequivocal stance and refuses to compromise the enduring values that lay at the foundation of the Alliance. "The Alliance does not seek confrontation and poses no threat to Russia. But we cannot and will not compromise on the principles on which our Alliance and security in Europe and North America rest" (par. 23).

In the Brussels Summit Declaration of 2018, the Alliance dedicates six paragraphs (4 to 9) to explaining its adverse attitude toward Russia, the cooperation mechanisms it decided to cease and the reasons for doing so.

> "While NATO stands by its international commitments, Russia has breached the values, principles and commitments which underpin the NATO-Russia relationship, as outlined in the 1997 Basic Document of the Euro-Atlantic Partnership Council, the 1997 NATO-Russia Founding Act, and 2002 Rome Declaration, broken the trust at the core of our cooperation, and challenged the fundamental principles of the global and Euro-Atlantic security architecture." (par. 4)

The "Warsaw Declaration on Transatlantic Security" (2016) and the "Brussels Declaration on Transatlantic Security and Solidarity" (2018) both contain identical formulations expressing NATO's willingness to continue cooperation with Russia, despite the interruption of cooperation mechanisms and annulment of previous agreements. Paragraphs 6 and 7 respectively, read "We continue to aspire to a constructive relationship with Russia, when Russia's actions make that possible". Obviously, cooperation with Russia will restart under certain conditions imposed by NATO. Although the phrasing does not contain an explicit conditional clause introduced by "if", the subordinate announced by "when" has the effect of creating a provisional context. By anchoring the condition on the background of a temporal clause, NATO expresses its wishful thinking that Russia will at some point comply with international law, and peaceful cooperation will be resumed. This discursive strategy is very efficient for communicating and reinforcing the Alliance's non-confrontational and cooperative attitude toward Russia, which by no means should be transformed into a foe. NATO seems to have adopted the "keep your friends close and your enemies closer" doctrine, in a world that has become increasingly less stable and predictable.

*NATO and the "war on terror"*

International terrorism has exposed the Euro-Atlantic community to a multifaceted threat that requires a comprehensive strategic approach that also involves NATO, in its dimension as a security organization. Although there have been a series of debates within the Alliance regarding the extent to which NATO should contribute to anti-terrorist actions, with some members arguing for a wider engagement and others opting for more modest roles, all the allies agree that international terrorism is a serious threat and have decided to approach the challenge through various means.

The initial debate regarding the extent of NATO's roles and missions echoed two opposing strategies to deal with terrorism: the "war" approach and the "risk-management" approach. In the immediate aftermath of the terrorist attacks of September 11, 2001, the Bush administration declared a worldwide "war on terror", involving a wide range of approaches: open and covert military operations, efforts to block terrorist financing, new security laws, etc. The war approach, especially favored by the United States, suggests a massive mobilization of resources in a joint effort that acknowledges boundaries on individual liberties at high costs. Washington summoned others to join in the fight against terrorism. The explicit linguistic polarization in the formulation "either you are with us, or you are with the terrorists" received harsh criticism for being an antagonistic ideology that, under the menace of fear and repression, is prone to create enemies and promote violence, rather than vindicating acts of terror and strengthening global security. The second approach, favored by the European allies, for which talk of war was deemed inappropriate, advocates the strategy of risk-management with emphasis on defensive, rather than offensive and preventing measures.

At the level of the Alliance, the argument about NATO's role in fighting terrorism was mainly underlined by the different perceptions European countries have had on terrorism throughout history. These range from social experiences with the poorly-assimilated domestic Muslim communities, historical and cultural ties with the Middle East and North Africa, different interpretations of the Israeli-Palestinian conflict, and even various degrees of anti-American views. Against this background, it is not

156

surprising that the allies have struggled to reach an agreement on how to best deal with the terrorist phenomenon. Agreement that terrorism is a serious threat and knows no boundaries has been, however, unanimous. While terrorism has been traditionally perceived and dealt with as a series of singular regional or national phenomena, modern day terrorism is defined as a single problem with multiple manifestations. The shift in perception and interpretation took place when governments understood the links between otherwise discrete manifestations of terrorism and started to focus more on a comprehensive and unified approach that valued broad cooperation inside and between security organizations.

The linguistic analysis conducted with specific attention to the discourse on "terrorism" has resulted in the identification of two distinct but fundamentally similar sub-discourses. One encapsulates NATO's approach to the terrorist threat as it had been defined and approached during the Cold War, with the main actors being the Soviet Union and the Warsaw Pact countries, the "enemy" for which NATO was initially designed. The second sub-discourse on terrorism encompasses the views and strategies that characterize the American-led global counter-terrorism campaign launched in response to the terrorist attacks of September 11, 2001.

One of the first documents that vigorously condemn terrorism, seen as a "flagrant violation of human dignity and rights" calls for increased cooperation between the allies, who, in the words of the 1981 "Declaration on Terrorism" reiterate

> "... their deep concern over the suffering inflicted on innocent people as well as the negative impact such criminal offenses have on international relations. ... Thus condemning energetically these activities as a flagrant violation of human dignity and rights, they [the allies] stressed the need for more co-operation in this field." (par. 1)

This declaration represents the cornerstone for the Final Communiqués of the NAC or of the DPC issued between 1981 and 1988, all of which contain at least one paragraph that makes direct reference to terrorism "in all its manifestations".

Example 1

"The Allies are profoundly concerned over the acts of terrorism which recur in several of their countries. They strongly condemn all such acts and solemnly appeal to all governments to wage an effective struggle against this scourge and to intensify their efforts to this end." (Final Communiqué of the North Atlantic Council 1982, par. 15)

Example 2

"The Allies reiterate their abhorrence and condemnation of recurring terrorist acts which menace democratic institutions as well as the conduct of international relations. The Allies reaffirm their determination to pursue all necessary efforts to combat and suppress crimes of terrorism." (Final Communiqué of the North Atlantic Council 1983, par. 14)

Example 3

"Terrorism is a serious concern to all our Governments. We are not prepared to tolerate this threat to our citizens and to the conduct of normal international relations. Our Governments are resolved to work together to eradicate this scourge and urge closer international co-operation in this effort." (Final Communiqué of the Defence Planning Committee 1986, par. 12)

Example 4

"We reiterate our condemnation of terrorism in all its manifestations and reaffirm our determination to combat it. We believe international co-operation to be essential in the eradication of this scourge." (Final Communiqué of the North Atlantic Council 1988, par. 12)

These four examples are illustrative for the seventeen documents that the Alliance issued in the 1980s as both a strategic and as a discursive response to the issue of terrorism. The overarching attitude of the allies, collectivized by pronominalization ("we", "our") or capitalized nouns ("the Allies", "Governments") is expressed by the speech acts embedded in the predicative constructions, most of which are modified by a strong adverb ("are profoundly concerned", "strongly condemn", "solemnly appeal", "our determination", "are resolved", "urge"). The synonymy of signal phrase verbs such as "reaffirm", "reiterate", "remain" stands for the constancy the Alliance wishes to transmit in what regards its approach toward terrorism. Semantically, the discourses are populated with explicit or symbolic references to the concept of "terrorism", denoted by indexical replacements throughout the text ("scourge", "crime", "threat", "menace").

The examples above illustrate parallel discursive strategies of reifying integrative and adversarial power, both of which are manifested in language through a constant and solid use of lexical concordances. Constructed in this manner, the discourse becomes a powerful weapon, carrying a dual task: on the one hand, it galvanizes the allies to join their efforts in eradicating, combating, and fighting terrorism; on the other hand, it is used to support the opposing attitude with illustrations of "abhorrence and condemnation" for the recurrent terrorist acts. More than expressing a merely discursive adversarial attitude, such texts represent one of the Alliance's mechanisms of encouraging cooperation and unity for the protection of shared values, such as democracy and integrity.

The second strand of sub-discourses on terrorism is reflected in a series of communicative events that were expressed by NATO public documents after September 11, 2001. All official texts issued since that event pivots on one central idea: the new threat has spread internationally and is totally different from the traditional terrorism promoted by the Soviet Union and Warsaw Pact countries. The new challenge extends beyond localized phenomena and takes the war to a new level, in which the fight is asymmetrical, the enemy is an entity of fluid networks, and the ideological struggle opposes Islam and the Western world. Driven by the desire to establish a new order in the Middle East and the Gulf area, these Islamic extremists hope to eliminate Western influences on local regimes and impose their own principles. The menace of Islamic terrorism is more difficult to contain because its reach is more global, more lethal, more adaptable, and more volatile than the influence achieved by the traditional terrorist groups of the 1960s, 1970s, and 1980s.

For NATO, fight against terrorism has become a top priority. Agreement has been reached regarding the nature of the problem, and all members have decided together on the most appropriate military and political responses. The first response to this new type of terrorist threat was issued in the immediate aftermath of the September 11 attacks. At the Ministerial Meeting of the NAC, held in Brussels on December 6-7, 2001, NATO foreign ministers issued a document entitled NATO's Response to Terrorism. The text starts with a strong condemnation of the terrorist attacks that radically changed the security architecture of the whole world: "The terrorist attacks of 11 September were an outrage against the entire world" (NATO's Response to Terrorism 2001, par. 1). The same paragraph continues with a justification of the measures NATO will take from that point forward in order to combat the phenomenon: "We are responding to bring to justice those responsible for these crimes, and to prevent them from taking innocent lives in future" The strategies NATO forged in response to the terrorist attacks of September 11 represented a critical reference point in the history of the Alliance. It was for the first time since the validation of the Washington Treaty fifty-two years prior that Article 5 was invoked. The article enshrines the principle of collective defense, stipulating that "an attack against one ally is considered an attack against all". The text of the article reads:

> "The Parties agree that an armed attack against one or more of them in Europe or North America shall be considered an attack against them all and consequently they agree that, if such an armed attack occurs, each of them, in exercise of the right of individual or collective self-defence recognised by Article 51 of the Charter of the United Nations, will assist the Party or Parties so attacked by taking forthwith, individually and in concert with the other Parties, such action as it deems necessary, including the use of armed force, to restore and maintain the security of the North Atlantic area." (Washington Treaty Art. 5)

Invocation of Article 5 was no easy task. The officials were dealing both with strategic and linguistic dilemmas. In an article published by NATO Review in 2006, Edgar Buckley tells the story behind NATO's appeal to Article 5 on September 12, 2001, just 24 hours after the terrorist attacks against the United States. The author, who at that time was the Assistant Secretary General for Defence Planning and Operations, remembers that a great deal of thought was put into deciding whether the planes crashing in the Twin Towers and in the Pentagon building could be defined as "armed attacks". After the debate, the present officials agreed there was enough moral and legal ground to activate Washington Treaty's collective defense provisions. The next step, Buckley recollects, was to back up this decision by researching earlier NATO documents and communiqués in order to find supporting policy statements. In the author's opinion, "referring to existing agreed language is an important step in facilitating consensus" (par. 11). As part of the research, the 1999 Washington Summit Declaration and the Strategic Concept, in particular, were examined for specific references that would support the upcoming approach with previously agreed-upon policy statements regarding terrorism.

160

This example is indicative of the importance that NATO officials themselves attach to language when drafting essential policy documents. Such a practice illustrates the fact that the people who are responsible with designing strategies and doctrine at the level of the Alliance do consider language powerful and, in addition to concepts and ideologies, they also carefully select the linguistic elements they construct discourses on.

As a consequence, the text of "NATO's Response to Terrorism" makes legitimate reference to the North Atlantic Treaty, and the text of the Strategic Concept adopted at the 1991 Washington Summit.

> "We reiterate our determination to combat the threat of terrorism for as long as necessary. In keeping with our obligations under the Washington Treaty we will continue to strengthen our national and collective capacities to protect our populations, territory and forces from any armed attack, including terrorist attack, directed from abroad. We recognised this challenge in the Strategic Concept adopted at the Washington Summit, where we made clear that any armed attack on the territory of the Allies, from whatever direction, would be covered by Article 5 of the Washington Treaty and where we singled out terrorism as a risk to the security interests of the Alliance. Meeting this challenge is fundamental to our security." (NATO's Response to Terrorism 2001, par. 15).

These intertextual references support the legitimacy the Alliance needed in order to validate its response to terrorism. Discursively, the ideological journey NATO embarked on in its attempt to combat the terrorist phenomenon is substantiated by the same linguistic mechanisms identified in the documents issued before the 2001 attacks. Similar formulations indicate that the Alliance has remained faithful to its credo, both conceptually and discursively. However, the weight of the predicative structures is intensified by the usage of stronger adverbial modifiers ("categorically reject", "resolutely condemn"): "We categorically reject and resolutely condemn terrorism in all its forms and manifestations" (par. 2). The entire document is infused with references to terrorism and terrorists and describes that institutional and cooperative mechanisms NATO will activate in order to "combat this scourge". In its dual dimension, of illustrating both adversarial and integrative power, the first discourse against terrorism fosters international cooperation by assimilating NATO and the international community under the umbrella of a common goal. "Our" fight, a specific reference modified by the first-person plural possessive, becomes a generalized concept, "the fight of the international community", and is directed against an all-encompassing terrorist phenomenon that includes "the terrorists, their networks and those who harbour them" (par. 4).

Seven more documents, out of which four are ministerial communiqués and three are declarations issued in the aftermath of the 2002, 2012, and 2017 Summits, contain similar reiterations of the Alliance's stance regarding terrorism and measures to combat it. The 2001 "Statement on Combating Terrorism" was issued during the December 2001 ministerial meeting at the level of ministers of defense in Brussels and is a continuation of the previous document in that it contains specific policy and operational references to how the Alliance can adapt its defense capabilities in order to combat terrorism in a more effective manner.

At the 2002 Summit, NATO "condemned unconditionally the terrorist attacks" and outlined its approach to fighting terrorism (Partnership Action Plan against Terrorism 2002, par. 1). The text of the document states the Alliance's goals: to help states deter, defend, disrupt and protect against terrorist threats from abroad. The basic strategy, outlined in NATO's military concept for defense against terrorism (MC 0472/1) and approved in November 2002, includes anti-terrorism defensive measures, counter-terrorism offensive measures, crisis management strategies, and military cooperation and coordination among member states as well as with international organizations, such as the European Union, the Organization for Security and Cooperation in Europe and the United Nations. The document was declassified in January 2016 and contains three parts outlining the definition of counter-terrorism and NATO's military role in combating it.

After the 2004 Madrid train bombings, NATO issued a "Declaration on Terrorism" during the April NAC meeting in Brussels. Using the same formulations as in the previous documents, the declaration expresses the allies' categorical rejection of terrorism, condemnation of the "atrocities" of "this scourge" and their strong determination to fight together this phenomenon "which challenges the values that unite us, most particularly freedom founded on the principles of democracy, individual liberty and the rule of law" (Declaration on Terrorism 2004, par. 1-2).

162

The two NATO-Russia Council documents, issued in 2004 and respectively 2011, extend the Alliance's internal strategies against terrorism to the framework of external cooperation with Russia. The first document, "NATO-Russia Action Plan on Terrorism" issued in 2004, was superseded by the "NATO-Russia Council Action Plan on Terrorism", in 2011. The opening lines of the two documents are identical: "The NATO-Russia Council categorically rejects terrorism in all its manifestations. Terrorist acts pose a direct challenge to our common security, to our shared democratic values, and to basic human rights and freedoms". In a dual exercise of integrative and adversarial power, the text condemns the acts of terrorism and calls for cooperation in the name of shared values and common security.

At the 2012 Chicago and 2017 Brussels Summits, NATO designed two more documents dealing with policy guidelines on counter-terrorism. These documents do not stride far from the previous ones and are the only public textual references to the Alliance's strategies in the "war on terror". Most of the documents containing operational policies remain classified to this date.

The 2018 Brussels Summit also mentions terrorism as a palpable menace of the present. Paragraph 10 of the "Brussels Declaration" reads:

"Terrorism, in all its forms and manifestations, continues to pose a direct threat to the security of our populations, and to international stability and prosperity more broadly. We categorically reject terrorism as it directly challenges the values that unite the Alliance. Our solidarity and determination will prevail. We are committed to continue the fight against terrorism, which has to be tackled through a coherent, significant, long-term effort by the international community as a whole, involving a wide range of instruments and actors." (par. 10)

The discourse against terrorism is characterized by the same elements identified in previous formulations. Adversarial language is condensed in the reiteration of the condemning attitude that runs throughout all the documents dealing with this phenomenon ("categorically reject"). Again, terrorism, in its universal acceptation, is seen as a "threat" to stability, peace and security. The fundamental values "that unite the Alliance" are once more emphasized and conceptually utilized here to promote the notion of cooperation and unity, by galvanizing the efforts of "the international community as a whole" in the fight against terrorism.

By and large, the textual references to terrorism and the Alliance's stance and actions against it are all permeated with similar linguistic elements. The lexical analysis indicated an essential host of words instilled with the concept that terrorism is a modern day atrocity. Given the similar formulations that typify all the exemplified documents, the conclusion is that the lexical pool from which NATO extracts its formulations is a finite one. However, while the choice of exact same words may be an indication of the fact that the lexical universe of military discourse is fairly limited, this may also account for discursive consistency and an informed communication strategy to intentionally eschew precious constructions, complex synonymy and fuzzy formulations. Simple seems to be the key word and the best approach to disseminate a message that does not need stylistic embellishment to transmit a fundamental idea: terrorism is bad, and it needs to be fought against.

## 3.3. The Discourse of U.S. Predominant Power

The analysis that informs this section of the paper starts from the assumption that NATO is traditionally perceived as an American-led organization, with most of the strategic policies adopted by the Alliance stemming from U.S. initiatives. The concept of integrative power, exploited in the previous section, is based on the premise that unity sometimes involves accepting U.S. leadership and, by extension, acknowledging United States' predominant role in NATO. The work hypothesis substantiating the critical analysis of the discourse of U.S. predominant power is that the Americans make use of the legitimate, referential, and expert dimensions of power in order to assert their influence on NATO doctrine and strategies.

The first indication of the Unites States' interest in enforcing European security in the aftermath of World War II is represented by the well-known Marshall Plan, which was given the name of his initiator, George Marshall. In a speech delivered in June 1947 at Harvard, Marshall points out America's essential and unconditional role in assisting European postwar recovery and the belief that world peace and stability logically stems from the United States' involvement: "It is logical that the United States should do whatever it is able to do to assist in the return of normal economic

164

health in the world, without which there can be no political stability and no assured peace" (par. 7). The British Foreign Secretary George Bevin's initiative to consolidate the restoration of Europe in close cooperation with the Western powers materialized in the Brussels Treaty, signed on March 17, 1948, a document considered to be the forerunner of the North Atlantic Treaty. Moreover, Bevin's proposal received immediate support from the United States in the form of President Truman's act of peacetime conscription, which validated the presence of U.S. occupation forces on the territory of Germany until the peace in Europe was secured. In the midst of the 1948 political tensions in Prague and Berlin, the Americans felt the need to make their intentions more transparent. Clarification came as the Vandenberg Resolution, adopted in 1948, a document that stated two of the main philosophies that will later be regarded as the foundation of the Washington Treaty. The first principle emphasized the fact that no security treaty signed by the United States would automatically indicate that the country must go to war (a right expressed and maintained by the constitutional mandate of the Congress); the second championed the idea that security must flow both ways, in that the other parties of the treaty would not have one-sided benefits.

The six-paragraph document synthesizes the main principles of consultation and cooperation that were to represent the pillars of the emerging security Alliance. It is also an expression of American referent and expert power in drafting key concepts underlying the values the future North Atlantic Treaty Organization will hold unchanged throughout its development. The Resolution pivots on the provisions of the United Nations Charter, a fundamental document from which the Washington Treaty itself extracted its core ideologies a year later. The document begins with affirming the principles of "international cooperation" and "international peace and security" and continues with enumerating the objectives of the American policy in a very straightforward and organized language.

"Whereas peace with justice and the defense of human rights and fundamental freedoms require international cooperation through more effective use of the United Nations: Therefore, be it Resolved, That the Senate reaffirm the policy of the United States to achieve international peace and security through the United Nations so that armed force shall not be used except in the common interest." (The Vandenberg Resolution 1948, par. 1)

Based on this framework document and also on article 51 of the UN Charter, the document establishing the need and role of the North Atlantic Treaty Organization came into being on April 4, 1949. Nevertheless, the notion of an-American led plan for European defense was received with a negative attitude by some of the European powers. In May 1952, France, Italy, West Germany, and the Benelux countries signed the European Defense Community (EDC) Treaty. Already mentioned and analyzed as a source of adversarial power in a previous section of the chapter, this European initiative becomes specifically relevant in this context, given the fact it was perceived as an attempt of the Western allies to create a European Army that would enforce a parallel plan for collective European defense, a move that was perceived as a challenge to the American supremacy and interests on the international scene. In order to secure the founding concepts of the Treaty, the Americans felt the need to emphasize the notion of structured defense and to integrate any plans for European defense within the broader framework of the newly founded Alliance. Dean Acheson, the then U.S. Secretary of State remarks in 1953 that West European unity can only exist at the center of an Atlantic Community and insists that it is exactly this hierarchical configuration that will avoid "disunity and weakness throughout the Atlantic community" (7). The official's intervention represents an attempt of the Americans to safe lock their hierarchical power and make sure that the Treaty's collective defense conceptions are not undermined by individual powers (although re-collected in another form, but away from the U.S. scrutinizing eye).

Against this backdrop, the balance of power tilted in favor of the U.S.-led NATO, which immediately came up with a solution for continental European defense. The void created by the subsequent demise of the EDC (ultimately rejected by the same Frenchmen who had initiated it) had to be filled up by a similar move. The issue of West Germany, the bone of contention whose unstable position in Europe was the main source of the French rejection, needed a viable approach. The 1954 London conference was dedicated to finding a feasible way by which to best associate the German Federal Republic with Western nations on a basis of full sovereignty. The solution NATO proposed was the creation of the West European Union (WEU) and of a WEU Agency for the Control of Armaments. The main purpose behind this initiative was to soften the French resistance by

166

alleviating any residual fears about German rearmament. In virtue of its close association with NATO, the WEU was endowed with a similar vision and analogous powers. It was perceived as a European integration instrument, made possible, as the U.S. representative, J.F. Dulles, pointed out, by the North Atlantic Treaty. Hierarchical positioning was once again reinforced, and America regained the dominant power it had lost with the rejection of the EDC. Under the umbrella of the same hopes and promises embedded in the rhetoric of the Treaty, the WEU was meant to eliminate Franco-German hostility and "to create a new Europe" (Dulles 1955:685). Through the WEU, the United States aimed at promoting European identity that was allied with and receptive to American leadership. Nonetheless, the very notion behind a continental defense left some room for slow disengagement of Europe from Atlantic control.

The evolution of events up to the year 1955 created the possibility that a continental conception of defense might be possible, a theory that has driven most of the imbalances in the power dynamics during the Cold War. This background proved very fertile for the re-emergence of a pluralist vision of postwar order, which, as David Calleo (1987) argues, ended when the United States assumed direct leadership for European defense. As we shall see in the decades to come, pluralism did not disappear. Or at least not the conceptual manifestation assuming its existence. In the years between 1949 and 1955, they were instrumental in fueling the national motives for supporting NATO and, despite conflicts of opinion or method, the Western allies had more reasons to agree than not. The British and the French benefitted from American support in rebuilding their devastated economies and cities; moreover, the U.S. offered them security against the threat represented by the Soviet Union.

During the Cold War, American rhetoric was always carefully constructed around the image of a threatening enemy represented by the Soviet monolith. U.S. officials' discourse of the period is infused with references to the negative influence the Soviet Union exerts globally, affecting the Unites States and the Free World equally. The Americans tried to maintain their decisional power in NATO by inducing the notion that the polarization between the Transatlantic Community and the Soviet Union stems from an ideological "battle for men's minds", located at the intersection between the mutually antagonistic free world and communist conceptions. The rhetoric of the period often invoked a conceptual framework in which the Cold War was a tussle between opposing civilizations that held divergent views about the nature of the individual.

A very illustrative example is the 1959 address of Allen W. Dulles, the director of the Central Intelligence Agency, regarding the Soviet military threat. The official's speech is permeated with references to the "us"/ "them" polarization and is constructed as a warning against the ideology of Communism, which threatens to take over the world, unless proper measures are taken against it. "Only a few weeks ago Khrushchev amiably advised us, as he left the United States, that Communism would in time take us over", Allen Dulles recalls in the beginning of his speech (par. 2). His discourse makes use of integrative power relations, insisting that "The United States and its allies of the Free World must continue to maintain a military defensive and retaliatory power such that no increase in Soviet military power could lead the latter to believe that they had gained clear superiority over us" (par. 17). The official's caveats are referential for the manner in which the Alliance built its nuclear power narrative to counteract the Soviet menace in the 1960s. In Dulles's words,

> "… the leaders of international communism [must not] misunderstand or miscalculate our posture today. They must not do so tomorrow. The prevention of misunderstanding is a continuing task. We must not slip into an attitude of complacency which might lead the Communists to have doubts about our intentions. They must not be allowed to feel that the threat of nuclear blackmail could be used to push us out of any position that is vital to our security, on the mistaken theory that it is not worth the risk of a nuclear conflict." (par. 20)

This paragraph is more than a warning. The use of the modal here, as an obligation equally extended to "we" and to "they", reflects the belief that it is imperative for the situation to be clearly understood by both parties, and that communication regarding the nuclear posture of both is paramount. The issue of the American nuclear policy was one of the many topics tackled by Dulles in his speech. As a testimony of the referent power of U.S. policies, such discursive references are faithfully echoed in the NATO documents of the period. For example, on the topic of the Cuban missile crisis, the Final Communiqué issued by the North Atlantic Council at the Ministerial Meeting held in Paris, in December 1962, reads "The recent attempt by the Soviet Union to tilt the balance of force against the West by secretly stationing nuclear missiles in Cuba brought the world to the verge of war. The peril was averted by the firmness and restraint of the United States, supported by the Alliance and other free nations" (par. 3).

The passive voice formulation in the second sentence of the paragraph attributes agency to the Americans, placing the effort of the Allies and other partners on the second place. Undoubtedly, in virtue of their nuclear capabilities, the United States was the NATO power most likely to counteract the nuclear threat represented by the Soviets. Their potency in this context is embedded in the discursive recognition that runs throughout the nuclear policy documents of the Alliance, with more than one hundred references to the American strategic and tactical nuclear assets during the period between 1962 and 1988.

The Americans were also in the lead in terms of defense policies, such as the Strategic Defense Initiatives (SDI), introduced by President Reagan. In early 1983, Reagan was still pursuing a campaign to renew the U.S. strategic leadership in NATO. The SDI, popularly known as "Star Wars", was a plan aimed at providing space-based defense against Soviet missiles. The SDI sparked controversial reactions both within the Alliance and from the Soviets. The latter claimed that the initiative was an escalation of the arms race and a violation of the Anti-Ballistic Missile Treaty, while the European allies feared that this completely new nuclear technology might undermine mutual deterrence. Plus, it placed the Europeans in an inferior position in relation to the Americans, to whom they had to turn to in search for protection, in exchange for valuable defense contracts offered to the European industries by the United States. Reagan's Strategic Defense Initiative was yet another attempt of the Americans to reassert their position as major power within NATO, but it resulted into a strain of both transatlantic and East-West relations and was finally set aside.

The importance of the American initiative was however acknowledged by NATO, and the Alliance dedicated discursive references to the significance of the strategic nuclear systems, which continue to be "an essential element of the Alliance's deterrent posture" (Final Communiqué of the Nuclear Planning Group 1988, par. 4). By using similar formulation, the Final Communiqués of the Nuclear Planning Group between 1983 and 1989 recognize the efforts made by the United States and by the United

Kingdom (the other NATO nuclear power) in maintaining credible the Alliance's policy of strategic nuclear deterrence.

Example 1:

"NATO's strategic forces are the ultimate deterrent to preserve security, peace and freedom. Therefore, we support the United States and United Kingdom efforts to maintain the credibility of their strategic nuclear deterrent capabilities." (Final Communiqué of the Nuclear Planning Group March 198,5 par. 2)

Example 2:

"We continue to support the United States and the United Kingdom efforts to maintain the credibility of their strategic nuclear deterrent capabilities; NATO's strategic forces are the ultimate deterrent in preserving security, peace and freedom." (Final Communiqué of the Nuclear Planning Group October 1985, par. 3)

Example 3:

"We expressed our appreciation for the efforts of both the United States and the United Kingdom to maintain the effectiveness of their strategic deterrent capabilities. We noted that strategic nuclear systems continue to be an essential element of the Alliance's deterrent posture." (Final Communiqué of the Nuclear Planning Group 1989, para. 5)

In the above examples, the core values of Alliance (security, peace and freedom) are reinforced by repetition in the language of the documents, while the initiatives of the United States are appreciated and supported by all NATO members as an acknowledgment of the American referent and expert power on the matter of nuclear deterrence.

The idea that stability and peace need to be secured through NATO's nuclear policies was not new to the lexicon of the Alliance. When he assumed presidency in 1977, Jimmy Carter's agenda was centered on promoting human rights as an instrument of foreign policy and aimed at strengthening America's defense and its relations with NATO. In a Report to the American people, the President outlined his vision by stating that U.S. foreign policy "should be based on close cooperation with our allies and worldwide respect for human rights" (1977:161). This new approach reiterated NATO's identity beyond a simple military and political alliance,

170

conceived as a safeguard for the protection of Western freedom and democracy and, at the same time, invested the Alliance with the role of securing human rights on a global scale. Carter carried this message to different NATO meetings, in an attempt to convince the European allies of the steady stance assumed by the U.S. in terms of its commitment to shared political and human values. At the opening ceremonies of the NAC summit in Washington, on May 30, 1978, Carter highlighted the idea that "human rights and human values are the final purpose and meaning of our alliance" (1).

The rhetoric of Carter's humane vision, which he had announced at the London meeting twelve months before his speech in Washington propelled the term "human rights" directly at the core of the Alliance's lexicon. For example, the Final Communiqué of the 1977 London Summit states the allies' recognition of "the aspirations of people throughout the world to human rights and fundamental freedoms" as "wholly legitimate" (Final Communiqué of the North Atlantic Council 1977, par. 11). A host of NATO documents, issued at the following Ministerial Meetings also emphasizes the importance of safeguarding human rights while pursuing the Alliance's stated security goals. Respect of democracy, freedom and the fundamental rights of the individuals is a salient value emerging from Final Communiqués NATO issued during 1986, 1989, 1991. "We have long sought a just and lasting order of peace in Europe, based on full respect for the human rights and political freedoms of all individuals, and on the security of all states from threats of aggression or intimidation" (par. 6), the Alliance maintains in the Final Communiqué of the North Atlantic Council meeting in Brussels, in December 1989, mirroring identical formulations from the other official documents on this topic. The all-encompassing extend of the Alliance's beliefs and practices in this regard resides in the use of absolute modifiers ("full", "all"), which testify for the global, overarching power of Carter's enduring vision and for the Americans' ability to prescribe lasting policies that are indeed reflections of the initially assumed roles that NATO remained faithful to throughout its ideological evolution.

In more recent history, NATO's commitments and programs has taken cooperation between the United States and its European allies to the outer limits of Europe and beyond. The Balkans offer an example where the Europeans pulled the United States into active military and political involvement outside the traditional perimeter of NATO but still inside Europe. The United States was determined to stay out of the conflicts raging in Croatia and Bosnia following the unraveling of Yugoslavia in 1991-1992. It was the bloodletting in Bosnia and the inability of the European forces deployed there under UN authority to control the situation that slowly drew a domestically oriented President Bill Clinton into more active involvement in Europe, culminating into the Dayton Peace Accord of 1995.

However, one important lesson the Americans and the Alliance extracted from this experience was the need for more flexibility. It is equally important that NATO be able to create opportunities for national ambitions and, at the same time, to encourage allied support for national policy when important interests are at stake. From the Americans' perspective: "The appropriate way of dealing with a security environment that is far more complex and fluid than it was during the era of Cold War bipolarity is to establish a more limited and flexible security relationship with the nations of Europe" (Carpenter 2000:37).

The materialized outcome of this new American-generated conceptual approach was discursively reified in text of the Alliance's Strategic Concept adopted in Washington in April 1999. Paragraph 10 of the Concept restates the meaning of the Alliance as a collection of nations "committed to the Washington Treaty and the United Nations Charter" and assents NATO's continued respect for "the legitimate security interest of others, and seek[s] the peaceful resolution of disputes as set out in the Charter of the United Nations" (The Alliance's Strategic Concept 1999, par. 11). This commitment is indicative of the Alliance's aim of building a security environment where NATO and other organizations, such as the UN, are "complementary and mutually reinforcing" (par. 25). In the same text, NATO recognizes the crucial role of the UNSC in maintaining security, stability, and international peace. As a consequence, NATO operations were placed under the authority of the UNSC or under the responsibility of the OSCE, while the Alliance was ready to commit its resources and expertise to these security institutions. By and large, the 1999 Strategic Concept advocates the need for a flexible approach under the framework of which NATO can enhance its cooperation to other institutions.

Nevertheless, the stipulations of the new Strategic Concept brought about different reactions. The French saluted and reinforced NATO's subordination to UN mandates. President Chirac's policy supported the idea that NATO should not be able to override the authority invested

172

in the UNSC. The French President interpreted NATO's compromise to undertake peacekeeping missions and other missions under the authority of the UN (paragraph 31 of the 1999 Strategic Concept) as a validation of a French policy reminiscent of de Gaulle's ambitions, which resulted in the conclusion that "Clinton could not ignore the French request for the UN to be acknowledged as having preeminence over NATO" ("Vrai Victoire" 1999:5). In reaction, the Americans refuted the French President's interpretation of events and politely argued that, while UN approval of NATO operations was welcome, it was not seen as necessary. The United States thus fueled the belief that NATO could act autonomously and did not necessarily recognize that the Strategic Concept tied NATO to the approval of the Security Council. Moreover, the fact that the UN has "primary" responsibility for international peace and security (The Alliance's Strategic Concept 1999, par. 31) left the door open for other actors if they wished to join in case the UN was unable to live up to the expectations. President Clinton's rhetoric on the occasion inscribed the American policy in values that were recognized by the democratic world, in that NATO's new Strategic Concept reaffirmed "our commitment to a common future, rooted in common humanity" (1999:360). In other words, if NATO chose to act outside a UNSC mandate, this would happen in virtue of old-fashioned national interests and, in addition to that, and given the Kosovo example, in order to protect the humanitarian values on which the Alliance had been founded according to the preamble of the UN Charter. The British placed themselves somewhere between the French and the Americans. Prime Minister Tony Blair used this straddling position to fashion a British general doctrine for intervention, coupling the Frenchmen's need of new guidelines for international cooperation and for new organizational structures of the international institutions with the importance of pursuing strategic or national interests, which he correlated with the U.S. views that justified the refutation of the UNSC consent.

In January 2001, when George. W. Bush took office, U.S. foreign policy experienced a turning point. At the time, NATO was going through a radical transformation and was about to become a security organization coping with new "challenges". At a NATO conference in June 2001, the U.S. Secretary of Defense, Donald Rumsfeld, told the NATO defense ministers that "we must prepare together for the new and quite different challenges we will face in the new century" (par. 9). The next decade certainly raised quite different challenges for the Alliance.

President George W. Bush maintained his predecessor's commitment to Europe despite some pull out remarks he had made during his 2000 presidential campaign. On June 15, 2001, while delivering a speech at the Warsaw University, he stated: "I know that America's role is important, and we will meet our obligations. We went into the Balkans together and we will come out together" (Bush and Dietrich 2005:149).

The September 11, 2001 attacks on the United States radically changed NATO's security agenda. It was for the first (and only) time in the history of the Alliance that Article 5 was invoked. NATO's unprecedented invocation – a decision taken without any encouragement from the United States – marked a moment of great solidarity between the United States and its European allies. It was extremely important that all allies perceived terrorism as a serious threat and therefore endorse compatible strategies to deal with the phenomenon. The uncertainty came from the nature of the threat and the characteristics of the security environment. If the threat was clearly stated and understood, then the U.S. had a unique occasion to re-create NATO as an alliance based on unity and common purpose. On the other hand, if the phenomenon was seen rather as risk and not a real threat, then the United States would have to convince the European allies that NATO would be a better and more flexible coalition than the EU.

More than ever, the Americans strategically and discursively acknowledged the interdependence between NATO allies after the launch of their major deployment to Asia in the aftermath of September 11. NATO's Secretary General Lord Robertson concurs with this view. In a speech at the Moscow's Diplomatic Academy, on November 22, 2001, he compared the new threat of terrorism to the situation in the Balkans: "The challenges in Kosovo and Bosnia may have seemed far away, but the challenge of global terrorism is not. It threatens us right here at our doorstep. Far more than Kosovo or Bosnia, the attacks of September 11 brought home the lessons of our interdependence" (par. 29-30). Intertextually, the reference to "interdependence" travels back to J.F. Kennedy's conceptualization of the type of relationship binding the Alliance. Robertson's reiteration of the idea, forty years later is a further proof of the enduring power of American-generated principles.

The U.S. national security was definitely entering an era of radical transformation, a change discursively framed in the 2001 National Security Strategy of the United States of America: "The major institutions of American national security were designed in a different era to meet different requirements. All of them must be transformed" (ch. IX, par. 1). As far as the Alliance was concerned, the Americans were promoting a new policy of international cooperation. In support of this new orientation, Donald Rumsfeld argued in 2002 that either "the mission will shape the coalition" or "the mission will be dumbed down to the lowest common denominator" (24). All U.S. policy declarations made repeated reference to "threats" and "threatened values" in an attempt to remind NATO of the Cold War, when a threat to common values encouraged the members of the Alliance to stay united. President Bush even went as far as to state that "either you are with us or against us", suggesting the existence of two blocks in world politics, the opposition of which was a reminder of the ideological clash between forces of enlightenment and regression.

Furthermore, while preparing for the war in Afghanistan, the Bush administration clearly stated that it did not intend to rely on NATO but would rather seek "different coalitions in other parts of the world" (Yost 1998:177). The European allies interpreted America's message as an attempt to disengage from NATO, while manifesting the desire to choose its own allies elsewhere. The belief that NATO was no longer valued by the Americans was strengthened when Bush's administration decided to go to war in Iraq without the support of the two major European allies, Germany and France.

Despite disagreements between the United States and some of its European allies, NATO participated in the two U.S.-led main campaigns linked to the 9/11 events – Afghanistan and Iraq. The Alliance's infrastructure was used for the surveillance and protection of the continental U.S., international forces were drawn together in the theaters of operations in Afghanistan and Iraq, and operational budget-sharing allowed the Americans to transfer their troops from one theater (the Balkans) to another. The important distinction to be made here in terms of assigning the responsibility for strategic design and operational implementation is crucial for the understanding of power dynamics at the level of the Alliance. NATO's fight against terrorism was actually the United States' own war on terror, especially since the Alliance's two essential mechanisms, the NAC and the integrated command, played a negligible role in the Afghanistan and Iraq campaigns. It was in Washington that the strategy was designed; it was the U.S. central command that directed combat forces. This remark is critical in that it demonstrates the American predominance in NATO and the different types of referent, legitimate and expert power that the United States assumed during its anti-terrorism campaigns. The following observations about the events in Afghanistan and Iraq fully support this argument.

The Afghan campaign was launched on October 7, 2001, with a U.S. attack on Taliban forces. By December 2001, a new interim government headed by Hamid Karzai had already been established, and an International Security Assistance Force (ISAF) was placed in Kabul to secure the capital and the newly-installed government. The American-led campaign originated in President Bush's reaction to the September 11 events. The Americans had announced a global offensive approach just nine days after the attacks. "Every nation, in every region, now has a decision to make. Either you are with us, or you are with the terrorists. From this day forward, any nation that continues to harbor or support terrorism will be regarded by the United States as a hostile regime", the president noted (2001:53-54). Their intervention was fully supported by the allies. The British submarines, which were compatible with the American Tomahawk cruise missiles, participated from the very initial moments of the attack. Other allies offered various types of support, such as Special Forces or shared intelligence. The operation was joined by Canada, Germany, France, and other countries in the Middle East, Africa, Europe, and Asia, illustrating other nations' commitment to the justice of the American war on terror. The military operations were led from the U.S.'s Central Command's headquarters at McDill Air Force Base in Tampa, Florida. The impressive number of contributing countries (40 of the 70 involved countries sent military delegations at the Central Command) is illustrative of the political support and legitimacy of the cause, as well as a recognition of American leadership. Upon the invocation of Article 5 in the Washington Treaty, NATO allies adopted a series of concrete measures in order to assist the United States. It was an exercise of integrative power that generated cooperation and common security, uniting all allies under shared objectives. At the Istanbul Summit in June 2004, NATO's official discourse was built on the importance of the allied cooperation: "Contributing to peace and stability in Afghanistan is NATO's key priority" (Istanbul Summit Final Communiqué 2004, par. 4).

The second stage in the American-initiated fight against terrorism started with the invasion of Iraq, in March 2003, where the U.S.-led coalition overthrew Saddam Hussein and the Baath ruling party. Under the supervision of the coalition, an interim governing authority was established to secure democratization of Iraq. This intervention was legitimized by UNSC Resolution 1441 on November 8, 2002, under the UN Charter's Chapter VII. Although many nations felt the need for another resolution to justify an armed intervention, their desire was quite impossible to fulfill given the complicated diplomacy it would have involved. Nonetheless, U.S.-led forces did not wait for another legitimization and invaded Iraq on March 19, 2003. Operation *Displayed Deterrence* was an example of cooperation between coalition forces, with the Americans and the Dutch providing Patriot anti-missile batteries and NBC units to Turkey, the only ally bordering Iraq. This operation is particularly relevant since it came under Washington Treaty's Article 4, emphasizing the importance of consultation between allies, whenever "territorial integrity, political independence or security" of an ally is threatened (Washington Treaty Art. 4). However, not all the allies agreed with the Americans' strategy in preparing for the war in Iraq.

Perhaps no other event has demonstrated the power imbalances in NATO than the decision taken by France, Germany, and Belgium in February 2003 to block the Alliance's preparation for the defense of Turkey. In preparing for the war in Iraq, Bush's administration requested such actions under Article 4 of the Washington Treaty, fearing that without NATO's intervention, Turkey might be drawn into a greater war. The crisis was resolved by tasking NATO's Defence Planning Committee with taking the decision, given that France does not have a vote there. However, the opposition of the three countries, of which two are among the most powerful European allies, cast doubt on the credibility of NATO's security guarantee as stipulated in Article 5, thus questioning the very foundation of all the Alliance's commitments. The event bruised the U.S.-European relations and endangered not only transatlantic relations but also the security of the whole world. For the dynamics of the Alliance, this episode was not only the expression of the lack of a single, commonly-agreed upon threat and outdated military capabilities; it was indicative of a value and cultural gap that was eroding the bedrock of the Alliance in its dimension as a community of states committed to defending the values mentioned in the prelude to the NATO Treaty: "democracy, individual liberty and the rule of law".

The campaigns in Iraq and Afghanistan are illustrative of the belief that if projecting security and stability in areas that were beyond the Alliance's initial scope and vision was to be understood as an act of democracy, it automatically required broader cooperation between the United States and Europe. Playing the card of commonly shared values, U.S. Secretary of State Condoleezza Rice asked the Europeans to assist the United States in "making the pursuit of global freedom our overarching organizing principle for the century" (qtd. in Weisman 2005, par. 22).

Despite the many occasions in which the Bush administration promoted NATO as a central forum for transatlantic dialogue on important security issues, many Europeans doubted that the Americans were actually inclined to view NATO as an alliance of equal partners. Such views are mainly supported by the U.S. attitude toward its European allies in the weeks and months after September 11. In an exercise of predominant power, the Americans mostly informed their European partners about decisions they had already made, rather than seeking consultation before taking the decisions. This view fuels the skeptics' perception that the United States uses NATO as a "toolbox" providing assets and serving coalitions.

The approach the United States embraced during its campaign against terrorism is indicative of the Americans' struggle to maintain, justify and attract support for its efforts in the campaign against terrorism. Although the Americans may have succeeded to legitimize their operations, at least on paper, their slant regarding terrorism sparked a few debates and opposite reactions. While Germany and France initially resisted U.S. policy against Iraq in 2003-2004 (with President Chirac and Chancellor Schroeder arguing in 2003 that any decision on military force should be made by the UN security council), it was the Americans who were made responsible for the lack of unity and cohesion within the Alliance, in virtue of the fact that their campaign was seen as being ill-prepared and their interests divorced from those of the allies.

Despite the hesitancy of the allies, the U.S. continued their policy and were eventually able to influence the Alliance diplomacy. The Americans' argued in support of their approach by invoking two components of their policy design: one, that international order was at stake; second, that the United States would go in alone if need be. The first argument reminds of the traditional ideological struggle that opposes good and evil, and it was obvious that by focusing on international order, Bush's administration pursued this global fight. As for the second component, it seemed like collective security had been discarded in favor of a "coalition of the willing". Ever since planning the Afghan campaign, Bush told the then Secretary of State Colin Powell that "At some point we may be the only ones left.

178

That's ok with me. We are America." (qtd. in Daalder and Lindsay 2005, par. 11). By asserting the uniqueness of America, Bush also legitimized this go-it-alone approach, which was also valid under international common law according to which "states have the right to pursue self-defense" (U.N. Charter Art. 1). It was obvious that by its response to terrorism, the United States expressed its intention to lead and the willingness to let others join if they were capable to do so. Still, and although the Americans decided to by-pass the United Nations and intervene in Iraq without an UNSC mandate, they also strove to gain U.N. approval. Bush's address to the U.N. General Assembly on September 12, 2002 was a sign that the Unites States decided to seek cooperation the United Nations rather than to act individually. Nonetheless, Bush's appeal to collective engagement was actually a new type of multilateral action designed to accommodate a new structure of power. The administration believed that questions of international order should be entrusted to great powers. And, at that time, the only great power on the international arena was the United States. The advocated approach was an "American-style multilateralism" aimed at getting allies on board and at obtaining endorsement for the U.S. policies. "Americans prefer to act with the sanction and support of other countries if they can. But they're strong enough to act alone if they must", one of Bush's policy advocates, Robert Kagan, declared for the Washington Post in 2002. In fact, this declaration indicates a preference for a policy of coalition, based on American power. Despite the declarative inclination to cooperation, the United States started the war in Iraq without explicit authorization from the UN, sparking a heated debate both in the United States and among allies with regard to the unilateralist, or "unbound" nature of U.S. policy.

The events illustrated so far set the stage for an essential aspect of the discussion on U.S. predominant role in NATO and on the international scene. The issue at stake here is the distinction between two sometimes mutually exclusive and other times parallel American political tendencies: unilateralism and multilateralism.

Although multilateralism is essential for the American foreign policy, the United States' power and respect for its own sovereignty permit it to act unilaterally when its convictions and principles are under attack. In the words of Colin Powell, "we believe in multilateralism. But when it is a matter of principle, and when the multilateral community does not agree with us, we do not shrink from doing that which we think is right, which is in our own interest, even if some of our friends disagree with us" (qtd. in the *International Herald Tribune* 2002:3).

In the context of the analysis of unilateral versus multilateral decisions influencing NATO's strategies and approaches, it is essential to define the Alliance as the forum that offers the United States the greatest opportunity to exercise leadership in Europe. Probably the most illustrative example of American unilateralism, manifested as influence and dominance in NATO is to be found in the doctrine, strategies, and policies adopted in the aftermath of the September 11 terrorist attacks on the United States. On Independence Day 2003, George W. Bush clearly expressed his view of America's part as a global power on the international arena: "Without America's active involvement in the world, the ambitions of tyrants would go unopposed, and millions would live at the mercy of terrorists. With America's active involvement in the world, tyrants learn to fear, and terrorists are on the run" (par. 19). Against the background of the asymmetrical type of threat America was experiencing, the United States was, more than ever, in a position to assert its unrivaled military and political power. George W. Bush revolutionized America's foreign policy, and what made his vision groundbreaking was his willingness to use this power, even despite the strenuous objections of America's friends and allies. By promoting his own war on terrorism, Bush used American power to set the international agenda. He compelled others to follow, or at least to accept, his chosen course. Bush understood that the American muscle could be used to shape events but ignored the fact that America is not omnipotent and that his exercise of unilateral exercise of power was not enough to deal with the new type of threat. America needed the cooperation of others in order to achieve its goals; if it wanted to be followed by others, America's discourse of power had to focus on common interests, not only on national ones.

In a 2003 New York Times article, columnist Bill Keller observed that "America is a feet-and-Fahrenheit power in a metric world" (9). It accurately describes Bush's vision that the rest of the world be measured by U.S. standards. The president's language was imbued with this attitude as he painted the world in black and white and refused to accept the shades of gray coming from the overseas allies. His discourse promoted a clear-cut distinction between "good" and "evil", between those who were "for us" and those who were "against us", between those who "love freedom" and those who "hate the freedom we have". The enemy, Osama bin Laden, was to be found "dead or alive". These linguistic polarizations were further supported

180

by a plethora of metaphors and set phrases. The Americans' "war on terror" was a "crusade", much as the medieval campaigns legitimized by the fight against the paganism and heresy that dominated the Islamic world. As radical and audacious Bush's rhetoric might have been at the time, it helped galvanize American public opinion to endorse his campaigns.

Bush's discourse made it clear that only the countries that support the U.S. war on terror mattered to the Americans. As he reoriented America's foreign policy agenda to focus single-mindedly on defeating terrorism, Bush expected the rest of the world to follow his example. Countries who failed to do so were considered, in Donald Rumsfeld's words, to be part of the "old Europe". France and Germany were chastised for opposing the invasion of Iraq and, although Germany had significantly contributed to the U.S. war efforts in both Iraq and Afghanistan, it was never mentioned nor acknowledged for that in virtue of the initial conceptual opposition.

The Iraq experience underscored that how America led mattered as much as whether it led. Mary McGrory argued that America under Bush behaved like the "SUV of nations", angering even its closest partners, many of whom did not feel that they were equal allies but rather considered themselves to be an impediment for the reckless exercise of power the U.S. was exercising (2002:B7). As a consequence, this weakened their support and undermined their willingness to cooperate in dealing with common challenges. The most important foreign challenges the United States was facing – fighting terrorism, stopping weapon proliferation, encouraging economic prosperity, preservation political liberty – were also world problems, and the unilateral exercise of American power was not the solution. The premise of this unilateralism was the belief that if the United States led, others would follow, in virtue of their common values and interests. But the lessons of Iraq were that sometimes, when you lead, few will follow. Part of the opposition the Unites States encountered during its campaigns in Iraq and Afghanistan was due to the desire of the other allies to counter America and delegitimize its power. The more America's power was questioned, the less influence America would have.

Drawing on the lessons in Iraq and Afghanistan, Bush reoriented his foreign policy toward multilateralism, especially in dealing with the nuclear threat posed by Iran and North Korea. He finally understood that some issues are far more difficult to be tackled unilaterally and that sometimes a cooperative effort is the best option. The shift from unilateralism to multilateralism is not so much a matter of principle and reverse conceptual approach but a need for American actions to be endorsed and invested with resources, in addition to legitimacy.

Bush's unilateralism has not always described America's foreign policy. Actually, Washington has chosen differently many times before. Let us remember that the United Stated emerged from World War II as a predominant global power, but it chose not to impose an imperialistic view on the world. Franklin Roosevelt and Harry Truman created the United Nations to promote international peace and security and duplicated these efforts with the creation of the North Atlantic Treaty Organization. They recognized that American power would be more palatable and longer-lasting if it was absorbed into alliances and international security institutions that served the interests and purpose of other states as well. The Marshall Plan, for the implementation of which the Americans spent enormous amounts of money, was initiated to assist the restoration of the European countries that had been ravaged by war.

In the 20th century, America asserted itself as a global player not because of its victory in war but because it understood that it is more important to be a powerful promoter of peace.

Traditionally, America has tried to eschew the pitfall of unilateralism and exerted its authority with the help of international institutions. NATO relies on affiliated organizations that help extend its influence in a broader Euro-Atlantic security architecture (e.g.: North Atlantic Consultative Council, Euro-Atlantic Partnership Council, NATO-Russia Charter; NATO-Ukraine Charter, and NATO-Mediterranean Dialogue Partners). The Alliance also cooperates with different regional security organizations with responsibilities in Europe and worldwide (e.g. ANZUS, ASEAN, European Union, Organization of African Unity, Organization of American States, Organization on Security and Cooperation in Europe, and United Nations) or used to do so in the past (e.g. CENTO, European Defence Community, SEATO, Warsaw Pact, and Western European Union). These mechanisms of cooperation are the most legitimate way of binding the rest of the world into a U.S.-run global order, while maintaining the impression that consultation matters, and everyone's opinion is equally important. America understood that power is greater when it comes from working with friends and allies.

Another issue that deserves attention in the context of an investigation of the United States' predominant power in NATO's decisions relates to the

Alliance's process of enlargement. The question of NATO's enlargement has been a debated issue within and outside the Alliance, with the Americans being especially vocal in prescribing not only policies about the mechanism of the process but also behavior, when it comes to Russia's position regarding enlargement. High-level U.S. officials have argued that Russian interests are served by NATO enlargement because it will prolong the U.S. engagement in European security, promote stability in East-Central Europe, and ensure that Germany in particular remains "part of an integrated security structure" rather than pursuing "independent national security policies" (Slocombe, remarks to the Atlantic Council, qtd. in Yost 1998:208).

In what regards Russia's attitude toward the enlargement process, Secretary of State Madeleine Albright considers that "Russia, no less than the rest of us, needs stability and prosperity in the center of Europe" (1997a, par. 23). She also argues that Russia needs to learn to move beyond an adversarial worldview and explains that, in her assessment, Russia's disapproval of the enlargement "is a product of old misperceptions about NATO and old ways of thinking about its former satellites in Central Europe" (1998, par. 50).

The Americans maintained the view that, in a Europe composed of democratic states whose security is safeguarded by cooperative security structures, Russia should get rid of obsolete conceptions such as "buffer zones" or "dividing lines". It must also detach from the outmoded geopolitical vision according to which countries such as Poland or Estonia or Ukraine are regarded as buffer zones separating Russia from Europe. Albright continues by recommending that America's European allies should follow the U.S. example and encourage Russia's more modern aspirations to become a democratic country. Only then will it "play an important role in Europe – as a great power, and no longer as an imperial power" (Albright 1997b, par. 54).

Equally, in advising NATO to avoid a "threat-based" and "anti-Russian" approach to the enlargement, Deputy Secretary of State Talbott calls attention to the less provocative reasons for enlargement, "which Russia should accept and even support: the promotion of democracy, free markets, and regional stability" (1995, par. 48).

U.S. officials have made their point by arguing that the Alliance cannot allow its enlargement to be postponed or blocked by Russian objections.

In doing so, the United States not only defended its vision of international security, stemming from the fact that America has security interests in Europe but also prescribed policy for NATO and asserted its position as a European power and, more importantly, as a predominant power in the Alliance.

The above examples are typified by the existence of broad consensus between the American views and the beliefs of the Western allies. Broad consensus generates a need for unanimity over specific policies, especially major ones. However, the terms of specific policies do not necessarily flow automatically. For example, it is possible to accept that there should be U.S. nuclear weapons in Europe and still disagree about their numbers, types, and roles. Accepting American leadership does not mean an implicit acceptance of the direction in which the U.S. should lead, nor does it imply fully uncritical acceptance of Washington's whims at any given moment.

The problem with publicly accepting U.S. leadership and with being forthright about it being the basis of European security is twofold. On the one hand, commercial competition and disparate economic interests regularly lead to trans-Atlantic disputes. Western European governments have often taken positions on political issues that were at variance with those of the U.S. On the other hand, since the 1960s, with the Vietnam War, the Watergate scandal, Reagan's policies, and more recently Trump's "twitting", the Americans have lost much of the positive image it had previously earned in Europe by being the liberator from Nazism.

As a result of these factors, attaching the term "anti-American" to critics seems to be not only a convenient response but also a code for defending the necessity of U.S. leadership, without which NATO would barely be a reality. But what does it mean to be "anti-American"? In general, acceptable forms of criticism take U.S.'s good faith and intentions for granted and argue about the logic of a particular policy within the given terms of alliance unity. The resonance of these forms of criticism in European public opinion can inhibit governments operating in an American-led Alliance. Therefore, allies need to be constantly reminded that NATO would not be North Atlantic without the United States and that its basic concept is that of continued cooperation. As demonstrated in this section, language is instrumental in achieving this goal and in infusing different types of discourses with manifestations of power.

By and large, the exercise of U.S. predominant power is encapsulated in the following basic rule: new policies cannot be adopted in NATO without the United States' approval. When the Americans adopt a policy they want to see followed by NATO, whether it is their own devising or initially stemming from another member state, there begins a complicated and prolonged process. The players on the decision-making and decision-adopting board game are the U.S. administration, the Congress, and, last but not least, the national governments that represent the allies. While the administration takes the decisions that shape U.S. and implicitly NATO policies, the Congress is more interested in maintaining a balancing act between the Americans and the allies. It usually wants to know both that the U.S. administration is exerting proper leadership of the Alliance to which the allies are properly responsive, and that the allies have been duly consulted and are really asking for a particular policy, whether it deals with weapons or strategic innovations, for instance. On the other hand, the allies rarely act as a group. The imbalance results from the importance of different countries within the Alliance. The smaller countries, especially on NATO's flanks, carry significantly less weight than the larger and geographically central ones.

However, consent to U.S. policies is not automatic. It has to be reached after a long process of debating and discussing, especially since allied governments have their own agenda in both domestic politics and foreign affairs, which results in various degrees of interest in the discussed issues. What concerns the Germans may bore the British or anger the French. The dynamics of interests also brings about a dynamic of power, and each country (especially the major powers) wishes to assert its at the table of negotiations. One of the fixed rules of the game is that surface decorum be maintained. This includes giving the impression that the discussions are free and frank, especially during high-level meetings, as well as polite, and when decisions are disseminated to the public, the language used transmits unity and agreement. This is achieved primarily through activation of integrative power, by the exercise of which the discourse of unity is infused with morphosyntactic variations belonging to this particular semantic field: nouns (e.g. "unity", "solidarity", "cohesion", "cooperation", "consultation"), noun phrases constructed around the adjectival modifier "common" (e.g. "common destiny", "common values", "common defense", "common aim"), predicates expressing collective speech acts (e.g. "are united", "agree").

The analysis of the discourse Americans use in order to sway their allies' decisions generated the conclusion that, more than often, U.S. officials employ a wide range of communicative strategies. For example, helping allied governments over the hurdles of their own doubts or public opposition is made easier if issues are tactically re-framed in a way that appeals more to their traditional policies. In the case of the SDI, the usage of the word "modernizing" tactical nuclear weapons was a great adjuvant in sweetening the pill. It was basically an issue of producing and deploying new nuclear weapons but framing it as improving the nuclear "inventory", a collective noun that sounds far less dramatic than the word "arsenal", made the allies perceive the American initiative as being to their benefit and advancement.

Another useful device the Americans use in order to hold the wavering allies in line and undermine any public opposition in western Europe is to ensure that it is the allies who ask for something to be done, not the U.S. administration that foists it upon them. The best example in support of this is the Marshall Plan. When Secretary of State George Marshall made the speech that announced U.S. readiness to fund a coordinated program of economic reconstruction, his concluding sentence was key to this approach. "The initiative, I think, must come from Europe", Marshall cunningly admits in his Harvard speech on 7 June 1947 (par. 7). Furthermore, in the formation of NATO itself, Marshall had agreed with the British Foreign Secretary Ernest Bevin on the need for an alliance but asked him to provide the initiative. Having the Europeans initiate policies invests the allies with a sense of responsibility and power of decision. Subsequently, these "European initiatives" are re-shaped during negotiations to correspond more closely to U.S. preferences and policies.

None of these tools and "schemes" would be efficient had it not been for the language itself. All NATO documents, final communiqués, strategic concepts and communications, orders and memoranda, from the highest to the lowest level are in English. With both the Americans and the British being stout supporters of the superiority of English within the Alliance, the language itself becomes a vehicle of power, and, for the two nations for whom English is the first language, it has clearly been a decisive advantage. Their domination is ensured in all talks, in virtue of the communication strategies they inherently possess. Since the differences between languages are not purely a matter of semantics, reduced to the use of different words to describe the same things, but more essentially, a conceptual difference, the framework of discussions is constantly set in terms that are more amendable to the American way of thinking than to any other.

# Conclusion

## The Rhetoric of Power Dynamics in NATO's Ideological Evolution

The analysis deployed in this study was informed by a three-level analysis of NATO official documents, grounded in the examination of the social, cognitive, and linguistic levels of discourse, with stress on the relationship between language and power. Offering a complete answer to the research questions entailed the identification of a framework for the manifestation of power dynamics, first of all in practice and, secondly, in the discourse associated with it. Consequently, the investigation was double-layered: the social cognitive interface located and discussed key social and political contexts; the discursive construction analyzed the manner in which the rhetoric of power was employed in these contexts so as to balance the interaction between the members of the Alliance or between NATO and external actors.

### The social-cognitive interface

As a method of investigation, CDA typically goes beyond the classical study of the structural properties of text and relates these structures to social structures. Creating a broader social and cognitive framework for the investigation helps explain the reason and the meaning of a discourse. Therefore, discourse structures are directly linked to social structures via a complex socio-cognitive interface. The analysis mediates between shared social cognition (attitudes, knowledge, ideologies), societal structures and the text. The purpose of this mediation is to interpret and explain discourse in terms of social and political contexts. To this purpose, CDA is argued to be not a method in itself but a critical manner of conducting discourse analysis.

The critical investigation of NATO discourses from a social and cognitive perspective has allowed for the identification of several distinct periods in the Alliance's evolution, each characterized by specific – sometimes different and other times overlapping – power dynamics.

In its early years (1949-1955), the U.S.-European partnership that the newly emerged NATO represented was not so much about shared values, but mostly based on an edgy dependence on a superpower, as the war devastated countries of Western Europe were largely reliant on the United States in terms of both economic and military security. It is only in the next decade that the notions of "community", "partnership" and "functional cooperation" will be employed so as to help the transatlantic nations converge toward one another.

Between 1956 and 1966, a rigid application of the concept of interdependence, by which the United States assumed expert power and attempted to dictate the terms of partnership and responsibility produced the opposite effect. It resulted in the alienation of France and the loss of a powerful actor to support U.S. political and strategic conceptions across the Alliance. Kennedy's plan for the establishment of an integrated Atlantic Community under U.S. leadership proved incompatible with the initially declared postwar U.S. objective of a strong and united Western Europe. As a consequence, the strict emphasis on the rhetoric of unity limited the United States' ability to exert its sanctional power on intractable allies and offered the European nations a chance to assert their own will and interests, thus challenging the dynamics of power instituted by the Americans in their favor.

The years between 1967 and 1975 were characterized by the pursuit of a policy of détente, which only succeeded to undercut the very rationale behind the creation of NATO and, instead of installing harmony and concord within the Alliance, opened the door for divergent attitudes among the member states. With the advantages of a détente policy notwithstanding, the rhetoric of NATO would return, in the next decade, to the initial ideological agenda that has opposed East and West and further polarized the two worlds by depicting the Soviets as the personification of evil and the Alliance as the embodiment of human values, an organization embarked in a never-ending crusade against communism.

Between 1976 and 1985, the conceptual focus of the Alliance shifted from its initial purpose – protection against the Soviet invasion – to issues such as arms race, peace movement and engagement in areas beyond NATO's primary range of action. The preceding period of détente had broken the Iron Curtain and effaced the previously clear distinction between East and West. In the absence of a real enemy in the East, and while rhetoric struggled hard to create an adversary with the help of the vehement lexicon of the Anglo-American discourse, NATO's cohesion seemed to have been weakened. In an attempt to solve this apparent crisis, the Alliance invigorated itself conceptually, posing into a peace movement, an ideological diversion meant to redirect public attention away from the arms build-up. NATO also assumed a cooperative dimension, acting as a forum for consultation fostering a collective approach to out-of-area issues. Unity was still brittle, but the balance of power within the Alliance was restored. With Mikhail Gorbachev assuming power in the Soviet Union in March 1985, NATO was now faced with an ideological dilemma. This new leader, in Margaret Thatcher's words, seemed a man with whom the West could do business and established himself as a determined reformer who sought not confrontation, but cooperation. And this was the conceptual change that challenged the dynamics of power in Europe and in NATO in the following decade.

The decade 1986-1996 is typified by the end of the Cold War. Since inception, NATO was endowed with the ideological power and values of the West. Before the Cold War and under U.S. guidance, NATO strove to promote a conception of pan-European security inherently linked to the interests of the Americans to act as a counterattraction to the communist ideology. Although the end of the Cold War anticipated the configuration of a continent no longer split by ideological confrontation, it did not automatically generate an era of peace and stability. Despite the fact that the security environment in Western Europe improved drastically, the collapse of communism unbridled new dynamics in some areas of post-Cold War Eastern Europe. Nationalist conflicts, ethnic rivalries, and territorial disputes resurfaced creating enclaves of violence and instability in the states of the former Soviet Union and Yugoslavia. Throughout these happenings, the Alliance demonstrated its remarkable power by perpetuating and reinventing itself through rhetoric and new conceptions. The following events showed that for NATO, the United States and the member states who invested the Alliance with their loyalty and trust, there was life after threat.

Although in the late 1990s NATO was able to address a wide specter of initiatives, ranging from adopting a new Strategic Concept tailored to enable out-of-area actions to enhancing partnership through a continuous enlargement plan, the Alliance seemed to lack cohesion and constancy in the years between 1997 and 2000. With Russia and China opposing the Kosovo intervention, the allies had to bend to these two countries' wishes and intervene in the absence of a UNSC mandate. This move opened the debate for legitimacy and started to shape a new paradigm of humanitarian actions, which was slowly replacing the law of nations with a new model of collective security grounded on the idea of individual rights. The two schools of thought that opposed the European allies – who were strong believers in the idea that coalitions must be steered by shared principles and have UN support – and the U.S. – believing that coalitions are guided by risk-related interests and therefore not limited by principles – finally reached a compromising view in the formulation of the 1999 Strategic Concept. Bluntly put, NATO had to adapt to a new coalition model or perish. With the Americans at the lead, the Alliance started to implement the change, while confronting an emergent competitor – the EU – which, for many actors on the European political scene, was a more fitting instrument for the implementations of the new sorts of security missions.

The events in the period 2001-2009 showcased NATO as a renewed Alliance that accepted the transatlantic bargain between the European allies and the United States. According to this design, NATO became an instrument for the Europeans to help them build on the ability to cooperate with the United States and obtain improved capabilities. However, the configuration of the international scene as set by external events, particularly located and related to the Middle East proved divisive for the member states of the Alliance. The argument is grounded in a combination of geopolitical and social factors that made Europe politically, religiously, and demographically vulnerable and exposed in ways that the United States was not. Hence, Europeans were in their right to reject a possible gradual Islamization of Europe. In Tony Judt's words, Islam was but an abstraction for the American Administration under George Bush and only served as a conceptual back up to legitimize the so-called Global War on Terror (GWOT): "For the U.S., the Middle East is a faraway land, a convenient place to export America's troubles so that they don't have to be addressed in the "homeland". But the Middle East is Europe's "near abroad" … America's strategy of global confrontation with Islam is not an option for Europe. It is a catastrophe" (2005, par. 26).

Throughout the discussed period, there were several cases when the allied countries were in agreement and where points of view converged despite the sometimes-edgy political relations. Nonetheless, there were some points on which NATO members disagreed, but, as long as the two sides of the Atlantic did not directly harm each other's interest, it was only natural that they had different standpoints regarding the purpose of the Alliance, especially given that the new NATO was built on two pillars: one ideological – an abstract sense of collective fate, and the other one practical – a concrete sense of what needed to be done. While the ideology was commonly accepted and shared among the members of the Alliance, the practical part was what generated most disagreements. Despite the ebbs and flows characterizing the relations between the allies during this period, the most important takeaway from the Alliance's experiences is the concept of "unity in flexibility", which allowed different allies to provide military assistance at various levels of engagement and in different geographical settings. It is noteworthy to mention that the allies were willing to reach an understanding, thus preventing the Alliance from breaking apart at a crucial moment. The ideological "glue" binding the allies together was the belief that "Muslim totalitarianism" generated a "war between liberalism and the apocalyptic and phantasmagorical movements that have risen up against civilization since the calamities of the First World War" (Berman 2003:183).

The period after 2010 until the present is delineated by two strategic landmarks: the latest Strategic Concept (Lisbon, 2010) and the recent NATO Summit (Brussels, 2018). The reconfiguration of NATO's doctrine in 2010 was aimed at adapting the Alliance to an ever-evolving security environment, while remaining faithful to the traditional values and strategic objectives: collective defense, crisis management and cooperative security.

However, as the world is experiencing a power transition from a unipolar to a multipolar order, characterized not so much by "the decline of the West" but by "the rise of the Rest", the new configuration of international diplomacy has transformed the existing institutions of global governance into irrelevant institutions. Against this background, NATO's relevancy is increasingly questioned while Europe is making attempts to disengage from the western part of the Atlantic Treaty Organization. The constitution of an EU army, the Permanent Structured Cooperation (PESCO), has already been agreed upon by 25 (of the 28) European Union member states whose vote is motivated by the need to reduce Europe's traditional reliance on NATO. While the extent of the EU military cooperation remains unclear, PESCO's initial purpose is to create a framework for increased collaboration and more efficient spending of military funds in Europe. The initiative has generated a split between Europe and the United States, and while France and Germany show total support for a European army, NATO itself considers that PESCO will strengthen the Alliance and might even prove beneficial for the Americans. Future developments in the balance of global and European power will definitely shed some light on the uncertainties generated by this debated initiative.

Outside NATO's traditional framework, the balance of power was radically shaken by the 2014 Russian annexation of Crimea. This move resulted in the dissolution of the NATO-Russian Council and in the freezing of all open cooperation mechanisms between NATO and Russia. Russia's annexation of the Crimean Peninsula was labeled "illegal and illegitimate" by the Alliance, a characterization that has remained valid until now. All practical civilian and military cooperation between NATO and Russia is currently suspended, and the subsequent evolutions of the tense situation between the two countries have prompted security experts and politicians to fear a return to the Cold War. The apprehensions regarding the re-emergence of tensions between the two super powers are also fueled by President Trump's decision to withdraw the United States from the INF Treaty signed between Gorbachev and Reagan in 1987.

In what concerns the U.S. predominant power in NATO, it is cogent to conclude that the preponderant American influence does not mean and has never meant that the United States is able to put forward and push through any proposal, however unpopular or implausible. As an equal member of the Alliance, The United States needs support for its position, which materializes during consultations with the other allies. By virtue of the values NATO stands for, decisions have to be unanimous, and there is no room for dissension in the Alliance's rhetoric. This practice is even more crucial as it represents the backbone that sustains the cohesion and effectiveness of NATO. The Alliance has traditionally served as an instrument for consultation and for the development of a common approach to deal with matters of international security, and the discourse produced by and associated with the Alliance has always been framed so as to express clear ideas, realistic objectives, achievable missions and ultimately a strong image of NATO as an international organization. Despite the many internal ebbs and flows in the Alliance's development, NATO's usefulness has not been hindered. It continues to provide reassurance, to serve as a provider of services for the "coalition of the willing" and become a "legitimizer" for such coalitions in the absence of a UN mandate.

The analyzed discourses have demonstrated that, in its seventy years of history, NATO has ideologically evolved into an alliance "at two levels". In the background, we have seen the traditional rhetoric of 1949, a general commitment to the core values of the Alliance: mutual assistance, common defense, collective security. In the foreground, and increasingly visible nowadays, we are dealing with an enlarged and looser NATO, serving as a broad framework for occasional joint action but more often for the "coalition of the willing". Regardless of the many facets the organization might have taken during its evolution, one aspect remains undisputed: NATO has created something better than just a "balance of power". It succeeded to create a "community of powers" composed of like-minded states pursuing common goals: collective defense and cooperative security. Woodrow Wilson's attempt to create a balance of power system in the form of the League of Nations in the aftermath of WWI may have failed at the time due to a number of reasons, but I postulate that the essential cause was the lack of unity and coherence, albeit not ideological but definitely discursive. What NATO has achieved throughout its evolution and despite the numerous crises it has undergone is largely due, as this paper has attempted to demonstrate, to the power of language and to the rhetoric of unity and relational power that have glued the whole of the Euro-Atlantic community around a common security culture. Concepts such as "dividing lines", "buffer zone" or "spheres of influence" have one by one been debunked and sent to the dustbin of history, while NATO emerged as an increasingly strong and unified alliance. Following the same ideological thread set up by the United Nations back in 1943, NATO has reshaped the international configuration and transformed it into the world Cordell Hull had imagined seventy six years ago, a world where "there will be no longer need for spheres of influence, for balance of power, or any other of the special arrangements through which, in the unhappy past, the nations strove to safeguard their security or to promote their interests" (344).

## The discursive construction

The critical discourse analysis studied three distinct discourse strands encapsulating different dynamics of power relations (integrative, adversarial, and predominant). The examination was first and foremost a qualitative approach mainly focused on what makes the discourses powerful rather than on what linguistic features characterize them. The linguistic breakdown of the targeted discourses was conducted with the help of automated statistical analyses aimed at describing NATO discourse in a more measurable and quantifiable manner.

The analytical framework that informed the investigation of NATO official documents was based on a dual approach that applied both a diachronic and a synchronic examination of the discourses of power within the historical, social, and political context that generated them. Moreover, frequent references to values, norms, and beliefs characteristic to NATO as an organization helped recreate the theoretical nexus that espouses ideology, power, and discourse and facilitated an applicative interpretation of language structures and choices within this framework. For a more structured deconstruction of discourses and subdiscourses, each strand was disjointed into topical threads that collected textual references under thematic clusters.

As illustrated in the undertaken analysis, the three examined discourse strands contain linguistic manifestations of unity, opposition, and predominance. They condense and reiterate similar or opposing ideological stances; they generate and galvanize a wide range of moral values; they proliferate an abundance of linguistic elements in support for or against ideologemes like "common values", "human rights", "collective security", "cooperative defense", or, contrarily, "terrorism", "threat", "crimes", "criminal acts", and so forth.

The analysis revealed several key moments on the timeline of events where the discourse strands intersect, indicating that the official policies over nuclear issues, enlargement, or terrorism, are indeed connected in various meaningful ways. The different frames illustrating unity and opposition have not yielded an equivalent quantity of relevant samples, with the former being far more discursively populated than the latter. However, the disparity of results whose abundance favors an extensive analysis of discourses of unity to the detriment of the more limited instances of discursive manifestations of adversarial power supports the symbolic (and discursive) value attributed to consensus and cooperation within the Alliance, contrary to the narrow emphasis placed on expressions of opposition, albeit its rather implicit existence.

The present linguistic analysis traced the presence of semantic variations that distinguish the three types of discourses of power. Despite subtle differences, mainly consisting of re-lexicalizations of constantly used concepts, all examined NATO documents share a number of commonalities. First of all, they are typified by an unpretentious and straightforward syntax. Complicated structures are avoided, sentences are typically simple, and there are only few occasions when relations of

194

subordination are used as a syntactic linchpin in the structuration of longer paragraphs. Secondly, an examination of verb semantics illustrate powerful attitudes and beliefs, most frequently embedded in predicative constructions containing modal auxiliaries (e.g. "must", "should", "have to") or communicated through the use of performative speech acts endowed with illocutionary and perlocutionary force to express necessity (e.g. "stress the need", "urge"), volition and decision (repetitions of the modal value of "will", "are determined", "reiterate their determination", "are resolved"), rejection and condemnation (e.g. "reject", "condemn"), congratulations (e.g. "express our appreciation", "applaud", "salute") or warnings (e.g. "must not", "should not"). The dynamics of these formulations support the assessment that the Alliance is a living organism, a dynamic entity constantly concerned with transmitting powerful pro-active messages to both allies and adversaries and relentlessly exercising authority through the use of language to duplicate the use of military might.

In what concerns the dynamics of adversarial power, the analysis of NATO public documents has not yielded fruitful results. This is due to the fact that, although opposition existed and was manifested on different occasions by the allies, it was mainly conceptual and not discursively framed. Given the fact that the Alliance bases its strategic decisions on consensus, the conclusion is that NATO documents do not contain explicit linguistically formulated references to the various manifestations of adversarial power exercised by the member countries during NATO's history. As disclosed by the research, opposition remains primarily contextual and is mainly illustrated by the dynamics of power relations – in terms of attitudes, reactions, and positions – rather than by any mechanism that is language-related. However, this gap could be filled by looking at political discourses that illustrate the various reactions of NATO member countries officials in the context of the identified issues of opposition. While the political discourses employed as examples do not belong to the primary corpus of investigation, they have been selected as secondary sources, in the hope that they transpire conceptual antagonism through language.

In sum, the qualitative analysis realistically answered the main research question in that it identified discursive patterns of power relations and power dynamics in NATO official documents. The invalidation of the secondary research question targeting materializations of adversarial power relations and the conclusion that there are few discursive manifestations thereof actually supports the first hypothesis. NATO is, indeed, an enduring alliance whose seventy-year validity is, in addition to its ability to transform, adapt, and reconfigure in the face of new challenges, largely due to the power of the language utilized in reifying relational power through the discourse of unity. The rhetoric of integrative power has kept the Alliance coherent and cohesive under the umbrella of common values, granting the success of NATO's enduring role in international security. In what concerns the manifestations of U.S. predominant power and its leading role in NATO, the validation of the third hypothesis does not come as a surprise. When the internal power balance tilts, it does so in favor of the United States, in virtue of its predominance in NATO. The innovative finding here is not the conclusion that the United States has a predominant role in NATO but that it is enforced, among other things, by the discursive materialization of three types of power: referent, expert, and legitimate.

Since the object of analysis is a form of institutionalized discourse which is subordinated to a composition structure and fixed conventions, it was only natural that the corpus be subjected to a quantitative investigation that offered a more in-depth description of the targeted documents. To this aim, the research also focused on a detailed statistical study conducted so as to compare NATO discourses between 1949 and 2018 with regard to what makes their writing style specific.

The complexity indices identified by the qualitative analysis reflect the variables that were essentially different between subjects. The results expose statistically interesting and significant differences in terms of the degree of word elaboration (length and polysemy count), the number of unique verbs per paragraph, the Age of Acquisition (AoA) score per paragraph, as well as the number of words within multiple lists, per such as: Means GI (words denoting methods, acts or objects utilized to attain goals), Academ GI (words related to academic, intellectual or educational matters), Space GI (references to spatial dimensions), Virtue GI (culturally-defined virtues, values, goals), etc.

In time, some differences were observed between the integrative and adversarial discourses based on the word lists extracted from the GI dictionary. The average number of words from list Means GI used in integrative discourses has increased over the years, while in adversarial discourse fewer words regarding motivation for goals' attaining were used. Such dynamics are indicative of a more specific focus placed on the power of cooperation and coordination between NATO member states in what regards their shared utilization of resources and methods to attain common goals. As predicted, the NATO's discourse is characterized by an exponential augmentation of linguistic references to cooperative defense and shared responsibility for peace and security as the Alliance has grown and expanded over time. Conversely, adversarial type documents registered lower reference to shared practices and common objectives, given that this motivational discourse is rather unifying and relates to integrative power and not to discourses that target confrontational power relations.

Words related to academic field, intellectual or educational matters (Academ GI), have declined drastically in integrative discourses after 1991. This might be interpreted as a powerful indication that NATO considered the public of its discourses had received enough education in terms of abstract concepts and values related to security, stability, and cooperation throughout the 41 years since the foundation of the Alliance. After 1991, the focus shifted toward more practical procedures (especially mentioned in the Strategic Concepts) and hands-on measures that would stabilize the fluid post-Cold War environment. Nevertheless, the adversarial discourses started to use more words related to this category over the years, and, although the increase wasn't high, it directs to a valid belief that countries situated outside the traditional NATO framework needed to be educated about what the Alliance represents in order to better understand its role and relevance for global security. This linguistic manifestation of referent and expert power is directly correlated with the increased use of words indicating knowledge of location and spatial relationships in integrative discourses (Space GI list) that pinpoint specific nations and countries as recipients of NATO's integrative power. The increase is mainly located in the discourses after 1991 when the Alliance sought to expand its area of operations toward Eastern Europe (the ex-Communist bloc), the Mediterranean and the Middle East.

As expected, integrative discourses use more words related to virtue, with an increased occurrence over the years, especially after 1991 when the linguistic expression of common principles, ideals, and beliefs typifying the Alliance registered a surge that testifies for the importance of the core values promoted by NATO (Virtue GI list). Language makes visible the evolution of the Alliance from interdependence to community, then to partnership; from collective defense to integrated defense; from increased cooperation to international cooperation. In contrast with the discourse of unity, adversarial power discourses don't use so many words that indicate an assessment of moral approval or good wealth. The focus here is more on how to discourage detrimental behavior through military actions, while the attitude implicit in the text of the documents emanates disapproval and condemnation of different terrorist acts.

At the beginning of the analyzed period (1949-1990), both the discourses of unity and those of opposition used approximately the same number the words referring to emphasis in terms of frequency, causality, validity or accuracy. Over the years, these two types of discourses go in completely opposite directions: while the integrative discourses started using more and more words from overstated list, their usage in adversarial discourses began to reduce drastically (Ovrst GI list).

As predicted, words indicating power, control or authority were abundantly employed in the two types of discourses, with an increase in both over time (Strong GI list). We can observe that the growth of strong words became more accelerated in integrative discourses after 1991, while the adversarial discourses registered very slow progress. This discrepancy can be attributed to the changes in power dynamics that manifested after the end of the Cold War. Multiple references to control and authority are used in the discourse of unity as the conceptual glue relating the existence of the Alliance to its enduring role for the preservation of peace and stability. Especially after 9/11, when the global security environment was radically transformed and reshaped by the surge of terrorism, the language of the official documents needed to produce a stronger impact both within and outside the Alliance.

A high variance was observed between the two types of discourses concerning the use of words that express quantity, including also numbers (Quan GI list). While in the integrative discourses these types of words started to be more and more used, in adversarial discourses their number decreased. In practical terms, this difference can be translated, for instance, by the accent placed by NATO, at different time periods, on the specific quantities of conventional and nuclear capabilities, whose numbers oscillated from period to period, depending on the various treaties the Alliance was involved in (Nuclear Non-Proliferation Treaty – 1968, Intermediate-Range Nuclear Forces Treaty – 1987, Mutual Balanced Force Reduction – 1973-1989, Treaty on Conventional Armed Forces in Europe – 1990, Arms Trade Treaty – 2014, etc.)

Words belonging to the fields of economy, commerce, industry, or business, including collectivities, roles, and references to money were used in both adversarial and integrative discourses, with a rapid growth for integrative discourses, and an easy growth for adversarial discourses (Econ GI). The usage of such words attests NATO's increased implication in economic assistance programs both within and outside the Alliance and the enlarged number of activities and list of recipients over the years, and especially after 1991.

In addition to using various word lists to analyze the dynamics of lexical properties in NATO, the statistical analysis has revealed other features that differentiate between the two types of discourses. For instance, the number of unique verbs per paragraph increased over time in both adversarial and integrative discourses, allowing for an interpretation related to the significance placed on speech acts and on transmitting attitudes and standpoints. The occurrence of verbs of opinion, of positive or negative appreciation, injunction verbs, verbs of demanding and verbs of enunciative modality has registered an increased frequency especially in the discourse of opposition, where an accelerated and high growth was identified. In addition to their semantic value, these verbs contribute to the structural complexity and elaboration of adversarial discourses, where the manifestation of power is more concentrated on expressing the Alliance's condemning and disapproving attitude toward its adversaries and their deeds.

The AoA (Age of Acquisition) score illustrates the complexity of words in relation to the age at which they are acquired. During the first analyzed period, adversarial discourses used more complex words, but their complexity decreased over the years, ending with the employment of simple words in 2018. NATO realized that pretentious language may not be effective when communication has to be straightforward and clear and gradually gave up using complex abstract notions by 2018. Conversely, the complexity of words increased in the case of integrative discourses, which were formulated in simpler terms in 1949 but become more and more elaborate, in direct correlation with the complexity of the topics NATO needed to address in its discourses of unity.

The cohesion and coherence indices reveal a slow and steady evolution of the adversarial discourse throughout the period, while the integrative discourses recorded a radical boost since 1949. The visible evolution in the language of unity accounts for a more organized discourse characterized by a more efficient use of linking devices, connectives and subordination mechanisms, which offer the more recent NATO texts a better local and global coherence, and ultimately optimized comprehension and readability.

The main goal of the quantitative analysis was to demonstrate that the operationalization of the concepts of integrative and adversarial power has suffered discursive modifications visible in NATO documents produced during the Cold War and in the years after the end of the Cold War. The findings of the critical discourse analysis conducted earlier in this chapter offered an explanation of the reason why these changes occurred and located them on the Alliance's historical, social, and political timeline. Paralleled with the exhaustive qualitative analysis, the diachronic examination of NATO discourses offers a broad image of the evolution of the language employed by the Alliance and explains the dynamics of power as illustrated in integrative and adversarial discourses. As internal and external power dynamics intertwine with the evolution of the Alliance and ultimately shape its development, discourse adapts, adjusts, alters, diversifies, or evolves, revealing a direct and active relationship between language, power and ideology.

The present security environment is undoubtedly unpredictable and extremely fluid. In this context, NATO faces a double jeopardy: a disparity in the power balance within the Alliance (due to the PESCO initiative, for example) and the re-emergence of bigger threats outside its borders (the risk of nuclear war with Russia to the east, the open door for China's implication in a potential arm race, the large-scale migration and terrorist initiatives flowing in from the south – Middle East and Africa, the proliferation of weapons of mass destruction, the increase in cyber-attacks or the various environmental challenges that bear security implications). The dynamics of power will remain as active as ever, with unpredictable consequences that will impact the position of the United States in NATO and on the global strategic map, the unity of the Alliance on the brink of the rising tensions with Russia, the solidarity of a Europe that is slowly but surely detaching from the Americans.

In the context of the renewed confrontations mentioned above, the Transatlantic Alliance might need to restate and reinforce its relevance once again. The language of power is expected to also suffer modifications, not only structural but also semantic; the power of language might be the mechanism through which NATO will restore its significance in the global security configuration.

Based on the geo-strategic configurations of the future, some scenarios are worth investigating both from a social-cognitive and from a discursive perspective. A wider range of inter and intra-alliance behavior is to be expected. Within the Alliance, the collective dynamics might display variations. Depending on the outside forces acting on the organization, the allies might either choose to act in unison (if faced with an external threat, e.g., Russia or China) or split in divergent directions (if some support the status quo while others seek revision). However, if the division is deep, there will be a fracture inside the Alliance (e.g., U.S. versus Europe); if the rupture is modest, the Alliance might find a way to accommodate divergence and embrace new mechanisms of cooperation (e.g., the PESCO initiative). It will be extremely interesting to analyze the language by which NATO will materialize these changes of attitude and behavior, both internally and externally. Such scenarios create a fertile ground for the manifestation of power relations, hierarchization, leadership, predominance, consensus, and adversity. The discourses of power could be further taxonomized into textual strands depending on the relations generated by the new power dynamics: alliance, concert, coalition, each being distinguished by specific features and linguistic devices. This new approach might shed more light into the mechanisms of any organization, from the perspective of the interaction between internal and external actors.

Further investigations into the realm of NATO discourse can reveal new dimensions of military language. In virtue of its context-related specificity, critical discourse analysis is relevant at any given time, for any given situation, on any given type of discourse or institution. Further explorations of the function of language and discourse enables change: individual and/or collective, positive, and constructive, pro-active and dynamic transformations of once traditional epistemological positions, concepts and procedures. Qualitative and quantitative studies of the language could disrupt longstanding notions of power and locate new patterns and dynamics; or at least, such practices may validate the already identified ones. Either way, there is enough room for creativity and innovation, even if military language has traditionally been perceived as fairly limited, extremely technical, impenetrably coded, and often boring.

The present investigation of NATO discourse from the perspective of power dynamics commends itself in virtue of its contributing efforts to the deliberation over the future of the Alliance. The two fault lines in this dispute run between two schools of thought: one group who believes that the Alliance has become irrelevant and predict a bleak future for NATO;

the other who still thinks that NATO has a meaningful future. My study aligns with the latter in that it tried to demonstrate why and how NATO has endured and will continue to do so.

One of the objectives of the study was to demonstrate that NATO's enduring purpose and function has remained valid in the seventy years of the Alliance's existence largely due to the galvanizing power of language. Despite the many internal and external crises that challenged the Alliance's raison d'être to the point of virtually nullifying it, NATO has remained a coherent security institution able to encourage shared attitudes and responses within an organization otherwise typified by heterogeneity and energetic interactions between its members. The Alliance's continuity and essential role in the global security configuration has been constantly fueled by the use of integrative power. The present investigation has demonstrated that the organization's discourse represents the legitimate locus for the manifestation of power relations within and outside the Alliance. Last but not least, NATO discourse can be perceived as a resourceful model worth emulating by other organizations wishing to adopt new strategies for the improvement of their institutional communication.

Language is not power, but it definitely encodes power. With this axiomatic connection in mind, the overall conclusion of the analysis is that NATO discourse can be considered an essential mechanism for the social construction of the ideology of power.

# Works Cited


Angelakis, Tom. "Russian Elites' Perception of NATO Expansion: The Military, Foreign Ministry and Duma." *Briefing Paper no. 11*, May 1997, International Security Information Service Europe.

Ashton, Nigel J. *Kennedy, Macmillan and the Cold War: The Irony of Interdependence.* Palgrave, 2002.

Barker, Chris and Galasinski, Darius. *Cultural Studies and Discourse Analysis: A Dialogue on Language and Identity.* Sage, 2001.

Berman, Paul. *Terror and Liberalism.* W.W. Norton & Company, 2003.

Biber, Douglas. "Corpus-based and Corpus-driven Analyses of Language Variation and Use." *The Oxford Handbook of Linguistic Analysis*, edited by Bernd Heine and Heiko Narrog, Oxford University Press, 2012, pp. 159-191.

Carpenter, Ted G., editor. *NATO's Empty Victory: A Postmortem on the Balkan War.* CATO Institute, 2000.

Chifu, Iulian, et al. *The Russian Georgian War: A Trilateral Cognitive Institutional Approach of the Crisis Decision-Making Process.* Curtea Veche Publishing House, 2009.

Daalder, Ivo. H. and Lindsay, James. M. *Bush's Foreign-Policy Strategy: Is the Revolution Over?*, 14 Oct. 2005, www.brookings.edu/opinions/bushs-foreign-policy-strategy-is-the-revolution-over/. Accessed 22 February 2018.

Dascălu, Mihai. *Analyzing Discourse and Text Complexity for Learning and Collaborating.* Springer, 2014.

Dascălu, Mihai, et al. "ReaderBench: A Multi-lingual Framework for Analyzing Text Complexity." *EC-TEL 2017, LNCS 10474*, edited by Élise Lavoué et al., 2017, pp. 495–499. DOI: 10.1007/978-3-319-66610-5_48.

Fairclough, Norman. *Critical Discourse Analysis.* Addison Wesley, 1995.

---. *Language and power.* Pearson Education, 2001.

Gervasi, Vicenzo and Ambriola, Vicenzo. "Quantitative Assessment of Textual Complexity." *Complexity in Language and Text*, edited by Merlini L. Barbaresi, Plus, 2002, pp. 197–228.

Ghadessy, Mohsen, editor. *Registers of Written English: Situational Factors and Linguistic Features.* Pinter Publishers, 1988.

Grosser, Alfred. *The Western Alliance: European-American Relations Since 1945*. Continuum Publishing Group, 1980.

Habermas, Jurgen. *Erkenntnis und Interesse*. Suhrkamp, 1977.

Henderson, Nicholas. *The Birth of NATO*. Westview Press, 1983.

Jenkins, Peter. *Mrs. Thatcher's Revolution: The Ending of the Socialist Era*. Cape, 1987.

Judt, Tony. *A History of Europe Since 1945*. Penguin Books, 2005.

Keller, Bill. "Does not Play Well with Others." *New York Times*, 22 Jun 2003.

Lieven, Anatol. "Russian opposition to NATO expansion." *The World Today*, vol. 51, no. 10, 1995, pp. 196-199.

McGrory, Mary. "Pit-stop Presidency." *Washington Post*, 27 Oct. 2002.

Ploae-Hanganu, Mariana. *Terminologia şi limba comună (Pentru o bază de date terminologice)*. Romanian Academy Publishing House, 1992.

Thomas, Ian. *The Promise of Alliance: NATO and the Political Imagination*. Rowan and Littlefield Publishers, Inc, 1997.

Van Dijk, Teun A. "The Discourse-knowledge Interface". *Critical Discourse Analysis. Theory and Interdisciplinarity*, edited by Gilbert Weiss and Ruth Wodak, Palgrave Macmillan, 2003b, pp. 85-110.

---. "Ideological Discourse Analysis." *New Courant*, vol. 4, no. 1, 1995c, pp. 135-161.

---. *Text and Context: Explorations in the Semantics and Pragmatics of Discourse*. Longman, 1977.

Wang, Yuan and Guo, Minghe. "A Short Analysis of Discourse Coherence." *Journal of Language Teaching and Research*, vol. 5, no. 2, 2014, pp. 460-465.

Yost, David. *NATO Transformed: The Alliance's New Roles in International Security*. United States Institute of Peace Press, 1998.

Zakaria, Fareed. *The post-American World*. W.W. Norton & Company, 2009.

**Secondary Data**

Acheson, Dean. "The North Atlantic Pact: Collective Defense and the Preservation of Peace, Security and Freedom in the North Atlantic Community." *Department of State Bulletin*, 27 Mar 1949.

---. "Address to Congress." *Department of State Bulletin*, 5 Jan. 1953.

Albright, Madeleine. "Enlarging NATO." *The Economist*, 15 Feb 1997a.

---. Prepared Statement before the Senate Armed Services Committee, 23 Apr. 1997b, https://1997-2001.state.gov/ statements/970423.html. Accessed 17 April 2018.

---. Prepared Statement before the Senate Foreign Relations Committee. *The debate on NATO enlargement.* U.S. Government Printing Office, 7 Oct. 1997c, https://www.gpo.gov/fdsys/pkg/ CHRG-105shrg46832/ html/CHRG-105shrg46832.htm. Accessed 17 April 2018.

---. Press conference at NATO Headquarters, https://1997-2001.state.gov/ statements/1998/981208b.html. Accessed 17 April 2018.

Blair, Tony. Speech at NATO's 50th Anniversary, 8 Mar 1999. 12 January 12 2018, http://www.ukpol.co.uk/tony-blair-1999-speech-at-natos-50th-anniversary/. Accessed 17 April 2018.

Boniface, Pascal. "Le débat français sur l'élargissement de l'Otan." *Relations Internationales et Stratégiques 27,* Autumn 1997.

Bush, George. Remarks at the Rome NATO Summit, 8 Oct. 1991. *European Wireless File.* USIS, U.S. Embassy, London.

---. "The Future of Europe", remarks at the commencement ceremony at Boston University, 21 May 1989. *Department of State Bulletin,* 17 Jul. 1989.

Bush, George W. "Independence Day Speech", 4 Jul. 2003, https://georgewbush-whitehouse.archives.gov/news/ releases/2003/07/20030704-1.html. Accessed 23 February 2918.

---. *News conference,* 14 Nov. 2001, www.nytimes.com/2001/11/14/world/ bush-putin-summit-2-presidents-words-new-relationship-moves-antiterrorism.html. Accessed 16 April 2018.

Bush, George. W. and Dietrich, John. W. *The George W. Bush Foreign Policy Reader: Presidential Speeches and Commentary.* M.E. Sharpe, 2005.

Carter, John. *Report to the American People,* 2 Feb. 1977, transcript of radio and television broadcast. *Department of State Bulletin,* 28 Feb. 1977.

---. Remarks at the opening ceremonies of the North Atlantic Council Summit Meeting in Washington, 30 May 1970. *Department of State Bulletin,* 1 Jul. 1978.

Charette, Hervé de. Press Conference after the North Atlantic council Meeting. *Propos sur la Défense 40,* 30 May 1995.

Clinton, William. "News Conference." Transcript in *Washington Post,* 8 Mar. 1997, p. A11.

---. "Remarks at the Close of the North Atlantic Treaty Organization 50th Anniversary Summit." In *Public Papers of the Presidents of the United States: William J. Clinton,* 1999.

Cohen, William. Prepared Statement before the Senate Committee on Armed Services. *Department of State Bulletin,* 27 Apr. 1997.

De Hoop Scheffer, Jan. "NATO's Istanbul Summit: New Mission, New Means". Speech by NATO Secretary General at the Royal United Services Institute, London, 18 June 2004.

Dulles, Allen W. Address before the National Association of Manufacturers, 64th Congress of American Industry, 4 Dec. 1959, http://infoshare1. princeton.edu/libraries/firestone/ rbsc/mudd/online_ex/adulles/ adulles_text.html. Accessed 20 April 2018.

Dulles, John F. "Address at the Annual Luncheon for the Associated Press, 1953." *Department of State Bulletin*, 30 Apr. 1956.

---. "Statement on the Sixth Anniversary of NATO." *Department of State Bulletin*, 25 Apr. 1955.

Eagleburger, Lawrence S. "The Challenge of the European Landscape in the 1990s". Statement before the Subcommittee on European Affairs of the Senate Foreign Relations Committee, 22 Jun. 1989, www. accessmylibrary.com/article-1G1-8139861/challenge-european-landscape-1990s.html. Accessed 5 November 2017.

Eyal, Jonathan. "NATO's Enlargement: Anatomy of a Decision". *International Affairs (Royal Institute of International Affairs 1944-)*, vol. 73, no. 4, Oct. 1997, pp. 695-719.

"France upbraids US as simplistic". *International Herald Tribune*, 7 Feb. 2002, pp. 1-4.

*Hansard*, 13 December 1979, col. 1542.

Havel, Vaclav. "NATO's Quality of Life." *New York Times*, 13 May 1997, p. A21.

Helms, Jesse. United States Senate. Committee of Foreign Relations. *The Debate on NATO Enlargement*. US Government printing Office, 1998.

Hoagland, Jim. "Gorbachev on Tour." *Washington Post*, 11 Oct. 1996, p. A21.

Holbrooke, Richard. "America, a European Power." *Foreign Affairs*, Mar./ Apr. 1995. pp. 41-42.

House of Common Debates, Canada, 1984/4.

Humphrey, Hubert. Address to the NAC, 1 May 1967. *Department of State Bulletin*, May 1967.

Hull, Cordell. Address to joint meeting of both Houses of Congress, 20 Nov. 1943. *Department of State Bulletin*, vol. 9, no. 230, Nov. 1943.

Iklé, Fred. "How to Ruin NATO." *New York Times*, 11 Jan. 1995, p. A21.

Kagan, Robert. "Multilateralism: American Style." *Washington Post*, 13 Sept. 2002, https://carnegieendowment.org/2002/09/13/multilateralism-american-style-pub-1065. Accessed 17 September 2017.

Kennan, George. "A Fateful Error." *New York Times,* 5 Feb. 1997, p. A23.

Kennedy, John F. "President Pledges U.S. Support of NATO." *Department of State Bulletin,* 6 Mar. 1961.

Kissinger, Henrry. "NATO: Make it Stronger, Make it Larger." *Washington Post,* 14 Jan. 1997, p. A15.

Kohl, Helmut. "Statement to the Bundestag", 21 Nov. 1983. *Bulletin 7,* 20 Dec. 1983, pp. 7-9.

---. "Ten-point program for overcoming the division of Germany and Europe, 28 Nov. 1989. *Bulletin des Presse- und Informationsamtes der Bundesregierung (Bulletin of the Press and Information Office of the Federal Government),* 29 Nov. 1989, reprinted, edited by Volker Gransow and Konrad Jarausch. Verlag Wissenschaft und Politik, pp. 101-104.

Lord Ismay, Hastings L. *NATO, the First Five Years 1949-1954.* NATO archives online.

Lukin, Vladimir. "Izvestiya." In *Foreign Broadcast Information Service/ Central Eurasia,* Daily Report, 12 May 1995, p. 22-23. Marshall, George. "Speech at Harvard University", 5 Jun. 1947, http://www.oecd. org/general/ themarshallplanspeechatharvarduniversity5june1947. htm. Accessed 25 October 2017.

Mauroy, Pierre. "France and Western Security." *NATO Review,* vol.5, 1983 p. 23-25.

Odom, William E. "History Tells Us the Alliance Should Grow." *Washington Post,* 6 Jul 1997, p. C3.

Reagan, Ronald. Remarks to Officers of the Department of State and the Arms Control and Disarmament Agency (ACDA), 14 Oct. 1986. *Department of State Bulletin,* December 1986.

---. Speech to American Evangelical Leaders, 8 Mar. 1983. *Department of State Bulletin,* April 1983.

Robertson, George. "NATO after September 11th". Speech to the Pilgrims of the United States, New York, 30 Jan. 2002, www.nato.int/ docu/ speech/2002/s020131a.htm. Accessed 6 February 2018.

---. Speech at the Moscow's Diplomatic Academy, 22 Nov. 2001, www.nato. int/docu/speech/2001/s011122a.htm. Accessed 17 April 2018.

Rocard, Michel. "Otan: attention, danger!" *L'Expres,* 13 Mar. 1997, p. 94-95.

Rodman, Peter. "Four More for NATO." *Washington Post,* 13 Dec. 1994, p. A27.

Roth, William. "Report on the new NATO." *Christian Science Monitor,* 15 Oct. 1988, p. 21-23.

Rutten, Maartje. "From St. Malo to Nice: European Defence: Core Documents". Institute for Security Studies of Western European Union, May 2001.

Rumsfeld, Donald. H. "Prepared remarks at the North Atlantic Council (NAC-D)", 7 Jun. 2001, Brussels.

---. "Transforming the Military," *Foreign Affairs* vol. 81, no. 3, 2002, pp. 20–32.

Rühe, Volker. Speech to the Yomiuri International Economic Society, Tokyo, 28 May 1997.

---. *The New NATO.* Lecture at John Hopkins University's Paul H. Nitze School of Advanced International Studies, American Institution for Contemporary German Studies, Washington D.C, 30 Apr. 1996.

Schmidt, Helmut. "Report on the State of the Union, address before the Bundestag on 20 March 1980". *Bulletin 4*, 25 Mar. 1982.

Schmitt, Eric. "Senate Reject Bid to Create a NATO Unit to Resolve Conflicts." *New York Times*, 29 Apr. 1998a, p. A14.

---. "Senators Reject Bid to Limit Costs of Enlarging NATO." *New York Times*, 30 Apr. 1998b, p. A14.

Schultz, George. News Conference at NATO Headquarters, 9 Dec. 1988. *Department of State Bulletin*, February 1989.

Shanker, Tom. "Bonn rebuffs U.S. over NATO role for Russia." *Chicago Tribune*, 10 Sept. 1994, p. 2.

Shihab, Sophie. "La Russie veut couper court à toute nouvelle extension de l'Alliance atlantique." *Le Monde*, 26 Mar. 1997, p. 2.

Solana, Javier. Speech at the Royal Institute of International Affairs, London, 4 Mar. 1997, www.nato.int/docu/speech/1997/s970304a.htm. Accessed 28 April 2018.

Stoltenberg, Jens. "NATO's Vital Role in the War on Terror." *The Wall Street Journal*, 25 May 2017, www.wsj.com/articles/natos-vital-role-in-the-war-on-terror-1495665078. Accessed 12 May 2018.

Surikov, Anton. "Special Institute Staff Suggests Russia Oppose NATO and the USA". *ASVAB 1017*, Conflict Studies Research Center, Royal Military Academy, 1996, pp. 3-7.

Talbott, Strobe. *The State of the Alliance. An American Perspective*, 15 Dec. 1999, https://www.nato.int/docu/speech/1999/s991215c.htm. Accessed 12 March 2018.

---. "Why NATO Should Grow." *New York Review of Books*, 10 Aug. 1995, www.nybooks.com/articles/1995/08/10/why-nato-should-grow/. Accessed 17 April 2018.

"Vrai Victoire" (editorial), *La Croix*, 26 Apr. 1999.

Weisman, Steven R. "Rice Calls on Europe to Help Building a Safer World." *New York Times*, 9 Feb. 2005, www.nytimes.com/2005/ 02/09/ world/ europe/rice-calls-on-europe-to-join-in-building-a-safer-world.html. Accessed 13 February 2018.

Yeltsin, Boris. "Secret letter on NATO expansion", published in full in an unofficial translation in the Prague newspaper *Mlada fronta Dnes, 2 Dec. 1993. Foreign Broadcast Information Service/Central Eurasia,* Daily Report, 12 May 1995.

# Military Documents

### NATO official documents

North Atlantic Treaty, Washington, 4 April 1949.

NSC-68 – A Report to the National Security Council by the Executive Secretary on the United States Objectives and Programs for National Security, 14 April 1950, reproduced in *Naval War College Review*, May/June 1975.

Study on NATO Enlargement. North Atlantic Treaty Organization, 1995, www.nato.int/cps/en/natohq/official_texts_24733.htm. Accessed 12 March 2018.

Summit documents

Final Communiqué of the North Atlantic Council, London, 10-11 May 1977.

Declaration of the Heads of State and Government participating in the Meeting of the North Atlantic Council, Bonn, 10 June 1982.

Declaration of the NATO Heads of State and Government participating in the Meeting of the North Atlantic Council, Brussels, 2-3 March 1988.

"Conventional Arms Control: The Way Ahead" – Statement issued under the Authority of the Heads of State and Government participating in the Meeting of the North Atlantic Council, Brussels, 2-3 March 1988.

Declaration of the Heads of State and Government participating in the Meeting of the North Atlantic Council (The Brussels Declaration), Brussels, 30 May 1989.

London Declaration on a Transformed North Atlantic Alliance: Issued by the Heads of State and Government participating in the meeting of the North Atlantic Council, London, 5- 6 July 1990.

Developments in the Soviet Union, Rome, 7-8 November 1991.

Rome Declaration on Peace and Cooperation, Rome, 7-8 November 1991.

The Alliance's New Strategic Concept, Rome, 7-8 November 1991.

North Atlantic Cooperation Council Statement on Dialogue, Partnership and Cooperation, Brussels, 19-20 December 1991.

Declaration of the Heads of State and Government (The Brussels Summit Declaration), Brussels, 10-11 January 1994.

Partnership for Peace: Invitation Document issued by the Heads of State and Government participating in the Meeting of the North Atlantic Council, Brussels, 10-11 January 1994.

Founding Act on Mutual Relations, Cooperation and Security between
NATO and the Russian Federation, Paris, 27 May 1997.

Charter on a Distinctive Partnership between the North Atlantic Treaty
Organization and Ukraine, Madrid, 8-9 July 1997.

"An Alliance for the 21st Century", Washington Summit Communiqué
issued by the Heads of State and Government participating in the
meeting of the North Atlantic Council, Washington, D.C., 24 April
1999.

The Alliance's Strategic Concept approved by the Heads of State and
Government participating in the meeting of the North Atlantic
Council, Washington D.C., 24 April 1999.

NATO-Russia Relations: A New Quality, Rome, 28 May 2002.

Statement of the NATO-Russia Council, Rome, 28 May 2002.

Partnership Action Plan against Terrorism, Prague, 21-22 November 2002.

Decision Sheet of the Meeting of the NATO-Russia Council at the level of
Heads of State and Government, Rome, 28 May 2002.

Istanbul Summit Final Communiqué, Istanbul, 28-29 June 2004.

Policy on Combating Trafficking in Human Beings, Istanbul, 28-29 June
2004.

Declaration on Alliance Security, Strasbourg/Kehl, 3-4 April 2009.

NATO Summit Guide, Lisbon 2010.

Active Engagement, Modern Defense – Strategic Concept for the
Defense and Security of the Members of the North Atlantic Treaty
Organization adopted by Heads of State and Government, Lisbon, 19
November 2010.

Summit Declaration on Defence Capabilities: Toward NATO Forces 2020,
Chicago, 20 May 2012.

NATO's policy guidelines on counter-terrorism, Chicago, 21 May 2012.

Wales Summit Declaration, Wales, 4-5 September 2014.

The Wales Declaration on the Transatlantic Bond, Wales, 5 September
2014.

Warsaw Declaration on Transatlantic Security, Warsaw, 8-9 July 2016.

Brussels Declaration on Transatlantic Security and Solidarity, Brussels, 10-
11 July 2018.

Brussels Summit Declaration, Brussels, 10-11 July 2018.

**Ministerial meetings final communiqués**

Final Communiqué of the North Atlantic Council, Paris, 13-14 December
1962.

Final Communiqué of the North Atlantic Council, Paris, 15-17 December 1964.

Final Communiqué of the North Atlantic Council, Paris, 14-16 December 1965.

Final Communiqué of the North Atlantic Council, Luxemburg, 13-14 June 1967.

Final Communiqué of the North Atlantic Council, Bonn, 30-31 May 1972.

Final Communiqué of the North Atlantic Council, Brussels, 12-13 December 1974.

NATO Declaration on Atlantic Relations, Ottawa, 18-19 June 1974.

Final Communiqué of the North Atlantic Council, Brussels, 11-12 December 1975.

Final Communiqué of the North Atlantic Council, Brussels, 9-10 December 1976.

Final Communiqué of the North Atlantic Council, Brussels, 7-8 December 1978.

Report on Future Tasks of the Alliance (*Harmel Report*), Paris, 13-14 December 1967.

Final Communiqué of the North Atlantic Council, Brussels, 15-16 November 1968.

Final Communiqué of the North Atlantic Council, London, 11 May 1977.

Final Communiqué of the Defence Planning Committee, Brussels, 15-16 May 1979.

Final Communiqué of the North Atlantic Council, The Hague, 30-31 May, 1979.

Final Communiqué of the North Atlantic Council, Ankara, 25-26 June 1980.

Final Communiqué of North Atlantic Council, Brussels, 11-12 December 1980.

Final Communiqué of the North Atlantic Council, Rome, 4-5 May 1981.

Declaration on Terrorism, Brussels, 10 December 1981.

Final Communiqué of the North Atlantic Council, Brussels, 9-10 December 1982.

Final Communiqué of the North Atlantic Council, Paris, 1-2 June 1983.

Final Communiqué of the North Atlantic Council, Brussels, 8-9 December 1983.

Washington Statement on East-West Relations, Washington D.C., 29-31 May 1984.

Final Communiqué of the Defence Planning Committee, Brussels, 4-5 December 1984.

Final Communiqué of the North Atlantic Council, Brussels, 13-14 December 1984.

Final Communiqué of the Nuclear Planning Group, Luxembourg, 26-27 March 1985.

Final Communiqué of the Defence Planning Committee, Brussels, 22 May 1985.

Final Communiqué of the Defence Planning Committee, Brussels, 1-2 June 1985.

Final Communiqué of the Nuclear Planning Group, Brussels, 29-30 October 1985.

Final Communiqué of the North Atlantic Council, Brussels, 12-13 December 1985.

Final Communiqué of the Defence Planning Committee, Brussels, 22 May 1986.

Final Communiqué of the Defence Planning Committee, Brussels, 1-2 December 1987.

Final Communiqué of the North Atlantic Council, Brussels, 9-10 December 1987.

Final Communiqué of the Nuclear Planning Group, The Hague, 27-28 October 1988.

Final Communiqué of the North Atlantic Council, Brussels, 8-9 December 1988.

Final Communiqué of the Nuclear Planning Group, Almansil, 24-25 October 1989.

Final Communiqué of the Defence Planning Committee, Brussels, 28-29 November 1989.

Final Communiqué of the North Atlantic Council, Brussels, 14-15 December 1989.

Final Communiqué of the Nuclear Planning Group, Kananaskis, 9-10 May 1990.

Final Communiqué of the North Atlantic Council, Brussels, 17-18 December 1992.

Final Communiqué issued at the Ministerial Meeting of the North Atlantic Council, Brussels, 1-2 December 1994.

Final Communiqué of the Ministerial Meeting of the North Atlantic Council, Berlin, 3-4 June 1996.

Final Communiqué of the Ministerial Meeting of the North Atlantic Council, Brussels, 10-11 December 1996.

Final Communiqué of the Meeting of the North Atlantic Council in Defence Ministers Session, Brussels, 17-18 December 1996.

Final Communiqué of the North Atlantic Council, Brussels, 8 December 1998.

NATO's Response to Terrorism - Statement issued at the Ministerial Meeting of the North Atlantic Council, Brussels, 6-7 December 2001.

Final Communiqué of the Ministerial Meeting of the North Atlantic Council, Madrid, 3-4 June 2003.

Declaration on Terrorism issued at the Meeting of the North Atlantic Council in Foreign Ministers Session, Brussels, 2 April 2004.

NATO-Russia Action Plan on Terrorism, Brussels, 8-9 December 2004.

Final Communiqué of the Ministerial Meeting of the North Atlantic Council, Brussels, 8 December 2005.

Meeting of the NATO-Russia Council Chairman's Statement, Brussels. 14-15 June 2007.

NATO-Russia Council Action Plan on Terrorism – Executive summary, Berlin, 14-15 April 2011.

Statement of the NATO-Ukraine Commission, Brussels, 1-2 April 2014.

Statement by NATO Defence Ministers on Ukraine, Brussels, 26-27 February 2014.

Joint Statement of the NATO-Ukraine Commission, Brussels, 2 December 2014.

Joint Statement of the NATO-Ukraine Commission, Antalya, 13-14 May 2015.

**Other (non-NATO) official documents**

UN Charter, San Francisco, 1945, https://treaties.un.org/doc/publication/ctc/uncharter.pdf. Accessed 14 May 2018.

The Vandenberg Resolution, U.S. Senate Resolution 293, 80th Congress, 2nd Session, 11 June 1948, www.nato.int/ebookshop/video/declassified/doc_files/Vandenberg%20resolution.pdf. Accessed 14 May 2018.

Joint Statement on Franco-German Consultations of 4-5 February 1980.

European Council Summit, Cologne, 3-4 June 1999, www.europarl.europa.eu/summits/ kol1_en.htm. Accessed 17 May 2018.

National Security Strategy of the United States of America, September 2001.

# Bibliography


Bradley, Margaret M. and Lang, Peter J. *Affective Norms for English Words (ANEW): Stimuli, Instruction Manual and Affective Ratings.* The Center for Research in Psychophysiology, University of Florida, 1999.

Calleo, David. *Beyond American Hegemony: The Future of the Western Alliance.* Basic Books, 1987.

Crossley, Scott A., et al. "Predicting Human Scores of Essay Quality Using Computational Indices of Linguistic and Textual Features." *15th International Conference on Artificial Intelligence in Education,* edited by Biswas, Gautam. et al., Springer, 2011, pp. 438–440.

Dascălu, Mihai et al. "Cohesion Network Analysis of CSCL Participation." *Behavior Research Methods,* vol. 50, no. 2, 2018, pp. 604–619. DOI: 10.3758/s13428-017-0888-4.

Garson, David G. *Multivariate GLM, MANOVA, and MANCOVA.* Statistical Associates Publishing, 2015.

Geis, Michael. *The Language of Politics.* Springer-Verlag, 1987.

Ghadessy, Mohsen, editor. *Registers of Written English: Situational Factors and Linguistic Features.* Pinter Publishers, 1988.

Golovin, Boris and Kobrin, Roman. *Linguistic Foundations of the Theory of Terms.* Vysshaya Shkola, 1987.

Gorbachev, Mikhail. *Perestroika: New Thinking for our Country and the World.* Harper & Row, 1988.

Kress, Gunther R. and Hodge, Robert I.V. *Language as Ideology.* Routledge, 1993.

Kuzio, Taras. "Poroshenko Could be the President to Take Ukraine into NATO." *The Hill,* 18 Mar 2018, http://thehill.com/opinion/international/378579-poroshenko-could-be-the-president-to-take-ukraine-into-nato. Accessed 19 March 2018.

Lasswell, Harold D. and Namenwirth, Zvi J. *The Lasswell Value Dictionary.* Yale University Press, 1969.

Manning, Chris. D. and Schütze, Hinrich. *Foundations of Statistical Natural Language Processing.* MIT Press, 1999.

McNamara, Danielle S., et al. "The Linguistic Features of Quality Writing." *Written Communication,* vol. 27, no. 1, 2010, pp. 57–86.

*NATO 2020: Assured Security; Dynamic Engagement.* 21 May 2018, https://www.nato.int/strategic-concept/strategic-concept-report.html.

Nelson, Jessica, et al. *Measures of text Difficulty: Testing Their Predictive*

*Value for Grade Levels and Student Performance.* Council of Chief State School Officers, Washington DC, 2012.

Page, Ellis. "Analyzing Student Essays by Computer." *International Review of Education, vol. 14, no.* 2, 1968, pp. 210–225.

Resnick, Lauren B., et al., *Perspectives on Socially Shared Cognition.* American Psychological Association, 1991.

Rheindorf, Markus and Wodak, Ruth. "Borders, Fences, and Limits – Protecting Austria from Refugees: Metadiscursive Negotiation of Meaning in the Current Refugee Crisis." *Journal of Immigrant and Refugee Studies,* vol. 16, no. 1-2, 2018, pp. 15-38. DOI:10.1080/15562948. 2017.1302032

Rühe, Volker. "Shaping Euro-Atlantic Policies: A Grand Strategy for a New Era." *Survival,* vol. 35, no. 2, Summer 1993, pp. 129-137.

Schellig, Thomas C. *The Strategy of Conflict.* Literary licensing, LLC, 2011.

Thatcher, Margaret. *NATO Review 31* no. 3/4, 1983.

Tognini-Bonelli, Elena. *Corpus Linguistics at Work.* John Benjamins, 2001.

Trăușan-Matu, Ștefan et al. "PolyCAFe–automatic Support for the Polyphonic Analysis of CSCL Chats." *International Journal of Computer-Supported Collaborative Learning,* vol. 9, no. 2, 2014, pp. 127–156. DOI: 10.1007/s11412-014-9190-y.

Trăușan-Matu, Ștefan et al. "Supporting Polyphonic Collaborative Learning." *E-service Journal, Indiana University Press,* vol. 6, no. 1, 2007, pp. 58–74.

Wodak, Ruth. et al. *Discourse and Power.* Wien: Deuticke, 1987.

Wresch, William. "The Imminence of Grading Essays by Computer – 25 Years Later." *Computers and Composition,* vol. 10, no. 2, 1993, pp. 45–58.

www.ingramcontent.com/pod-product-compliance
Lightning Source LLC
LaVergne TN
LVHW011006200726
843509LV00011B/1012